PRINCIPLES OF CLASSICAL JAPANESE LITERATURE

THIS BOOK IS BASED ON CONFERENCES
SPONSORED BY THE JOINT COMMITTEE ON
JAPANESE STUDIES OF THE SOCIAL SCIENCE
RESEARCH COUNCIL AND THE AMERICAN
COUNCIL OF LEARNED SOCIETIES
WITH SUPPORT FROM THE JAPAN-UNITED STATES
FRIENDSHIP COMMISSION

PRINCIPLES OF CLASSICAL JAPANESE LITERATURE

❖

SUMIE JONES
KONISHI JIN'ICHI
MEZAKI TOKUE
EARL MINER
NAKANISHI SUSUMU
NOGUCHI TAKEHIKO
MAKOTO UEDA

❖

EDITED, WITH AN INTRODUCTION, BY

EARL MINER

❖

PRINCETON UNIVERSITY PRESS

Published by Princeton University Press, 41 William Street,
Princeton, New Jersey 08540

In the United Kingdom: Princeton University Press, Guildford, Surrey

Library of Congress Cataloging in Publication Data will be
found on the last printed page of this book

ISBN 0-691-06635-3

Publication of this book has been aided by a grant from the
Paul Mellon Fund of Princeton University Press

This book has been composed in Linotron Aldus

Clothbound editions of Princeton University Press books
are printed on acid-free paper, and binding materials are
chosen for strength and durability

Printed in the United States of America by Princeton University Press
Princeton, New Jersey

DESIGNED BY LAURY A. EGAN

CONTENTS

PREFACE

THE ORIGINS of this study include the practice of Japanese literary study that has developed over the centuries or, more exactly, our interpretation of the practice as it exists today. The four Japanese authors are, of course, the best interpreters of that practice among the seven of us. The other three of us received our higher education in the United States, so that our interpretation of that practice has been affected by two other influences. One is North American practice in study of Japanese literature. That is no single enterprise and certainly replicates, in many respects, features of Japanese practice. Yet in little more than a quarter of a century a distinct American practice has been developed. During the same period, no similar advances have been made in the American study of the great literatures of Korea, India, and the Middle East. And no counterpart in scale exists in the study of Japanese literature in other places. Since three of the four Japanese authors have intimate knowledge of American approaches and methods, this factor functions for almost the entirety of this book, and the result is, to that extent, a testimony of our indebtedness to the work of many North American colleagues as well as to Japanese practice. The other influence involves the practice of literary study here in literatures other than Japanese. Assumptions about Japanese literature and how to study it have been affected by approaches to American, English, and European literatures.

These contextual matters have not involved deliberate decisions on our part so much as the inescapable historical situations in which we have prosecuted our work. We have had, however, two specific aims. One has been to combine the Japanese practice with the North American. Those of us from the United States (and Makoto Ueda also taught some years at Toronto) have sought to approach classical Japanese literature in ways that would honor both Japanese and American understanding. For their part, the four Japanese authors have sought to consider the interests of

American readers. In this joint effort, effected by lengthy discussion among us of each of the seven chapters, we have sought to use two related but distinct kinds of understanding to make some advance on, as well as synthesis of, both. Our second aim has been to offer a more explicit conceptualizing of the subjects dealt with. Quintilian distinguished three kinds of narrative: fable, argument, and history. There may be more fabula here than we intended, and we certainly have not sought to denigrate historia in the terms that are current in much contemporary Western criticism. But, to continue this adaptation and redefinition of Quintilian's terms, we have been most concerned with argumentum. That is, we have aimed at explicit conceptions of our subjects, conceptualizings that others might argue with, adapt, or build on in their own study of that conceptual entity, "classical Japanese literature."

Classical Japanese literature is often studied in other contexts, whether to elicit similarities, or, more often, to provide contrasts. The usual contexts are those of modern Japanese literature, of Chinese literature, and of Western literature. For example, modern and classical Japanese literature are often thought to be quite distinct entities, and the fact that the classical runs for many centuries to 1868, and the modern only from 1868 to the present, suggests a very great difference in conception. In recent years, attempts have increased to seek the origins of modern literature in later classical literature, particularly for fictional prose narrative.

The presumed distinctions between the classical and modern in Japanese literature seem to vanish when Japanese literature is compared with Chinese. The dominant Han Chinese rationality (however tempered by Taoism and Buddhism), Confucian morality or prudery, Chinese ideas of the political function of the poet—not to mention the absence of so much that seems Japanese—all function to highlight differences between Japan and China. Yet when traditional Western literature is considered, Japanese and Chinese literature seem far more similar. In East Asia (including Korea), it was not considered necessary that literature be fictional, and the rhetoric has been more one of norms than of forensic debate. Outside the Western literary parish, and not only in East Asia, varieties of affectivism and expressivism have defined the nature of literature. The principle of mimesis was an exotic and alien import into late nineteenth-century Japan.

There is an undoubted irony in the fact that, as some current Western literature and criticism have taken on antimimetic features, they have seemed more and more to resemble the nonmimesis of East Asia. Such resemblances are often superficial, but they have made classical (and modern) Japanese literature easier to teach. Grown accustomed to a Samuel Beckett or Robbe-Grillet, Western readers do not psychologically require conclusive endings, consistent narrative patterns, tidy representation, and other features of the so-called classic realistic (Western) novel.

Any discussion of these matters is bedeviled by problems of terminology. The usual Japanese for "classical Japanese literature" is "Nihon koten bungaku." "Nihon" here means "Japanese," and the "koten" or "classical" has already been touched on as a distinction from the modern. A greater problem is posed by the presumed equivalence between "bungaku" and "literature." Far from meaning "literature" as imaginative writing, "bungaku" has strong overtones of "literary study," or Literaturwissenschaft. This is true also but less obviously so in English. "Comparative literature" obviously means "comparative study of literature," since nobody writes in "comparative." By the same token, a department of English literature engages in *study* of that literature (along with American and other varieties of literature in English). Except for its "creative writers," it does not mean a department given to the making of English literature. "Bungaku" also has a wider sense inclusive of political and religious writings that are not usually part of the modern English meaning of "literature."

The "bun" of "bungaku" is one Sinified, Japanese pronunciation of the character read "wen" by Chinese. (The Japanese also have a second Sinified pronunciation, "mon," and two non-Sinified readings, "fumi" and "aya"; all three bear in some slightly different fashion on Japanese conceptions.) There is also the Japanese "bungei," or "literary art," "literary accomplishment," which is in some ways closer to "literature" in modern English usage. There is great importance in the fact that in China "wen" and in Japan "bun" differ from Western notions of literature in that the East

Asian terms presume that "literature" is defined primarily by lyrics, lyric-related prose, and certain kinds of historical writing.

Despite these assumptions shared in China, Japan, and Korea, there are great differences among them in temporal scale. Extant Chinese poetry reaches back well into the pre-Christian era, whereas the earliest Japanese works we possess date from about A.D. 500. There is another difference. Until modern times, Japan and Korea received from China, whereas the Chinese felt themselves blithely self-sufficient providers of the exemplary. Yet all priority and distinctness does not belong to China. There is no Chinese precedent for the *Genji Monogatari (The Tale of Genji)*. That is, its appearance antedates anything comparable in China, and none of the great Chinese works of prose fiction that followed was written by a woman.

All the differences provided by contexts require that the study of classical Japanese literature involve establishing our terms of context, our principles of study. In recent years students of classical Japanese literature in the West have felt the need to possess not just a context but also such principles. Not long ago Westerners felt that we should apply Western critical methods to Japanese literature, and no doubt we must continue to do so, if only to make the literature understandable to nonspecialists. Any simple-minded application of the approach suffers, however, from the fact that Western methods are just that, Western, and thereby their application or imposition distorts the literature studied. We have come to see with increasing clarity that Japanese literature must be understood by Westerners as well as by Japanese in terms of the principles that made possible its creation. As a result, the ideal requirements for study of Japanese literature are truly formidable. The student should possess thorough acquaintance with Japanese language and literature, thorough knowledge of Japanese historical and other indigenous culture, thorough knowledge of the Japanese reception of Korean and Chinese learning, thorough knowledge of at least one other literature than Japanese, as well as—finally—thorough grounding in literary theory, Japanese as well as Western.

That ideal can be realized by none of us. So simple and sober a principle has led the seven authors of this book to approach the impossible in a joint effort. Each of us has written a chapter that was discussed at length by the rest. Because our discussions were conducted almost solely in Japanese, they were unusually frank and critical.

The principles of classical Japanese literature we discussed are at once plural and far from exhaustive. In Japanese terms, we have taken pains to identify principles of conception (kokoro) and of expression (kotoba). These might be formal, as with the properties of sequentiality; they might be institutional, as with the practice of aesthetic recluses; or they might be interpretive, as with Edo and earlier ways of reading monogatari (prose fictional narrative). It will be observed that we have made too little of Japanese dramatic literature, and that much else might have been considered. But seven chapters can cover only so much ground, only so many principles of classical Japanese literature. If we have succeeded in communicating some major portion of our own interest and excitement, the ends of this book will be well served.

E. M.
Princeton, 1983

ACKNOWLEDGMENTS

THE JOINT COMMITTEE for Japanese Studies of the Social Science Research Council and the American Council of Learned Societies supported this work with initial funding and with a recommendation to the Japan-United States Friendship Commission, which provided the grant of money that made possible the meetings of the authors and other expenses. Because this book would not have existed without their support, these two agencies deserve the first and fullest acknowledgment.

Although it has not been possible to include the work of two members of our group—Professors Araki Hiroyuki of Hiroshima University and Susan Matisoff of Stanford University—we greatly benefited from their presentations and from their comments on chapters included here.

Our meeting in August 1981 at the University of California, Berkeley, was greatly assisted by Professor James A. Matisoff; and our Washington meeting at the Woodrow Wilson International Center for Scholars in April 1982 was made possible by the help of Dr. Ronald A. Morse, head of the East Asian program at that Center. We are deeply indebted to them both.

The period of the grant from the Japan-United States Friendship Commission included the executive secretaryships of Francis B. Tenny and Richard A. Ericsson, Jr. We are grateful for their assistance.

The staff membership of the Joint Committee for Japanese Studies also changed during the period of the grant, and all three—Dr. Ronald Aqua, Dr. Sophie Sa, and Dr. Theodore C. Bestor—gave invaluable assistance. I wish to express my personal thanks to the other members of the Joint Committee for Japanese Studies for their faith in this work and to Ron Aqua for his crucial assistance.

I must express my thanks to the translators of the Japanese chapters for this English version. They have done excellent work with complex material. Whenever any question arose, I made a point of raising it with the individual authors, who have seen copies of the edited writing if they desired it. I am grateful to the other authors for putting up with many questions over a considerable period of time.

Robert E. Morrell of Washington University gave generous assistance on problems of Buddhism and literature.

Ann Sherif's assistance in reading proof was invaluable for its care and intelligence.

As an editor of work by others, I felt it wise to ask for vetting of my own chapter, and Thomas Reed provided me with very helpful suggestions. The two readers for Princeton University Press assisted with numerous suggestions. Both urged me to revise most of the translations more than I had been inclined to do, and I think they were right. One stigmatized a number of errors, particularly in Buddhist matters. The other urged that I separate from the preface accounts of the contexts and aims of the individual chapters. I did not feel it possible to intrude on the authors of chapters and on readers to the extent recommended—a few prefatory pages to each essay. But I have followed the spirit of the recommendation by reducing the preface to general matters and transferring to an introduction a sequential account of those contexts and aims we have had in mind. I am grateful for all these suggestions.

Finally, I take pleasure in thanking my friends Gail Ullman, who edited the manuscript for the printer, and Laury A. Egan, who designed the book. Their intelligent care for matters large and small has put me in their debt.

PRINCIPLES OF CLASSICAL JAPANESE LITERATURE

INTRODUCTION

❖

BY EARL MINER

THE PREFACE has touched on the aims of this book. Here, an attempt is made to account for each chapter, giving some description of its ends, its relation to other chapters, and its place in the intellectual scheme of this book.

The sequence of the chapters was partly decided at our final meeting. That is, the order of the first two chapters was set and the remainder left to my discretion. After considering various topical groupings, I settled on a more or less chronological scheme based on the literary subject dealt with. That decision derived from a belief that a chronological ordering is easier to follow. It also seemed to make fortuitous topical sense, even while honoring continuities and breaks between chapters as well as their subjects.

The first two chapters are more explicitly theoretical than are the five following. Yet the author of each chapter has sought, and has been urged, to isolate a practice, an issue, a method, or a way of thought that would represent some issue vital to classical Japanese literature. We have aimed at giving explicit conceptual status to whatever subject is treated. The Japanese have so long prized the implicit, the hinted, or the unstated, that some Japanese scholars have found an explicit "argument" uncongenial. This inclination has been reinforced by native tastes for the particular and by the positivist German scholarship that has greatly influenced literary study in Japan. The prizing of the implicit grows from centuries of teaching, or learning, by example. Rather than propound abstract concepts—as Pope does in his *Essay on Criticism* and Wordsworth in his preface to *Lyrical Ballads*—Japanese critics have commonly made exemplary collections or have worked otherwise by example. By memorizing exemplary poems and writing on their model, an individual is recognized as a poet. Theatrical training has been very similar. No one could accuse Zeami (1364-1443) or Komparu Zenchiku (1405-ca. 1470) for failing to be abstractly theoretical about nō, but then as now practical instruction has been by example from youth. The same has held true for the comic interludes of nō, kyōgen, and for actors on the popular or kabuki stage.

For these reasons, Japanese have tended to look on abstract or theoretical discussion of literature as a rather bloodless enterprise, preferring instead an approach they term "daihyōteki." As a daihyō is a representative for another person or of a group, so "daihyōteki" has "representative" as its major dictionary meaning. Common usage and context frequently imply "excellent," "outstanding," or even "normative." This range of meaning is probably best suggested in English by "exemplary." The "representative" example of this conception of criticism in this volume is surely the chapter by Mezaki Tokue.

Since these qualities of thinking have sound intellectual basis and are so congenial to Japanese, I have made no effort to alter the essays by cutting, for example, the number of examples cited to demonstrate a point. My violence has far more often been intrusion, as indicated by square brackets in the text and signaled notes or parts of notes. Although it has seemed desirable to try to retain the style of thought of contributors, as the example of Japanese authors here is meant to show, I have intervened with some frequency in the translators' versions. It is one thing to translate a single chapter. It is quite another to see various chapters as part of a whole. Much is left of the varying styles of the translators in their response to the originals.

CHAPTER 1. MINER As has been said, the chapters by Makoto Ueda and myself were ordered second and first by group decision. By now there is no use apologizing for having written the longest chapter or for having dropped more names and titles than did my fellow authors. Literary collections have interested me for over a quarter century. Konishi Jin'ichi introduced the importance of waka (court poetry) collections to Robert H. Brower and me at Stanford in 1957 and 1958. We were excited to discover that the royal poetry collections were integrated by increasingly complex means, that hundred-poem waka sequences were made to employ such integration, and that those means were drawn on and extended by both varieties of linked poetry, renga and haikai. Matters of general knowledge (and various resources in English as well as Japanese) that are taken for granted now did not exist so short a time ago.

The discovery that Japanese collections were integrated was of interest for literary, aesthetic reasons. It also led me, in the study of seventeenth-century English poets, to understand orderings in poetic collections of the well known (Jonson, Herbert, Milton, Dryden) and the less familiar (Herrick, Habington, Stanley, Vaughan, etc.). The discovery has also had a long-delayed effect best represented by the close of the chapter. While at the Woodrow Wilson International Center for Scholars and revising the chapter, I found the atmosphere of so many bright social scientists led me to new thought. Was not the literary collective principle correspondent to major features of Japanese society? Answers to that question will be found in the sections on ideology and on the collective and the individual.

CHAPTER 2. UEDA Although the first chapter does not ignore sequence, this second chapter offers a large-scale taxonomy of sequences and sequential ordering in premodern Japanese literature. Someone as well versed in modern Japanese literature as Makoto Ueda might also have dealt with modern literary examples. In fact his third epigraph and passages in this chapter do just that. Getting things in suitable sequence (and knowing what suits is an art in itself) offers "a structural principle of Japanese literature." Ueda defines sequence as "a structural principle that is characteristic of Japanese literature that attains an overall artistic unity—or semblance of unity." It is described in opposition to plot, "in which the law of causality unites all the parts into a whole." (Noguchi's chapter employs similar distinctions for prose narrative, monogatari.) Ueda identifies six types of sequence ranging from repetition to qualitative progression. His range of literary example is impressive in its choices from both Japanese and English literature.

Makoto Ueda shows that certain, no doubt simple, matters have considerable explanatory power. Even repetition requires succession, sequence. Above all, he demonstrates beyond question that sequentiality is of unusual importance to Japanese literature, often in the relative absence of plot or at the expense of plot. (His explanation has obvious bearing on the first chapter.) His insight is one that many people seem to have felt, or to have recognized tacitly. His chapter provides an excellent example of what we sought in working together on this book: a principle of evident importance, the development of the implications of the conception in Japanese practice, and implied bases for application to other literatures. Even before one reaches the end of this chapter, additional illustrations spring to mind. When Izanagi no Mikoto and Izanami no Mikoto first go around the pillar in their mating ritual, she speaks first. Apparently a female deity should keep her mouth shut till spoken to, since the result is the birth of a misshapen Leech Child. When he speaks first the next time, the results are far better.

In distinguishing among the types of sequence in his taxonomy, Ueda remarks that in Japanese poetry narrative sequence is relatively scarce and that even in prose narratives of considerable length "structural principles other than the narrative are often involved." One reader of this illuminating discussion finds that Ueda's first and last kinds of sequence—repetition and qualitative progression—offer an interpretive method not only for Japanese literature but also for a great deal of recent Western narrative from *Finnegan's Wake* to novels (or antinovels?) by Robbes-Grillet and Beckett. As Ueda well says in a modest understatement, "When applied with discretion, my categories might lead to some interesting discoveries in classical Japanese literature." Quite apart from the theoretical and practical connections his chapter has with the first, fourth, and last chapters, the statement just quoted surely has wide application to modern Japanese literature as well as to other literatures.

CHAPTER 3. NAKANISHI This chapter deals with a spatial and local conceptualizing that offers a counterpart to the collective and sequential emphases of the preceding two chapters. Nakanishi's concern is with the substitution of place and space for what we now consider temporal, as also with interchanges between the two. In English as well, "before" and "after" are ambiguously spatial and temporal. "She marched before the marines in the parade" is at once temporal as to occurrence and spatial as to visual observation. Nakanishi knows this well, but he also knows that in later writing that is not mythic Japanese emphasized temporalities. Whatever else it was taken to be, and however subtle its philosophy, Buddhism was popularly taken to emphasize causality, a temporal sequence of cause and effect. It is no accident that Ueda emphasizes classical literature informed by Buddhist thought and Nakanishi literature prior to that dominance. It also can be no accident that Nakanishi is one of the leading Japanese critics of Kakinomoto Hitomaro, who writes as if Buddhism did not exist in his time, and of the first great collection of Japanese poetry, the *Man'yōshū*, in which much of the poetry shows no Buddhist influence.

Beginning with evidence that ancient Japanese conceived of time and death spatially, Nakanishi Susumu asks why this should be so, showing how involved time and space were in their thought. The answer comes in part in terms of connections of the names of deities and of place names. If matters as immediate as place and as mysterious as deities were so considered, then it is likely that intermediate conceptions would be similar. He shows that the final stage of life is considered in terms of a place, real or mythic, the lintel between life and death, as it were. These considerations lead him to a proposition that will surely be taken as a major and daring suggestion. This concerns the michiyuki or set travel-piece that was an inheritance from Japanese myth to late classical writing. "I believe," he says, "that since the age of the myths, michiyuki offered a form of the delineation of the process toward death." The claim is substantiated by examples from passages in Japanese mythology to drama in the Edo period, and he gives counterpart examples of michiyuki leading to death and back to life or through a metaphorical death to a metaphorical rebirth of a crown prince to his role as sovereign.

Nakanishi's argument involves a Japanese conception of contiguities. In ancient thought, this involved spatial stages for what we and later Japanese would consider temporal sequence. In other terms, these contiguities reveal the enduring Japanese desire to think in terms of gradations rather than of absolute polarities in the Western sense of gods and human individuals, life and death, time and place. As he shows, the deities (kami, etc.) can die. Other evidence shows that people could become, or were (in the case of sovereigns), deities. Mountains, streams, and trees might have, or be, deities. The four provinces now prefectures of Shikoku were thought of as four place-divinities. If places have life, and life is identified with place, then the spatializing of what we think temporal is altogether natural. At one degree of generalization, this kind of graduation relates to Ueda's concept of sequence, especially of qualitative sequence. In other respects, Nakanishi offers an ancient and obverse counterpart to Ueda's evidence from later literature.

CHAPTER 4. NOGUCHI In this chapter, the spatial metaphor is developed very complexly with other matters. Noguchi's subject is "the substratum constituting 'monogatari,' " or prose fictional narrative, particularly the greatest work of Japanese literature, the *Genji Monogatari (The Tale of Genji)*. Using historical and therefore temporal insights, particularly those of Hagiwara Hiromichi (1813-1863), he discusses strata in the "structure" of monogatari. In one sense his complex discussion addresses a simple question: how could Heian ladies read the *Genji Monogatari* with such ease, whereas modern Japanese readers as well as Western readers of the original must labor with such difficulty to understand what is conveyed by the ceaselessly flowing style?

Two explanations stand out from his complex account. One, using Hagiwara Hiromichi, posits that they could, and we must, read in terms of "strata" that represent structural principles distinct from plot. These principles he likens to the skeletal, whereas plot is fleshly. The second explanation involves a speaking narrator for, as he points out, "monogatari" means both a person (mono) relating (katari) and a matter (mono) being related (katari). He well shows that narratorship is at once simple and enormously complex, that our "distance" from characters may be less when we are given access to their innermost thoughts, even while that involves the most "distant" reaches of a narrative that necessarily requires an intervening narrator. During our Berkeley meeting, Noguchi mentioned, without adversely criticizing it, the view of some Japanese critics that in addition to first-person (daiichi ninshō) and third-person (daisan ninshō) narrative, there is also personless (muninshō) narrative. In this mention and in features of his discussion, Noguchi shows how traditional and current Japanese discussion of narrative have anticipated much that is debated in current Western theory of narrative. In discussing the increasing complexities of narration in the *Genji Monogatari* he speaks sometimes of "polyphony." As far as I am aware, this conception derives from his study of the *Genji Monogatari* rather than from Western criticism (by Bakhtin, for example). Be that as it may, this chapter will be read with close attention by anyone interested in the complex issues of narration or in the *Genji Monogatari*.

CHAPTER 5. MEZAKI Whereas Nakanishi and Noguchi stress spatial and schematic matters, this chapter and the next make more of historically based concepts. A cultural historian, Mezaki Tokue seeks to account for the continuities that persist in literary-cultural change and the changes that alter the continuities. Focusing on aesthetic reclusion, he posits some distinctions, particularly between shukke (leaving the family) and tonsei (escaping the world). The former, older concept implies leaving home, usually at a young age, to enter a temple for the duties of a priest. These include numerous kinds of ecclesiastical offices. But a priest also was able, in principle, to mingle with all conditions of people, however high or low. The tonseisha, the escapers of the world, were people who entered religion after experience of the secular world. Among them were those in whom Mezaki is particularly interested, the suki no tonseisha, or aesthetic recluses. In time, as Mezaki says, and as the next chapter shows, the practice of the tonseisha would lead to a near identification of religious and literary pursuits.

This group of religious poets can be traced back to Kisen (fl. ca. 810-824). By the time of Nōin (988-1058?) we can discern a pattern of reclusion, foot-travel, and poetry (or other arts). Mezaki shows that, after some generations of preparation, individuals in the twelfth century gave tonsei practice its definition. The principal writers discussed are Kamo no Chōmei (1155-1216), a (very difficult) poet and author of a prose classic; Yoshida Kenkō (ca. 1283-after 1352), whose account of his life and his hut has long been esteemed as a principal classic in prose; and above all Saigyō (1118-1190), details of whose life and examples of whose verse Mezaki sets forth in admiring detail. If popularity is the criterion of poetic importance, Saigyō is a member of a trinity of Japanese poets including Kakinomoto Hitomaro and Matsuo Bashō.

Western notions of the "direction" of history postulate the future. In important respects, Buddhism does also. But in East Asia the past is the usual norm. There the major cultural value lies in what has precedent, which is to say in the past. If in Europe there has been concern with the seemingly endless rise of the middle class, in Japan the concern lies with the seemingly endless decline of the court. Asian concern with the exemplary purity of the past contrasts remarkably with Romantic and post-Romantic concern with the new. The tonseisha and, in particular, Saigyō offer past norms of reference to judge the present or, rather, to offer what matters.

This chapter has very close connections with the first. A Saigyō is venerated for having cut himself off from the collective social world of his time, as very few Japanese can do or perhaps really wish to do. Only the enduring presumption of the importance (the representativeness!) of integrated social groups can account for the special place accorded a Saigyō. It is part of the creative paradox of Chōmei, Kenkō, and Saigyō that their reclusion was marked by frequent returns to the Japanese collectively defined society. Saigyō certainly prized his reclusion. Equally certainly, he enjoyed a priest's freedom to move. It is doubtful that he would have taken orders unless he knew that by doing so he would be able to enter the court and meet with the more humble. On one of his journeys, he visited the bakufu (military government) in Kamakura, where he discussed military matters, court kickball, and surely also poetry. In such fashion do the suki no tonseisha like Saigyō reveal the tension between their desires for religious seclusion and for merging with that living collection we term society.

CHAPTER 6. KONISHI Beginning where the preceding chapter left off this chapter shows that by the Kamakura period religious idealizing of the role of the poet brought the seemingly separate recluses into union with social ideals in a troubled age. The collective genius of Japanese cultural constraints made the ideal of the recluses part of larger social ends. Konishi sets forth the ideological or conceptual basis of that integration in terms of michi or vocation. "Michi" is a highly value-laden word: the Chinese character so given in Japanese reading is also read in Sinified fashion "tō" (cf. Shintō, the michi of the native deities) or "dō" (cf. Butsudō, the michi of the Buddha). There is also the Chinese conception set forth in the same character as "tao," used not only of the "michi" of Taoism but also of those of Confucius and the Buddha.

The michi ideal has long interested Konishi as an important feature of medieval Japanese experience. In this chapter, his range is very broad. He begins with the mythical material treated by Nakanishi and goes on as far as nō. The chapter combines a wealth of detail with a clear line of argument. In his first two sections, Konishi shows that the aesthetic recluses discussed by Mezaki—along with many other medieval Japanese—dedicated themselves to the vocation of poetry (kadō or uta no michi). Konishi also shows that the michi chosen did not need to be poetry. It could be whatever one's family was known for. The individual and the household held interests in common. (The powerful sense of the collective shows yet again.) This search for a common ground, this attempt to discover what might be done, and this sense of dedication were, as Konishi shows, responses to the common belief that the nation was disintegrating and that the final stage of the Buddhist Law had come. Instead of fleeing to retirement, like Mezaki's recluses, those of a later generation sought to discover religious devotion in their daily work.

In the last section of his chapter, Konishi deals with the expressive results of this dedication to michi. Like Mezaki, he is mostly concerned with poetry. But he deals with nō as well as with waka and renga (linked poetry). This unusual coincidence of religious and secular ideals offered definition for human endeavor in, as well as for hopes amid, many a cause for despair. The michi ideal may be compared in this respect with the Jōdo (Pure Land) Buddhism that Hōnen (1133-1212) instituted or, it may be better to say, separated from Tendai Buddhism. By revering the name of the Buddha and reciting it with honor, or by dedication to one's station in the world, one had hopes either of rebirth in the Western Paradise or enlightenment. The interest Konishi shows in michi is not, however, simply an important historical matter. The poetry that this dedication produced may be, as some think, the greatest Japan has known. There is no question but that it is the most profound.

CHAPTER 7. SUMIE JONES The court and its values had long seemed to outlast its rivals. But genuine, definitive change did occur by the time of the Edo or Tokugawa regime that finally pacified a war-weary nation at the beginning of the seventeenth century. The order was a sufficiently radical change to require a new legitimacy. (The sovereign and nobility continued to exist, but more in name than even as ritual center.) The Edo bakufu found its source of legitimacy in neo-Confucianism of a kind known in Japan as Shushigaku, or the teaching of Chu Hsi (1130-1200). If there had been any major continental thought that, over the centuries, had seemed to be alien to Japan, especially to writers, that was Confucianism. Now that a revived version of it was declared orthodoxy, it suffered the fate of all orthodoxies. That is, it required application to actualities, which meant that it required interpretation. There were disputes among adherents of Shushigaku, and there were alternative versions of neo-Confucianism energetically proposed, if never with success in overturning the official version.

One rival version proposed was Yōmeigaku, another neo-Confucian school based on the teaching of Wang Yang-ming (1472-1529). There were yet others, particularly kogaku, an alleged pristine Confucianism. The appeal to a true, old version is particularly East Asian, given the habit of locating value in the past. But like the Protestant Reformers in England, those who sought a pristine Confucianism were interested in change. The major kogaku proponents are usually identified as Yamaga Sokō (1622-1685) and Itō Jinsai (1627-1705). Today neither of these holds nearly as much interest as Ogyū Sorai (1666-1728) who, depending on one's definition, is another proponent of kogaku or a figure to himself. Sumie Jones chooses him as her representative of Edo neo-Confucianism, pairing him with an extraordinary polymath, Hiraga Gennai (1728-1779).

Sumie Jones does not spend time rehearsing the neo-Confucian disputes that are likely to seem as remote to us as some early Christian or Islamic debate. She addresses herself instead to language, which is not only a topic of very warm debate in the West but also an issue that had to concern a Sorai reinterpreting Confucian classics and a Gennai who was a gifted literary author. Debates among neo-Confucianists involved strong support of, as well as opposition to, the orthodoxy of the regime and its official savants. (As usual, personality played a large part in seemingly purely intellectual disputes.) Along with such debate, there was genuine turmoil among writers of prose fiction, whose aims were not congenial with those of a rationalistic, repressive government. This situation is the one that Jones terms "language in crisis." "Language" has more than one meaning here. It includes the Chinese of the Confucian and neo-Confucian writings and the Japanese of actual life. It also involves the Japanese of literature, which is yet another thing from official pronouncements and philosophizing. Moreover, it is at the heart of Sorai's efforts to control the uncontrollable issues of interpretation and Gennai's subversive playing of brilliant, intelligent games with language in an age when games were the last thing the official philosophers had in mind. Above all "language in crisis" refers to conflicting aims over what should be thought and felt in the use of language.

Sorai sought pristine meaning in Confucian writings set down in Chinese. Because the bakufu prohibited travel out of the country, Sorai's grand program was conducted without any experience of Chinese as a living language. As Jones shows, Sorai used main strength to break through the language barrier, at least to his satisfaction. His efforts and intellectual gifts have made him one of the most problematic of Japanese thinkers. There are many rival versions of Sorai, since interpreting the radical interpreter is no easy task. In Jones's view, Sorai sought to abolish the multifariousness of language. If he had enjoyed the status of a Cardinal Richlieu, the result might have been the establishment of a body like the French Academy to oversee control of Japanese. He had no such power, however, and his efforts to resolve linguistic and philosophical conflict only intensified the "crisis" that he hoped to resolve.

Gennai is also difficult to describe in brief, but for very different reasons. Of him we may say, as of Sorai, that there is many a Gennai. But with him, the variety is due not so much to the interpreters of him as to the many roles he played. He stood above his contemporaries in study of Dutch, botany, electricity, painting like that of the West, along with a variety of other subjects, including literature in particular. He distrusted any simplistic, literalist conception of language. Jones gives some examples of the famous Hiragaburi, or Hiraga style, in which the author offers a stream of words requiring double or triple interpretation by his willful plays with meaning. Gennai posits multiplicity of meaning against Sorai's attempts to define the single truth of words and sentences. To Sorai's earnest, he opposes double entendre, other puns, outrageous predications, and sexual innuendo—all subversive not only of the efforts of Sorai but of orthodox neo-Confucianism. Logically speaking, both Sorai and Gennai could not both be right. But as Samuel Jonson wrote, "Inconsistencies cannot both be right but, imputed to man, they may both be true" (*Rasselas*, ch. 8). It is in this sense that these two striking figures contribute to the truth of experience in Edo Japan. That truth was not so much a resolution as an exploration of "language in crisis."

After so much seriousness in the preceding chapters, and in Sorai, Sumie Jones's wit and that of Gennai provide a close suitable to her Edo subject. For the whole book, her chapter offers a suitable ochi (fall or resolution) like that which resolves comic Edo monologues, rakugo. Looking back to earlier chapters, we observe how radical an alternative these Edo writers provided to Mezaki's aesthetic recluses and Konishi's devotees of vocation. Her concerns resemble, although at an extraordinary distance in kind, the philological interests of Nakanishi and the concern with methods of interpretation dealt with by Noguchi. Ueda's taxonomy of sequences would certainly provide interesting means of discussing these writers' major works, and in particular Gennai's masterpiece of prose fiction, *Fūryū Shidōken Den (The Dashing Life of Shi-*

dōken). All that need be said of the relation of the first chapter to this concluding one is that Sorai and Gennai were, in their different ways, devoted collectors.

Our seven chapters deal with principles fundamental to Japanese literature and other expressions of human experience throughout the classical period. We do not pretend to have exhausted the meanings of the principles themselves, or the range of important principles. Just as we worked by discussion of the major aims and the details of each other's work, so we hope to evoke further discussion by others. If this is the first time that four Japanese and three Americans have joined to make a book treating literary matters of some importance, it will surely not be the last. We look forward confidently, expectantly, to other joint studies that will range farther on what Sidney called the zodiac of wit than any single author can aspire to do.

It remains to say that, as editor and introducer, I have reviewed all the chapters, editing them with some care, sending questions to authors, and seeking approval for changes. I have taken an especially active part in revising the translations, so that the versions seen here may include mistakes of my doing rather than faults of the translators. It will be observed that individual authors have their own ideas about presentation of, say, poems, and that there is some inconsistency. The translators have also chosen somewhat different means. I have not chosen to intervene beyond a certain point, thinking that no serious problem is posed and that the variety may preserve something more precious, the individual styles of the other authors and the individual gifts of the translators.

n of either a collection or of literature. In twenty scrolls
over 4,500 poems by named or anonymous poets have
erved. Because no single method of compiling is used
tly, various compilers must have been involved. For that
umerous notes and other evidence show that this collec-
on earlier collections no longer in existence. One need
panese to be excited by this first great collection of the
Japan. As a collection, however, it must yield in impor-
he *Kokinshū* (ca. 905-920), the first of the royally com-
anthologies (chokusenshū) and of the collections of twenty-
s (nijūichidaishū). As is well known, it resembles the
ū in consisting of twenty scrolls and in including Japa-
ns by writers past and present (as its full title, *Kokin-*
implies: *A Collection of Ancient and Modern Japanese*
Apart from many wonderful poems, it is a watershed of
s in its arrangement. Each half, consisting of ten books,
th esteemed kinds of poem. The first starts with books
asons (1-2 Spring, 3 Summer, 4-5 Autumn, 6 Winter),
cond half begins with poems on Love (11-15). The re-
sections in each half deal with poems on other topics like

ors of the *Kokinshū* might vary considerably, but all are
arranged. No doubt it is hard for the human mind to put
any collection that is not ordered in some fashion. But
shū model is topical, not chronological; a given poet's
not all appear together or in order of presumed com-
Few Japanese can appreciate how unusual this is, but
o full counterpart of the *Kokinshū* model either in India,
orea, or the West.
inciples of this model are progression, association, and
. A progression might involve that of the four seasons
velopment and fluctuations of love. Since there would be
ems on the autumn moon, compilers sought such sub-
ons as geographical ordering of places where the moon
Ordering by small progressions led to the development
tion, so that an autumn poem on frost might be followed
umn poem on withered plants. As we read sequentially,

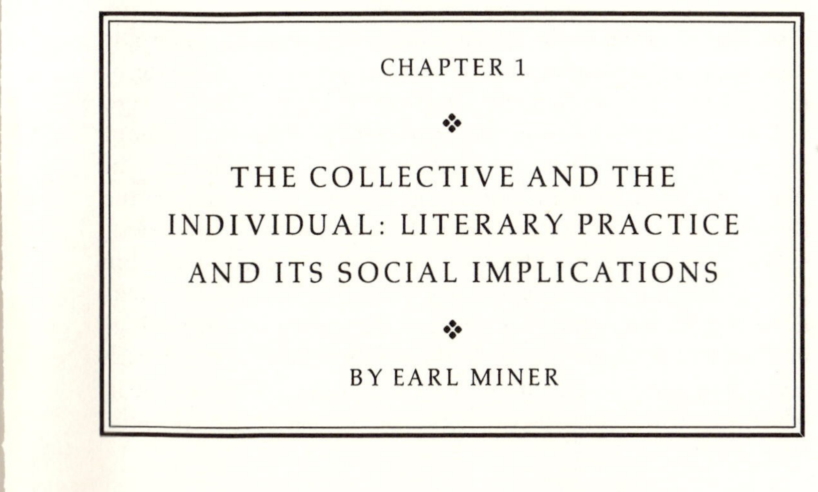

CHAPTER 1

THE COLLECTIVE AND THE INDIVIDUAL: LITERARY PRACTICE AND ITS SOCIAL IMPLICATIONS

BY EARL MINER

"Collections: The Old *Man'yōshū*. The *Kokinshū*."
—SEI SHŌNAGON, *The Pillow Book*

In 1424 at the court of Gosukō In, preparations were made for a linked-poetry (renga) party on the Seventh Night Festival (Tanabata). By contemporary standards, the place where poetry would be composed was suitably decorated.

> Two pairs of screens stood in the apartments. From them hung three scrolls inscribed with the name of Sugawara Michizane, and also one painting with side panels of plum branches, and one hanging scroll depicting Hotei, with its side panels of birds and flowers. A variety of utensils was grouped on a shelf nearby. On another table, a number of flower vases was lined up. The decorations resembled a pattern.[1]

[1] *Kammon Gyoki*, 1424, Month VII, 7; as in Akazawa Eiji, ed., "Jūgoseiki ni Okeru Kinbyōbu ni Tsuite," *Kokka*, 849 (Dec. 1962), p. 579, n. 8. Cited by and quoted from (with slight revision) Gail Capitol Weigl, "The Reception of Chinese Painting Models in Muromachi Japan," *Monumenta Nipponica*, 35 (1980), 264. In the quotation: Sugawara Michizane is the divinified patron of writing; Hotei is one of the Seven Divinities of Good Fortune. For a discussion relating Japanese art and poetry in collective terms, see Yoshiaki Shimizu, "Seasons and Places in Yamato Landscape and Poetry," *Ars Orientalis*, 12 (1981), 1-14. See also the chapter below, Ueda's "Taxonomy of Sequences."

That the decorations should be taken to make up a pattern is significant, since all that display was not casual but evidence of the Japanese "taste for enjoying works of art in ensemble" (Weigl, p. 268). A pattern or ensemble of related but different works of art is a kind of collection, on whatever scale. The multiplicity of things in restricted space testifies to the love of display in the Muromachi period. The instinct to arrange various items exemplifies the principle of collections in Japanese literature and life from earliest times to today—from that "Old *Man'yōshū*" mentioned by Sei Shōnagon to displays of calligraphy or other things in a department store today. Is there another country in which seven spring and seven autumn plants are painted together, or in which its earliest form of writing—man'yōgana—takes its name from a collection?

The Centrality of Collections in Japanese Literature

"Japanese literature" (Nihon no bungaku) is a modern concept, just as in the West the modern meaning of "literature" does not emerge until the eighteenth century. Early Japanese wrote about particular kinds: uta, monogatari, nikki, -ki, etc. After the Chinese example of wen, Japanese bun, fumi, and other equivalents designated two kinds of esteemed writing: a poetry fundamentally lyric, and prose historical writing of certain kinds, whether in Chinese or in Japanese. A distinction arose later between the Japanese standard and nonstandard—between prestigious and popular or vulgar literature. The standard came to have such names as ushin and ga. The nonstandard naturally had more names: haikai, mushin, zoku, kyō, etc. In what follows I shall move from the narrow definition to postulate all kinds presently considered literary.

Only two kinds of Japanese writing have always been thought serious by Japanese: history and the kind of poetry—waka—associated with the court. To these we can add only composition in Chinese. Every other kind that came to be thought standard (mo-

nogatari, renga, nō, kyōgen) w
mere pastime. For centuries onl
labeled anonymous (yomibito s
mattered as to name, as to wri
significant that waka poets were
is not true of literary kinds that
not signed. Renga masters took
"names" may come to mind: Zea
are not their real names. Yet th
implies that by Edo times a far w
grown, even if the additions were
for this discussion is that, wheth
broader view of Japanese literatu
its history.

The abundant evidence ranges
fundamental features of Japanese
of illustration, there is a card ga
Year's, involving the *Hyakunin Issh*
Poets). The poems of this collect
cards with a part of the poems m
version. Although it seems unlik
collection in other national literat
example is merely illustrative. It i
Japanese literature should have be
main classical line of poetry shou
The first extant Japanese literary w
of these matters) is the *Kojiki* (712
of divinities and human creatures
also divine words and acts, legends
five works usually included in acc
ature, it is remarkable that all are
them we know a surprising amour
for conveying and collecting. Such
exist in other national traditions o
The last of the early five works,

[2] For the categories, including utamonoga
see Itō Sei, et al., *Shinchō Nihon Bungaku*

concepti
or parts
been pr
consiste
matter,
tion dre
not be
poetry
tance t
mission
one re
Man'y
nese p
wakas
Poems
collect
begins
on the
as the
maini
Trave
Suc
carefu
toget
the K
poem
positi
there
Chin
Th
suita
or th
seve
prog
was
of a
by a

we assume that the frost in one poem is the cause of withering in the next, although such a concept derives from the compilers' arrangement. In other words, the principle of collection was foremost, and this principle had a major, enduring effect on subsequent Japanese literature.

Court poets devised a number of ways of emulating the *Kokinshū*. One was the compilation of an unofficial anthology (shisenshū) on a scale like the royal collections. Another was a sequence of perhaps a hundred poems (hyakushuuta) modeled on all or some part (e.g. Love) of the *Kokinshū*. Such sequences became major means of composing poems on fictional topics, as did the poetry matches (utaawase), for which topics came to be set for matched pairs of poems. A striking example is provided by *The Poetry Match in Fifteen Hundred Rounds* (*Sengohyakuban Utaawase*, 1201-1202). We should note that Gotoba (1180-1239; r. 1184-1198) called this match to obtain poems for the *Shinkokinshū* (8th royal collection), which was then under compilation. Another kind of work of this general kind is the kashū which, according to conception or designation (歌集, 家集) might be either an individual's personal collection or a house selection. Whether the individual poet or some heir chose the poems, the aim might be completeness, emphasis on an idealized version of the poet's whole life, focus on youth (and love affairs) or age (and religious devotion), or collection of collections by an individual, or even selection of striking poems.[3] Some kind of order for parts or wholes or both was sought. For example, the personal collection of Sone no Yoshitada (fl. ca. 985), the *Sotanshū*, includes his *Maigetsushū*, 360 poems, one for each day of the year in the old calendar, a rare example of a purely chronological—calendrical—Japanese collection, although we cannot be certain that the poems were composed in the order of presentation.

The royal collections hold importance both as a model for kinds of integration (the seasonal arrangement holds for haiku to this day) and, more importantly, for the concept that collections should

[3] For an excellent discussion, see Phillip Harries, trans., *The Poetic Memoirs of Lady Daibu [Kenrei Mon'in Ukyō no Daibu Shū]* (Stanford: Stanford University Press, 1980).

be integrated. The concept influenced many other kinds of writing. The utamonogatari, which offer brief narrative prose contexts for poems, are among the first to adapt the collective principle, to a great extent by adapting the model of love sequences, or other kinds of poems in the royal collections, which used headnotes describing circumstances of composition. As we have seen, the principle can be traced retrospectively to the *Kojiki*. But the supreme exemplar of utamonogatari, the *Ise Monogatari*, collects episodes dealing (more or less) with the figure of a man of the past associated with the poet, Ariwara Narihira (825-880). The two others are the *Heichū Monogatari* (ca. 959-965) concerning Taira Sadabun, which has 150 poems in thirty-eight episodes; and the *Yamato Monogatari*, compiled a bit earlier (ca. 938-949), much the most miscellaneous in involving about 140 individuals in a wide variety of stories, although Love topics are among the most frequent.

Some detail and some generalization will clarify this kind of writing. In the eighteenth part of the *Kokinshū* (poems 971-72) there is an exchange of poems accompanied by prose between Narihira and an unnamed woman. With little alteration, this exchange became the 123rd episode of the *Ise Monogatari*. Simple enough: find enough sources and you have an utamonogatari. It is harder to understand why an individual work may go under the name of utamonogatari, poetic diary (uta nikki), or poetic collection (kashū). It is a question of the function assigned a work. An utamonogatari is taken as an arrangement of poems and their prose contexts by someone other than the poet. A diary is taken to be poems with even more prose context provided, or as if provided, by the poet. A kashū is a collection of poems, with or without prose contexts, by an individual poet and compiled, or as if compiled, by that poet. The functional distinction has importance, but, since the same work may go by two or all three of these functional designations, we arrive at the crucial postulate that all three are essentially collective in nature. This collective principle extends far beyond anthologies—a collective work need not have "shū" in its title—as we can now see in turning to other kinds.

Linked poetry in its earlier kind, renga, arose as a pastime among waka poets. (Eighteen renga stanzas by Gotoba are extant.) For a party, or after the rigors of composing waka, a few poets might gather to alternate in composing a sequence of stanzas. Like so much else in Japanese literature after waka, what began as game gradually became earnest. Although shorter sequences might be written, a hundred became the most prevailing, along with such multiples as a thousand or even ten thousand. The elaborate canons of renga need not concern us.[4] The crucial matter is that those rules developed from, and codified, ways of integrating waka collections, using instead of whole waka of the tanka form its upper stanza or three lines (in 5, 7, 5 syllables) and its lower (7, 7). Waka topics were also used, in adaptation.[5] In brief, a renga sequence resembles a royal collection in the central principle of arrangement by topics. The composing group (za), which is the counterpart of the compilers of a collection, does not of course have existing poems to choose from and arrange. The poets are present to compose new stanzas in their group. It is to us later readers that the completed sequence most resembles a waka collection.

Renga was not only understood to resemble waka collections in arrangement. It also took on serious (ga) status after the highborn nobleman and poet, Nijō Yoshimoto (1320-1388) wrote rule books, composed renga, and—naturally enough—compiled a collection of renga stanzas, his *Tsukuba Shū*. This is divided into twenty books modeled on the waka topics and anthologies. It also gives the preceding stanza (maeku) with the esteemed added stanza (tsukeku). The greatest of renga masters, Sōgi (1421-1502), made similar collections, the chief of which are his *Shinsen Tsukuba Shū* and *Chikurinshō*. The latter is in ten parts (as a couple of the royal collections had been). In one of the final of several orderings, Sōgi begins with four parts on the seasons. The second half begins with

[4] For a full account of the canons of renga, see Konishi Jin'ichi, *Sōgi* (Chikuma Shobō, 1971). In "The Art of Renga," Karen Brazell and Lewis Cook provide a considerably abbreviated translation of Konishi's account: *The Journal of Japanese Studies*, 2 (1975), 29-61. I offer a somewhat different version in *Japanese Linked Poetry* (Princeton: Princeton University Press, 1979).

[5] In waka, Miscellaneous (zō) designates poems in which no single topic (Spring, Love) predominates. In renga and haikai, any stanza without a seasonal topic is Miscellaneous.

two on Love. There follow another pair on Miscellaneous topics. The final book gives opening stanzas (hokku), and therefore of course does not offer prior stanzas.

In addition to its many debts to waka, renga offers a new principle. Its poets adapted from court music a three-part rhythm. The jo-ha-kyū involves a stately introduction (jo), a lengthy, more agitated development (ha), and a "fast" close (kyū). This rhythm was taken over by a wide variety of writings, most obviously haikai, the successor to renga. Well before haikai came into existence, however, the rhythm was adapted by nō, both for individual plays and for a given day's performance of five plays: making an integrated collection of a series of productions. Many of the plays for the puppet theater (jōruri) adapted the rhythm. If kabuki did not, it had its own annual sequence with the kaomise performance beginning the annual run toward the end of the year and so on to the nagori (a renga term for the last sheet of stanzas) performance at the end of the acting season. Some of these matters will be dealt with in more detail subsequently, but just as the collective principle could govern works assumed to have this or that authorial function, so could very different methods of integration assure integrity for diverse materials. For the moment, an example from haikai can best serve.

Among the more or less canonical seven collections of the Bashō school (*Shichibu Shū*), the most remarkable is *Sarumino* (1691). This "*Kokinshū* of haikai" consists of six parts. The first four include hokku (or at least stanzas in the 5, 7, 5 hokku form), but in the very unusual sequence of Winter, Summer, Autumn, Spring. The disorder can only have been deliberate, an example of haikai change (haikaika). Whatever else might be said of this strange order, it enables the compilers, in offering Spring stanzas last (instead of first), to include Flower stanzas at the equivalent place of the most important Flower stanza, the thirty-fifth in Bashō's favorite thirty-six-stanza sequence (kasen). In short the collection of hokku is ordered within each section along the lines of fluctuation familiar in a haikai sequence (and from waka of the eighth royal collection, the *Shinkokinshū*, onward), even including a few stanzas on Love featuring cats and their owners in a position equivalent to the development (ha) section. The fifth part of *Sarumino* includes four kasen, arranged out of order of composition to follow the unusual Winter, Summer, Autumn, Spring sequence of the hokku. Like the hokku sections, these also are arranged on the model of a kasen. That is, the first kasen, *Tobi no Ha mo no Maki (Even the Kite's Feathers)*, is a very regular one, representing an introduction (jo). The final one of the four, *Umewakana no Maki (Plum Blossoms and Fresh Shoots)*, is such a mixed bag that Japanese scholars have tended to ignore it, failing to see that it makes a fine fast close (kyū) for the four kasen considered as a collection modeled on a single kasen. The intermediate two sequences are brilliant kasen that explore the limits of haikai in a way offering a beautiful counterpart of the development (ha) of linked poetry. The very strange sixth part offers its own version of a kasen, even providing a version of the fast close (kyū) to the whole of *Sarumino*, ensuring that the entire collection is also designed on the kasen model.[6] Significantly enough the proper title of this compilation is *Sarumino Shū, The Monkey's Straw Raincoat Collection*, a work truly deserving (in the sense of both nouns) its fame as "the *Kokinshū* of haikai."

Once we grow alert to the collective principle in Japanese literature, we are apt to find that all works of importance and length are collections. In a sense that is true, since anything of a certain length will be a composite. My uneasiness with so wide a sense of "collection" leads me to take issue with Konishi Jin'ichi's thesis that it is a characteristic of Japanese literature that it contains no long integral works.[7] He holds that Murasaki Shikibu's *Genji Monogatari (Tale of Genji)* and Kyokutei Bakin's *Nansō Satomi Hakkenden (The Story of Eight Virtuous Heroes)* are not really long works but compilations of brief units. The issue applies to the whole range of Japanese prose narrative. The problem for me is

[6] For more evidence on this thesis, see (by Hiroko Odagiri and myself) *The Monkey's Straw Raincoat and Other Poetry of the Bashō School* (Princeton: Princeton University Press, 1981).

[7] Konishi Jin'ichi, *A History of Japanese Literature*, vol. 1 (Princeton: Princeton University Press, 1984), pp. 10-12. As can be seen, I view the problem as distinguishing the collective literary work from the composite or the episodic.

that the sense in which the Konishi thesis holds for Japanese literature would also make collections out of the *Odyssey*, the *Nibelungenlied, Don Quixote, The Adventures of Augie March*, along with many Indian, Chinese, and Middle Eastern narratives.

My fear is that so broad a conception of what is a collection explains too little by purporting to claim too much. I would like to consider a collection to be an assembly of comparable (that is coordinately rather than subordinately relatable) units that are distinct in authorship, as integers, or in similar radical fashion. By these criteria, neither the *Genji Monogatari* nor Rabelais' *Gargantua and Pantagruel* is a collection. Once we decide that, we are also able to say that both these examples may be collective in parts. In the *Genji Monogatari*, the second chapter, "Hahakigi" ("The Dwindle Bush"—most of these translations are my own), offers a gallery or collection of women in Uma no Kami's long disquisition. "Eawase" ("The Picture Match") presents an obvious counterpart to the poetry matches mentioned earlier. "Maboroshi" ("The Sorcerers"), the last chapter dealing with Genji, details his last year with events and poems ordered on the progression of seasons in a royal collection. We can go so far as to say—with some heightened appreciation—that "Tenarai" ("Writing Practice") offers us in title and action a non-utamonogatari, since Ukifune does not send her replies to the stream of poems presented her by others. And of course Rabelais rejoices in those lists of his, feats of enormous ingenuity, as when he sets forth that lengthy collection of games that Gargantua plays on going to the university. We are, I think, able to verify that parts of these two works are collective in nature because we are also able to falsify, to deny that the works are collective as total works. To pursue this a bit farther, it seems to me that we can say with assurance that few if any of the *individual* stories can be called collective in the *Konjaku Monogatari (Tales of Times Now Past)*, but that the whole is, as in fact we recognize in its full title, . . . *Shū (A Collection of Tales . . .)*. Similarly, if the longest works by Bakin are not collective as wholes, the *Ugetsu Monogatari (Tales of Rain and Moonlight)* by his contemporary, Ueda Akinari, unequivocally is a collection of nine stories. With such limits set to our sense of the collective principle in literature, we are able to draw comparisons with other literatures and consider the implications of what we discover.

A suitable transition to Chinese and other Japanese evidence can be found in adaptations of a Chinese collection very highly regarded in Heian times. This is a work known to Japanese as *Monzen (Wen Hsüan, Selected Compositions)*, which includes varieties of prose, rhyme-prose (fu), and poetry. The Chinese collection is distinctive for its designation of kinds for various examples (in Japanese, fu, ki, den, etc.). In 1706 there appeared a collection, *Fūzoku Monzen (The Popular Monzen)*, which used the same kind of labels for individual pieces but which was in fact a collection of haikai prose writings (haibun) of the Bashō school. By "haikai change," the elevated Chinese kinds were "lowered" to prose and to haikai. This was followed in 1718 by *Honchō Monkan* using similar classifications. From 1785 to 1823 there were published the parts of a work by Yokoi Yayū (1702-1783), *Uzuragoromo* (*Rags and Tatters)*. This work has been second in popularity among haibun only to Bashō's *Oku no Hosomichi (The Narrow Road Through the Provinces)*. For his short units, Yayū used the classifications established by the hallowed *Monzen* and by *Fūzoku Monzen*. In fact he added to them. The units themselves are chiefly made up of prose with frequent poetic conclusions—sometimes waka by others, perhaps a hokku by himself, or even his linked Chinese verse. With whatever counterexamples, it should be clear that Japanese writers from early to late classical times commonly used the collective principle to assemble large units from smaller. In their compulsion and their methods of integration, they distinguished themselves from writers in other traditions.

Chinese and Western Collections

The impulse to collect represents a human desire to preserve what is important—as tribal or sacred writings, as literature, as painting, or as other important achievements. Japanese were by no means the first people to wish to preserve. Since the Chou dynasty (sixth century B.C.), the Chinese have collected poems or songs on the principle that they exemplified the virtues or defects of rule. By the third century A.D., compilers were specifying not only authorship but topics of poems. In this period, aesthetic rather than solely moral criteria are introduced. Printing was invented in the seventh century, although it became widespread only after a lapse of four or five centuries. About the eighth or ninth century the Chinese version of the codex had come into use, and the oldest extant books (preserving much from earlier times) date from this time.

The details are special to China in certain respects. Chinese taxonomies differ from Western and even from Japanese. In particular, some writings classifiable as collections were given special status as classics (ching; J. kyō). These were held to have special moral—normally Confucian—value, although the same term was appropriated by Buddhists for sūtras (the dominant Japanese usage). In Han times (ca. 200 B.C.-A.D. 220), as early as the first century B.C., an academy had been formed and set about to tidy matters of writing. By *The New History of the T'ang Dynasty* (T'ang: 618-907), a taxonomic model had been set for ensuing histories. There were four parts: classics; history (shih; shi); philosophy (tzu; shi); and poetry in collection (ji; shū).

Poets signed themselves by styles (pen names or studio titles). Collections that are not classics were arranged both on thematic and prosodic lines. The prosodic kinds tend to be considered today as "genres," although in practice all are lyric or have lyric elements. Individual collections date from Han and Six-Dynasties (220ff.) times. In terms of official "histories," individual collections are a feature (as parts) from *The History of the Ch'ing Dynasty* (dynastic period 1616-1911). Fictional prose narratives were also collected.

By T'ang times, poetic collections may be ordered by "genre," chronology, or imputed quality. A typical anthology would have divisions by kind (e.g. fu) with chronological ordering, including dating when possible. The individual poet might issue three or four collections in a lifetime, selecting and ordering by kind (shih vs. fu), or by subject. After a poet's death, heirs or friends might reprint all as before. Or they might rearrange, perhaps changing order from the chronological to the generic. Highly popular poets such as Po Chü-i (772-846) would have their works collected during their lifetimes. Chinese sovereigns might decree anthologies, somewhat as in Japan. But in China, individual collections were more important than official anthologies. And from Sung times (960-1279), collections were often programmatic, to justify the practice of an individual, a school, or a critical concept.

Certain elementary comparisons with Japan are feasible. Collections were natural to Chinese (as well as Japanese) because of the Asian veneration of precursors and, quite simply, because of the centrality of poetic composition in the culture. In China poetry was, however, but one of four kinds of esteemed writing, none of which involved prose narrative of the Japanese monogatari kind. In fact, prose narrative and drama mature later in China than in Japan, and the nature of collections varies. Chinese examples show a desire to preserve or make some evident point. Japanese collections preserve, but they are arranged to be enjoyed as collections. There are exceptions. The *Konjaku Monogatari Shū* mentioned earlier offers a Japanese version of the Chinese-style omnibus collection, although even here there are signs of care in arrangement.

In Western antiquity, the Alexandrians began real arranging. Callimachus, an Alexandrian, is thought to have been the first Greek poet to have collected his own poems, to have revised them for his collection, and perhaps even to have written a commentary on them. The basic Greek principles of collection involve occasion or chronology and a sense of pleasing variety. Pindar's odes are divided by the kinds of occasion celebrated. Poems on the oldest games, the Olympian, are set first, and the others follow in order of institution. Another principle, exemplified by Sappho's lyrics, is division by prosodic distinctions. Greek poetry was commonly read (like Japanese and Chinese) as if autobiographical: a fictitious first edition was devised of the *Argonautica* of Appolonius of Rhodes in order to fit with the supposed life. This urge might yield to other principles, for although Hellenists did try to date Greek tragedies, the major collection of the plays by Euripides is organized alphabetically by titles. As a collection of short poems, the *Greek*

Anthology most resembles certain Japanese and Chinese collections. Unfortunately, almost nothing is known of its ordering or circulation.

As might be expected, matters become clearer and tidier with the Romans. Prose as well as poetry more often appears in Latin collections, although it is often unclear who did the collecting or what the principles were. The physical length of a (poetic) book-roll continued to determine the scope of a book in a collection, something that has a more rigorous counterpart in Japanese linked poetry than in other Japanese or Chinese collections. Roman collections vary widely from real or pretended randomness to careful integration. It is not clear who organized the love elegies of Catullus. Ovid claims that his own love elegies (*Amores*) once consisted of five books instead of the known three. But that is taken as a joke.

Certain collections bear titles suggesting variety or randomness. The title of Statius' collection, *Sylvae* (and its Greek origin in hylē, raw material), suggests random matter. Similarly, Cicero is known to have had a collection, *The Meadow (Pratum)*, which is lost. The *Attic Nights (Noctes Atticae)* of Aulus Gellius has survived and does show variety. But each of the extant, various collections also seems to be suitably ordered—e.g. the books of Martial's *Epigrams*, issued one by one.

Horace and Virgil bring more complex schemes of order. The *Odes (Carmina)* of Horace appeared in a first book that is clearly arranged with great care. When he added two more books, he managed to incorporate the first into an order for all three parts. (The fourth book is separate.) Modern classicists have made most, however, of the order of Virgil's ten *Eclogues*. Balanced or paired groups have been identified. Numerological patterning has been claimed, and is fairly well accepted that Virgil introduces an acrostic version of his name. The extent of balance in a given book or in parts of the *Aeneid* has been much disputed, but everyone seems to agree that some kind of arrangement is involved, at the very least an Odyssean first half and an Iliadic second. These variously well-ordered Roman collections and other works seem to involve two kinds of principles. The proportional, numerological, and related schemes do not go well with Japanese procedures of progression, association, rhythm, and asymmetry. On the other hand the perhaps vague but very crucial idea of a suitable ordering of various materials is shared by Roman and Japanese practice.[8]

Religious scriptures are also collections, and in the West the most fully studied collection has been the Bible, the holy writings of the Jews and the Christians. The Jewish scriptures were assembled during times of crisis from the Babylonian exile of 587 B.C. into the second century of the present era. Although often involving very old materials, the Jewish scriptures were actually fitted into a canon not much before the Christian. They were divided into three parts: "The Law" (Pentateuch, Torah), "The Prophets," and "The Writings," of which the first has remained the most important in Judaism. Each part constitutes a collection of books that are themselves collections. The book of Psalms is clearly a collection of songs, although little else is agreed upon about it except that the present version is a selection. In calling their holy writings the "New Testament," Christians appropriated the Jewish Bible as an "Old Testament." The "old" foreshadowed the "new," and Christianity was taken to have fulfilled or superseded Judaism. Christian writings were also divided into three parts: the four "Gospels" or accounts of the life of Jesus, the "Letters of Paul," and the "Writings" (e.g. the general epistles, Hebrews, and Revelation—the last nearly rejected). The present contents were effectively set in a pastoral letter that Athanasius wrote for his diocese of Alexandria in 367. New Testament studies have tended to deal with individual books rather than the whole, but it is

[8] My information about Chinese collections derives from conversation with my colleagues, F. W. Mote and Andrew Plaks. Plaks, who also reads Japanese, remarked, "But there is nothing in Chinese like the *Kokinshū*." My information about ancient Western collections comes from conversations with two other colleagues, J.E.G. Zetzel and Nita Krevans (now at Cornell University), as also from three essays in *Arethusa*, 13 (1980): John Van Sickle, "The Book-Roll and Some Conventions of the Poetic Book," pp. 5-41; Matthew S. Santorocco, "Horace's *Odes* and the Ancient Poetry Book," pp. 43-57; and Zetzel, "Horace's *Liber Sermonvm*: The Structure of Ambiguity," pp. 59-77. I also thank Thomas G. Rosenmeyer and William Anderson for their letters. The possible multiplication of citations for this and the next note must be resisted, but see the notes to the three articles mentioned here.

generally agreed that the Christian as well as the Jewish scriptures make up ordered collections.

Scriptural collections differ from literary ones in that they involve a concern with genuineness much in excess of such concern about secular writings. Literary critics sometimes speak of a canon of esteemed writings, but the literary conception of a canon is metaphorically adapted from the religious, and the grounds of genuineness differ. A poem is considered "canonical" on the basis of authorship, text, or normative standards. Sacred writings are genuine if truly holy, and commonly only by reference to transmission by a holy figure or deity. In distinction to the canonical, there are apocryphal works that may be considered well worth reading but still not specially holy, and pseudepigraphical works deemed falsely attributed to biblical figures. The Judaeo-Christian tradition makes these distinctions with more zeal, if not rigor, than Buddhists have done with their holy writings. Yet for the sutras also, there are Mahayanist groups and Hinayanist groups, with differences between such major translations as those in Pali and in Chinese. In addition to these large collections, some sutras were joined in small groupings for various reasons, with Japanese sects often compiling their own special minicollections. In addition, some sutras were broken down into units presumed integral in themselves. In short, sacred writings are established more properly into canons than are secular collections, and, although they are ordered, the ostensible end of ordering is religious rather than literary. Yet literary principles are often involved. Also any given book of the Bible, Jewish or Christian, or Buddhist sutra is itself a collection of diverse teachings and other matters.[9]

In Renaissance Europe there are numerous examples of organ-

[9] Information about the Judaeo-Christian scriptures will be found in the following studies in English: the controversial work of Morton Smith, *Palestinian Parties and Politics That Shaped the Old Testament* (New York: Columbia University Press, 1971); Otto Eissfeldt, *The Old Testament, An Introduction* (New York: Harper and Row, 1965); the collection edited by Frederick E. Greenspahn, *Scripture in the Jewish and Christian Traditions* (Nashville: Abingdon, 1982); and Robert M. Grant, *The Formation of the New Testament* (New York: Harper & Row, 1965). For these matters I am indebted to my colleague John G. Gager. The standard version of the Buddhist Tripitaka in its East Asian version is *Taishō Shinshū Daizōkyō* (*Newly Revised Tripitaka of the Taishō Era*, 1924-1932; repr. 1962) in

ized literary collections modeled in various ways and, from Petrarch to Donne, sonnet sequences that are ordered by various means. Donne's *Corona* provides an obvious example: the last line of one sonnet provides the first of the next; and the final line of the last sonnet is the same as the opening line of the first. Certain sonnet collections, Shakespeare's for example, seem quite uncertain as to order and perhaps were once ordered differently. Very complex numerological symbolism has been argued for some sonnet sequences (and for other works). Of all these arguments, the calendrical seems the clearest, as will be obvious in Spenser's *Shepherd's Calendar*, which may be complex in other ways but still clearly follows the months, much as does Yoshitada's *Maigetsu Shū* in more detail.

Two seventeenth-century English collections deserve notice. George Herbert's collection, *The Temple*, has an initial sequence of place. He begins with the "Church-Porch," goes on to the doorstep, and then into "The Church." Often there are verbal links from poem to poem, and yet more often conceptual connections. Above all, Herbert shows the trials of the Christian soul, its devotions, and its final rest in Holy Communion. At the end of the century, John Dryden collected twenty-one poems, some original with himself, most translations, in a largely narrative work twice as long as Milton's *Paradise Lost*. The title, *Fables Ancient and Modern*, is remarkably similar in meaning—ancient and modern—to that of the *Kokinshū*. His ordering, like Herbert's, uses both verbal and conceptual links (like the kotobazuke and kokorozuke of Japanese linked poetry). But his essential unifying principle is thematic and is therefore dependent on an awareness of recurrence alien to Japanese collections. Because for Japanese collections we are expected to connect one poem with the next and to presume principles of progression and rhythm—but not echoes from a poem in one part of a sequence to a poem in another.[10]

---

100 vols. See also Gerald L. Bruns, "Canon and Power in the Hebrew Scriptures," *Critical Inquiry*, 10 (1984), 462-480.

[10] I have treated Herbert's sequence and his debts to emblem sequences in *The Metaphysical Mode from Donne to Cowley* (Princeton: Princeton University Press, 1969), and Dryden's in *Fables* in *Dryden's Poetry* (Bloomington: Indiana University Press, 1967). Many other sources, mostly essays, could be cited.

From these examples, it will be clear that integrated collections are not unique to Japan. The human mind resists disorder, and when we can discover no order, we seek to invent some scheme for finding it. Two major differences can be identified between Japanese collections and the others discussed here, whether Chinese or Western. Both in China and the West, chronological arrangement is far more congenial than in Japan. A modern Western anthology of poems almost always orders the succession by the chronology of poets' lives, and the examples from a given poet's work by chronology of composition. There are some few modern Japanese collections that are so ordered, but almost no classical ones. In the West, seeming disorder may be resisted by allegory. If Ovid's *Metamorphoses* seemed pagan and confused, its fifteen books were divided in the Middle Ages into separate fables (corresponding to episodes for the most part) and then treated allegorically for "morals." Japanese have a keen sense of time and are familiar with allegory. But it will be obvious to readers of Japanese literature that neither chronology nor allegory is a principle that is called on to make sense of collections. To make our own sense of these alternatives, we must inquire into the fundamental principles of collections.

Theoretical Principles of Collections

As with trees or dangers, we can recognize collections when we encounter them, but we find it difficult to explain what it is that we have seen. One easy distinction divides literary collections from those of furniture or paintings. Furniture or paintings may be collected at home for private use and enjoyment. Literary collections as we have been considering them resemble, much more, public libraries and art museums. That is, literary collections are meant to be available, in some degree to make public a number of poems, plays, or prose stories. For both the private and the public collections, mess or order may be in evidence. But for utility's sake, some kind of order will almost always be in use, even if it is not evident at first.

Literary collections also seem to differ from editions. An edition not only makes a collection public but is likely to introduce the works collected, establish a useful or accurate text, and explain what requires glossing. An edition has, therefore, additional purposes. An art museum may hang a given collection. To make clear the terms of that collection a catalogue will probably be produced to explain it. The assembled pictures resemble a collection of poems or stories. The catalogue resembles an edition. All these examples have in common diverse materials arranged in some suitable fashion.

Nothing said so far about literary collections enables us to say that a long poem like the *Aeneid* or a long prose work like the *Genji Monogatari* is not a collection. They also offer "diverse materials arranged in some suitable fashion." There may be some gain in deliberately misreading the *Genji Monogatari* or the *Aeneid* as a collection. But there is no gain from misreading when we are trying to understand what differentiates the *Genji Monogatari* from the *Konjaku Monogatari Shū*. All literary works of any length are assemblages of diverse matter. The difference between a collection and a narrative like the *Genji Monogatari* is that a collection brings together units that are supposed to be (or resemble being) capable of being appreciated in themselves as wholly discrete units, even if their meaning or beauty may be heightened by their being collected. In fact, it is in the nature of a collection normally construed that its constituents were not written with the knowledge that they would be included at just this point in a sequence of poems or stories and that there should be other candidates for a place in the collection. In addition, the piece collected might be written by only one person or one collaboration, whereas various compilers can collect that piece again and again in different collections.

A collection of stories like the *Yamato Monogatari (Tales of Yamato)* does have a sequence of units, but there is no story line running throughout that sequence (although there is in the individual stories). Whatever a story line may be, it involves the continuity of a group of characters, a chronological series, spatial matters. We observe that a given story line can be told in a variety of sequences. It can be rearranged. That is well shown by various retellings of myths, which may be begun at this or that point, and any necessary antecedent materials can be introduced later in retrospect. In fact a lengthy narrative will invariably disorder the continuous chronology, sometimes to very great extremes (e.g. Milton's *Paradise Lost*). Changing the sequence in which a story is related will change its emphasis, its meaning. But it need not change the story line at all, if necessary ingredients are kept. On the other hand, any change in a sequence by definition changes it. This shows us that sequence is a radical of literary extension more primitive or basic than story line and so (as we shall see) logically prior to it. It will be further evident that this distinction matters, because Japanese collections have sequential properties but not story lines.

The usual English term for story line is plot, normally translated into Japanese as suji. The implications of the two terms differ, however. Western plots are used to stress occurrence, causality, agency, and responsibility. Various Japanese suji may function so, but they are used far more to emphasize sequential flow, connection, association, and arrangement. Suji obviously resembles the arranged sequentiality of a collection more than a plot does. The causal implications of plots involve a given motive that leads a character to certain behavior. The actual sequence in which the plot of that motive-behavior event is narrated may, however, be a counterlogical one in which the author presents the effect (behavior) before its cause (motivation). This is particularly the case when an author desires to build up suspense: why did that happen? In logic and in life, no effect can precede its cause. But by use of memory, recollection, anticipation, and analysis we can make full literary sense of what is not logical in the sequence of the plot. Or again, two or more events may occur at the same time (as we see in the *Odyssey* and the *Genji Monogatari*), both in logic and in life, provided only that they happen to different people in different places. Such are the greater constraints on sequence than on plot, however, that two events occurring simultaneously cannot be narrated simultaneously in the necessary sequentiality of literature. One must be told before (or after) the other. These illustrations show that, *even in a plotted story*, sequence is a more fundamental radical than plot.

All kinds of verbal (and some other kinds of) expression are necessarily sequential, since if we are presented with all the words of the *Kokinshū* at once we shall hear only noise, just as words spaced infinitely in a sequence would give one sound followed by everlasting silence. In other words, all verbal expression is continuous in its telling or reading, although to be intelligible a long literary continuity will have numerous discontinuities (episodes, chapters, sentences, etc.). The element of discontinuity is stronger in a collection than in a plot. The stories in a setsuwa collection are sequential both as a collection of stories and as individually told stories. But the individual story has an integrity whose close marks a more decisive discontinuity than any in its story proper. Whether we think of a sequence in a collection or of a sequence in a story we know the elements of discontinuity and continuity by recognizing beginnings and endings. Lesser endings such as those of a clause or a sentence or an episode may have great importance, but their importance is one within the integral continuity of the sequence. The very beginning and the very ending are more radical, marking as it were the boundaries of the integrity of the sequence. When one unit is found to have ended, another is found to begin, until of course the sequence is taken to have ended.

If we ask whether continuity or discontinuity, beginning or ending, is the more decisive element, the answer should be apparent. Something can end only if it has begun, and only that which has been continued may be discontinued. Indeed, as we read through a sequence (whether with or without a story) we can never be wholly certain that a sequence, or a subunit of the sequence, *has* ended until we have established that a new something has begun. Some of the longer and early poems in the *Man'yōshū* adhere to a prosody in which a short line is followed by a long line in repetition. But there are also passages in which we suddenly find two short lines and then the longer. We discover that we must delay closing the expected sequential unit until we understand that it has ended by determining that a new unit has begun. What is so simple in this example will be found more complex in nō, where constituent elements (e.g. nanori, michiyuki, kuse) may be lengthened or abbreviated, sometimes be repeated, and sometimes be omitted. For a work as lengthy and as complex as the *Genji Monogatari*, it is no doubt impossible to give an adequate account of the conditions for its totality of beginnings and endings, of continuity and discontinuity.

Modern Western literary theory has made much of a distinction between the diachronic (that understood sequentially, i.e. temporally, serially) and the synchronic (that understood apart from the diachronic). As literary history has come to seem an invalid and useless study, criticism has made more and more of the synchronic understanding. Leaving aside various excesses in this attention to the nondiachronic, the synchronic accounts for the way by which we derive meaning from elements in the diachronic sequence of our experience of reading a work. Without a synchronic understanding (i.e. exercise of memory, anticipation, and synthesis), we would have, as it were, words unconnected, unrelated, all apart: nonsense. Yet this synchronic understanding depends on experience or knowledge gained diachronically. Once again we must observe logical priority: any synchrony depends on diachrony, just as plot depends on sequence, discontinuity on continuity, and ending on beginning. Linguists have aired similar issues.[11]

What we term synchronic is actually not a property of the sentence or novel but of actions of our minds, of mental operations as we pursue the verbal expression diachronically, serially (also matters of our minds). By use of memory, comparison, analysis, synthesis, and affect we are able to extract a something, a "whatness" that is a "synchronic" characteristic of that individual diachronic sequence. Simple seriality or sequentiality can hardly be a mental operation in isolation, for it would not allow us to dis-

[11] See Roman Jakobson and Krystyna Pomorska, "Dialogue on Time and Language in Literature," *Poetics Today*, 2 (1980), 15-27. Jakobson is concerned with the synchronic as the state of the language at a given time, and the diachronic as the changing character of the language. He argues that Saussure's rejection of diachrony "had categorically to be overcome" (p. 16).

tinguish one royal collection like the *Kokinshū* from another such as the *Shinkokinshū*. To say that our understanding of the diachronic or serial element of literature is logically prior to, and the foundation of, synchronic understanding of the whole or major parts is not to say that the synchronic is unimportant. By the same token, the fact that our understanding of discontinuity depends on our understanding of continuity does not deprive discontinuity of importance to use.

These distinctions show why collections are fundamentally more discontinuous than are single integral units such as a complete long poem or long prose story.[12] The kinds and relative importance of diachrony and synchrony differ in a collection from in a long story. The total purpose of a collection such as the *Konjaku Monogatari Shū* is to present the best and most edifying stories. The total purpose of a long story like the *Genji Monogatari* is to realize the greatest single-multiple complexity consistent with the serial presentation. Like the other matters discussed, this becomes obvious on reflection. But without making such theoretical distinctions we could hardly appreciate the special nature of Japanese collections.

Principles of Japanese Collections

Collective means of integration are simply more important to Japanese than other peoples. No other country of which I know makes so much of those collections, compendia, or dictionaries that usually go under the name of jiten. There are literary compendia (bungaku jiten), historical compendia (rekishi jiten), Buddhist compendia (bukkyō jiten), and so on and on including dolls (ningyō

[12] I would like it understood throughout that I consider the elements discussed here to be properties of our knowledge rather than of "texts." Continuities and discontinuities are things *we* know, and since texts are physical codings, they cannot properly be said to begin or end, to continue or discontinue. The distinction is literalist, probably pedantic, but it avoids the absurdity of much current Western personification of "texts" that are said to demand and to do other things that only human agents can do, even read themselves.

jiten).[13] There are standard collections of collections, as for waka poetry in *Kokka Taikei* or *Kokka Taikan* and its sequel, *Zoku Kokka Taikan*. (Surely there is no other country in which publishers bring out rival editions of dictionaries of old forms of the language [kogo jiten]?) These modern compendia had earlier counterparts. In the late Edo period, the 530 volumes or parts of *Gunsho Ruijū* were published (1779-1818) and a bit later the sequel in 1,000 volumes, *Zoku Gunsho Ruijū* (1822). We have seen that the first works of Japanese literature to appear are collections, and before them the most valued early books brought to Japan were Buddhist sutras, often in collections, and themselves collections. From ancient times to the present, Japan has been a nation devoted to collections. What other culture has so refined the poetic collection? What other nation distinguishes literary period by collections? Every Japanese responds to the Man'yō period (jidai), Kokin period, and Shinkokin period.

The more closely one looks at Japanese literature, the more extensive appears the practice of collection: again, a work need not have a title ending in shū to be a collection. *Minashiguri* is as much a seventeenth-century haikai collection as is *Sarumino Shū*. More than that, major kinds of literature not usually considered collections are such by any definition that I can conceive. There is zuihitsu, for which no exact English word exists (Japanese conceptions have varied over the years). Today the narrow sense of the term holds that it includes Sei Shōnagon's *Makura no Sōshi (The Pillow Book)*, Kamo no Chōmei's *Hōjōki (A Record of My Hut)*, and Yoshida Kenko's *Tsurezuregusa (Idle Jottings)*. We might (of course!) examine in the library a zuihitsu jiten that lists hundreds and hundreds of titles. But to stay with the narrower range, the three works named have in common their being collections of observations made by a single author. On such grounds, one cannot rule out Bashō's *Genjūan no Ki (Record of the Unreal Hermitage)*,

[13] An illustration: in his brief piece, "Compendia and I," Sugiura Mimpei writes of his lasting fondness for jiten. "Even now I like compendia [jisho]. It is not just dictionaries, but *The Encyclopedia of Japanese History*, *The Catholic Encyclopedia*, or biographical dictionaries—when you have them lined up on the shelf, somehow they engender a reassuring mood" ("Watashi to Jisho," *Hon*, 1981, no. 8, p. 27).

or, for that matter, what he called his "michi no nikki" (diaries of the road) such as *Oku no Hosomichi*.[14] If so, we must also include the diary literature of the court. In fact, there is no rule observable in Japan that collections must be made by a single person (those of waka are not) or represent a single point of view. For example, Nijō Yoshimoto's *Kyūshū Mondō (Kyushu Dialogues)* is not a single-piece work, and if Yoshimoto's work is a zuihitsu collection, there is no reason to exclude Chōmei's *Mumyōshō (Nameless Treatise)* any more than his *Hōjōki*, which is always included.

In short, collections make up a far higher proportion of Japanese literature than even Japanese themselves realize. That fact implies a relative lack of distinction between collections and noncollections. In an earlier section it was remarked that we can distinguish collections from editions. In England there are collections from the Middle Ages onward, but literary editions do not appear from English hands until the late seventeenth century, and then of Latin writers. Editions of Shakespeare, Milton, Dryden, and others appear only with the eighteenth century. (There is one exception: Chaucer, edited from the sixteenth century.) In Japan the distinction is harder to make. The *Man'yōshū*, the first poetic collection (eighth century), shows symptoms of editing in the interpolation of alternative textual readings, in the footnote commentaries on possible authorship or source from a previous collection, and in the obvious pains taken by Ōtomo Yakamochi to get good texts of provincial poems. For that matter, in the two prefaces to the first royal collection, the *Kokinshū*, we find theoretical, historical, and interpretive matter unlike anything in an Elizabethan collection such as *Tottle's Miscellany* or even in Ben Jonson's very careful presentation of his *Works*.

The inclusive point is clear. Some matters less clear may be more important, and for them the best evidence derives from the most obvious and most prestigious collections: the royal anthol-

[14] Eleanor Kerkham informs me that Bashō and his contemporaries referred to *Oku no Hosomichi* as a collection. Her forthcoming study of the work may touch on such matters. Meanwhile, it is quite clear that the second most popular example of haibun, Yayū's *Uzuragoromo*, is a collection by any definition.

ogies. We have seen that, although modern collections, especially in the West, are usually ordered chronologically, premodern Western and Chinese collections normally are not. The twenty-one royal collections beginning with the *Kokinshū* (ca. 905-920) may *use* chronology but *are not governed* by it. The six books of seasonal poems in a twenty-part collection followed seasonal chronology (from the beginning to the end of the year). They do not follow the chronology of the poets, beginning with the earliest and printing in succession all the poems included by that poet. (As a game or gesture, the Travel poems of the *Shinkokinshū* are arranged in part chronologically.) The chronology respected is that of the topics of the poems related to the temporal succession of the seasons.

The redisposal of poems by a single poet is equally marked among Love poems. The usual explanation for these four or five books holds that they begin with the man's point of view as he feels some agitation on learning of a desirable woman. The sequence goes on to his initiating correspondence and exchange of poems with the woman. There comes a love meeting. After that, the woman's view prevails. She waits for her lover to visit her. She regrets the increasing rarity of his visits, and regret turns to resentment and anguish over betrayal, and perhaps last of all a sudden recollection of a man she had otherwise forgot. In practice, however, matters are more complex. There is the greater fluctuation, agitation of renewed meetings and new partings. The man's view may enter at a very late stage.

The reasons for such agitation include the ever-shifting point of view. Each poem has a speaker with a viewpoint, but each poem has a different speaker. The resentful women of poems 1007 and 1008 are different women. The integration of the collections involves progressions from poem to poem and associations aroused by the progressions.[15] But there is no plot—only sequence. Western sonnet sequences and similar collections commonly employ a

[15] On the integration of the royal collections, see Konishi Jin'ichi, "Association and Progression: Principles of Integration in Anthologies and Sequences of Japanese Court Poetry, A.D. 900-1350," *Harvard Journal of Asiatic Studies*, 21 (1958), 67-127. This article has no exact counterpart in Japanese.

single "point of view" in a fashion that endows an *integrated* sequence with plot: the same speaker/narrator, the same other characters, the same general place, and a continuous temporal series. The integrity of the sequence of a waka collection is a principle that requires honoring topics more than plot or the canons of individual poets.

In this respect as well, renga and haikai resemble the *Kokinshū* model. The speaker imagined in a given connection of two stanzas is determined by that stanza added (tsukeku) to its predecessor (maeku), the two making up a new poetic unit (also termed tsukeku). With the addition, the new speaker may differ from the prior speaker (which had been determined just before by the now maeku) in age, sex, or other condition. In both waka and linked-poetry sequences, semantic connection of any plotted kind (character in time and place) breaks with each five-line unit. If units separated by twenty others seem alike, there is no semantic connection. None at all. There is no parallel, no motif, no recollection of an earlier similar image, no synchrony.[16]

In traditional Western literature we expect consistency in narratorship, or at least that has been the usual view. In Japanese collections we find that single identifiable personality dispersed in favor of multiple personality and narratorship on the individual level and integrity assumed to exist at the collective level. This strong tendency in Japanese literature is least visible in prose narratives (monogatari) and drama (nō—except for the shite role—jōruri, and kabuki). The *Genji Monogatari* certainly has a plot and a chief female narrator. But even here we observe a serial tendency in the relative absence of group scenes. (Major early Chinese prose narratives commonly portray many characters at a time.) Genji seems to visit women one by one, and they never seem to meet each other, even while living "together" in his Rokujō palace. Within a single sentence (or period or whatever the basic prose unit is taken to be), the narrator may move from one character's

[16] Haikai has a few exceptions. For example, in their duo, *Shi Akindo no Maki (Poetry Is What I Sell)*, Bashō and Kikaku almost repeat the first two stanzas in the last two. The few examples of such exceptions that I know involve beginnings and endings and all are in haikai rather than in renga or waka.

mind to another's, and from one character's remarks to another's. In fact, the point of view often seems neutral, involving both that of the narrator and of a given character or characters. The same thing occurs in a poetic diary like the *Izumi Shikibu Nikki (The Diary of Izumi Shikibu).* Similar things go on in nō, where very few characters are involved in encounters, commonly only two. A given character (or the chorus speaking on behalf of the leading character) may well step out of role to speak as if another character or to speak in the third person of the self.[17] It will be abundantly clear that Japanese literary collections represent assumptions at variance from Western collections.

Ideological Implications

To understand the implications of collections, we require conceptions even stricter than those defining a collection. If we do not, we may make such errors as presuming that Japanese literature includes nothing but collections, or that Japanese society is a collection in which individuals do not exist. There must be important implications of so striking a feature of Japanese literature, and something will be said here about a few that seem important as well as strictly definable. Consideration of some poetic collections will demonstrate their implicit ideological significance.

"Ideology" means many things. In what follows a very narrow definition will be used: ideology is the connection between literary collections and the power status of those who promote or compile them.[18] Those who deal with political philosophy agree that success requires both power and legitimacy. Certain acts, that is, certain codes or symbols or rites, legitimize power and provide it its ideological basis. In traditional societies, the establishment of power

[17] For examples, see Benkei's speech in *Ataka* on being asked for the subscription list and the endings of *Matsukaze* and *Tadanori.* See the chapter by Noguchi on narratorial procedures in the *Genji Monogatari.*

[18] Further discussion of the ideological features of classical Japanese literature will be dealt with in an essay ranging beyond collections and providing evidence from earlier and, in particular, from later times.

is often demonstrated by the founding of cities or courts, usually with a sacred center and economic or military advantage in the location.[19] The sacred center provides one kind of legitimizing. Laws may provide another. The institution of survey of the country (census and other procedures) both celebrates the ruler and provides ways of taxing or otherwise controlling the population. Japanese assigned little practical or symbolic importance to those walls that were so important in Europe (see Virgil, *Aeneid*, 1, 137). But the Romans were also keen on laws (*Aeneid*, 6, 809ff.; 12, 821ff.). In the West there are many such instances, as with the Code of Hammurabi and the Ten Commandments conveyed by Moses to his people.

Legal codes matter in Japan, but collections are also of wider ideological significance. They were used to celebrate or legitimize power, to console those who once had power, or to proffer a claim by those who aspired to power. That series represents, more or less, the historical sequence of the ideological implications of literary collections from earliest times to the end of classical literature. To cover so long a period in a rapid discussion would distort the balance of this inquiry. Perhaps it will be enough to deal with the evidence offered by the twenty-one royal collections, leaving earlier and later evidence for another occasion.

It is an exaggeration, but a pardonable one, to say that in the Heian period the tennō (now all male) reigned and a select group of the Fujiwara house ruled in the sovereign's name. The chief changes during the period of the twenty-one collections involved attempts to make substitutions for the Fujiwara and other hegemons. Given such historical circumstances, it is no accident that the first of the royal collections was compiled under the aegis of Daigo (r. 897-930), who became a model and a source of envy to his successors.

During the earlier reign of Seiwa (858-876), the ingenious Fujiwara succeeded in establishing two new court positions: that of sesshō or regent for a young sovereign, and that of kampaku or chancellor to "advise" a sovereign come of age. By these means

[19] See Paul Wheatley on the ancient Chinese city, *The Pivot of the Four Quarters* (Chicago: Aldine, 1971), a fascinating study.

the Fujiwara noblemen could control young tennō by getting them betrothed to their daughters. Since the next tennō would then be their grandson, and since family obligations were what they were, the Fujiwara got things their own way—most of the time and for some while.

Like his father, Uda (r. 887-897), Daigo sought to rule as well as to reign. For much of his reign he succeeded, at least symbolically. By playing off a powerful non-Fujiwara minister (none other than Sugawara Michizane, who features in the first quotation in this discussion) and the current Fujiwara potentates, he succeeded in neutralizing Fujiwara power for a time. In fact, after the first six or seven years of his long reign he did without regent or chancellor, a long continuance that had not happened for many reigns and would not happen again till modern times.

Anyone acquainted with earlier strong sovereigns would not be surprised to discover that Daigo prosecuted his reign with a series of remarkable collections. These began with history, the *Nihon Sandai Jitsuroku (The Actual History of Three Japanese Reigns).* As many have observed, the power to write authoritative history is a major feature of legitimizing rule. This collection may not be one of the major Japanese histories, but it served Daigo's purpose. By 921, he saw to it that the sacred court dances, or kagura, had been collected into a fixed repertoire. By 927 he had had compiled what may collectively be termed his *Engi Codes: Engi Kyakushiki, Engi Shiki,* and *Engi Kotaishiki.* In the first or second decade of the tenth century, he decreed and received the first of the twenty-one royally ordered collections, the *Kokinshū.*

We have already observed the genius and the influence of this collection. In addition, no other collection has held a similar place in court culture. When the nation was on the verge of collapse in civil warfare, Hosokawa Yūsai (1534-1610)—a political figure, warrior, waka poet, and critic—regarded his learning about the *Kokinshū* (Kokin denju) as not only his most valued possession but a sacred national treasure. As he prepared to do battle at momentous Sekigahara, he feared that this learning might be lost with his life. He took pains to transmit it to someone at the center of the court that had devised it, Prince Toshihito Hachijō no Miya.

In fact, much of that learning appears to have consisted of sterile rules and pendantic facts, but the point is that even on the eve of Ieyasu's seizing military control of Japan, the symbolic value of the *Kokinshū* conferred prestige and legitimacy upon the possessor. Waka would continue to be thought the central poetic art of Japan, even if creative energies had already passed to renga and would shortly be exemplified in haikai. It is no accident whatsoever that the fifth, and most highly regarded of the seven official collections of the Bashō school of haikai, *Sarumino*, should have been called by the school "the *Kokinshū* of haikai" (haikai no *Kokinshū*).

Over the centuries Japanese scholars have dealt with some of the things just mentioned and a myriad of others besides in their devoted scholarly study of the anthology ordered by Daigo. Yet they seem to have overlooked one of the simplest facts about the *Kokinshū*. It is anything but a Fujiwara collection, as later royal anthologies would become. There is not a single Fujiwara among its compilers. The only other possible designation for it, other than its proper title, would be one bearing Daigo's designation of his famous regnal era: the *Engi Shū*. By an agreement, if only tacit, between him and his compilers, the poets featured are chiefly those great earlier poets such as Ariwara Narihira (825-880) and Ono no Komachi (fl. ca. 850), along with contemporaries who either are not Fujiwara or, if Fujiwara, are chiefly those whom the powerful, select Fujiwara had squeezed out of main power. There are only about twenty named Fujiwara poets represented (there may have been others whose poems are designated anonymous). Of these twenty, all but three are people of low rank who might as well not have been Fujiwara, and in fact only one of those three held really high rank.

Daigo's success in personal rule was not complete and brought only a temporary challenge to, a diminution of, Fujiwara control. During the course of the next six royal collections, Fujiwara poets came to matter more and more, including among them many of the most important poets. Daigo's success remained a model for later sovereigns, however, and many of them chafed under domination by the Fujiwara. The highly capable Gosanjō (1034-1073) sought to counter Fujiwara power by working with the non-Fujiwara nobleman, Minamoto Tsunenobu (1016-1097), himself a gifted poet. But it was Gosanjō's son and successor, Shirakawa (r. 1072-1086), who devised a means to evade Fujiwara dominance. This was the insei or system of cloistered sovereigns, in which a given tennō would resign his ritualized rule after reaching maturity and then seek to exert some portion of real power from his cloistered position. As Shirakawa In, he thus managed to recapture for the royal house a degree of influence it had not enjoyed for many reigns. It is to be expected that such a new system of rule would produce innovations in the royal collections. Shirakawa In, whose period of cloistered rule extended from 1086 to 1129, ordered a collection toward the end of his life. He commissioned the son of Tsunenobu, the gifted if somewhat eccentric Minamoto Shunrai (or Toshiyori, ?1059-1129) to compile a collection that had several new features. One was its new and fancy name, *Kin'yōshū (Collection of Golden Leaves)*. A more radical departure was the brevity of the collection—only 716 poems, and in ten rather than twenty books. The contents were also new in some ways, including such things as a dozen or so tanrenga (short renga; in reality a waka written by two people). And Shirakawa In played a determined role in effecting the collection, rejecting at least two versions before being satisfied. The next collection followed somewhat similar lines. The retired Sutoku (1119-1164) commissioned the *Shikashū* (completed ca. 1151-1154), also in ten books and the shortest of the twenty-one royal collections with but 411 poems. The compiler he chose was Fujiwara Akisuke (1090-1155), a highly conservative poet and critic. But Sutoku seems to have ensured that there be good representation of innovating, non-Fujiwara poets, particularly Shunrai and Sone no Yoshitada (fl. ca. 985).

The political situation had become extremely volatile. Military insurrections had become common. Over a period of ten reigns the Taira and the Minamoto warlords were struggling to gain supremacy, with the Minamoto or Genji winning out and establishing a military government, bakufu, in Kamakura late in the twelfth century. The political situation was now complex and dangerous for the court, and in this heated atmosphere there emerged the highly gifted, ambitious, and nervous Gotoba (1180-1239).

When he came to reign at the age of three (r. 1183-1198), he was obviously in no position to become an instant Daigo or Shirakawa. But he abdicated as soon as he could, becoming Gotoba In and arbiter of the court for the next three reigns (1198-1221). Talented in poetry and music, he left behind a diary, poetic collections, critical writings, and above all, the eighth royal collection, the *Shinkokinshū* (completed in 1206, with later revisions). This is usually thought to include more great poetry than any other of the twenty-one royal collections. Gotoba was clearly a gifted, highly ambitious man.

Between him and his dreams of power, however, there now stood the bakufu in Kamakura, controlling much of the land. Foolishly hopeful that he could outwit the bakufu, Gotoba In plotted to overthrow it by allying himself with dissident military figures. The attempt was easily quelled by the bakufu. Gotoba and two tennō were sent into exile, where he continued to tinker with, or perfect, the poetic monument to his reign, the *Shinkokinshū*. This is the first of the twenty-one collections to use "new" (*Shin-*) in its title, and it is no accident that, in ideological terms, Gotoba had cast himself as a new Daigo and arranged to have a "New *Kokinshū*."

The next or ninth collection was compiled solely by Fujiwara Teika (1162-1241), one of Japan's three or four greatest poets and one of the several compilers of Gotoba's collection. Not that Teika and Gotoba got on very well. Teika agreed completely with nobody. What mattered most to him was, apart from the self-interest that we observe in all others but ourselves, his poetic art. He had the wit to see that Gotoba was headed for trouble. Earlier, during the Gempei wars, the great struggle between the Taira and Minamoto, he had echoed in his diary Po Chü-i's observation that the wars of the red and the white banners (of the two clashing houses) were no affair of his. The collection he put together was called the *Shinchokusenshū*. In the "Shin" he perhaps recalled for any who needed reminder that he had played a major role in compiling the *Shinkokinshū*. The rest of his title ("chokusenshū") emphasized that he (the first person to be a compiler of two collections) was offering a generic royal collection, since "chokusenshū" designates as much. If he hoped that his title would spare him criticism, he hoped in vain. Tongues wagged at court: Teika had included too many poems by writers from warrior families and the bakufu. Teika had his eye on his own interests. But he also had his eye on reality, understanding what Gotoba and others failed to realize: hereafter waka collections were to be founded on compromise with the military powers in an ideology of accommodation or they would have no feasible ideology, no realistic accommodation with power at all.

As we have been seeing, the political implications of royal collections were becoming very complicated as the gradual realignment of power created enormous social tensions. To add to the court's other troubles, problems of succession arose. The impatient potentates directing the bakufu (by now even the shoguns were being ruled by nominal advisers) decided with no doubt irritated practicality simply to alternate tennō from the two claimant lines. From 1336 to 1392, the rivalry was so serious as to give the period a name, Nambokuchō (the period of Northern and Southern Courts). The northern was the weaker of the two, and like the southern it advanced the claim not only to sovereignty but also to have the true poetic heritage from Teika. Weaker politically as it was, the northern was stronger in poetic quality, and the last two royal collections of real consequence were compiled by adherents to the northern line and to creative interpretation of Teika's legacy.

A partisan of both the political and poetic hopes of the northern line, Kyōgoku Tamekane (1254-1332) was ordered in 1311 by Fushimi In (r. 1287-1298) to compile the fourteenth collection. It is a testimony to his enormous energy and poetic as well as political purposes, that Tamekane should have succeeded so quickly (by 1313 or 1314) in completing the *Gyokuyōshū*, much the largest of the twenty-one collections. He gave it a fresh kind of title, a new perfection of ordering—and an ideology of forlorn hopes for power that recall Gotoba's. Tamekane succeeded with his collection; he also succeeded in being banished, recalled, and banished yet again.

One of the most artistically talented of all tennō, Hanazono (r. 1308-1318), saw into existence the last important royal waka collection. This is the seventeenth, the *Fūgashū*. It had long been thought that Hanazono himself compiled the collection, something now known to be literally untrue. He had the compiling done by Kōgon (r. 1332-1333), the first of the separate northern tennō. Hanazono did supervise the work carefully, and from his mind and brush came both the Japanese and Chinese prefaces, making the *Fūgashū* one of the few collections to resemble the *Kokinshū* in having both. His efforts show his literary talents (well demonstrated in the collection) and his ideological insight. His talents are otherwise testified to by his skill in various Japanese and Chinese studies, his learning in Zen Buddhism, and his abilities as calligrapher and also as painter. His insight would be clear if only from his diary, *Hanazono In Tennō Shinki*, which remains one of the most valuable historical resources for knowledge of his time. Along with other evidence, the title for what we may term his collection shows that he understood what Gotoba and Tamekane could not. The court's role is now almost as much arbiter of art and culture (*Fūga-*) as it is a legitimizing agent for noncourt sources of power that it was otherwise nearly powerless to control. This is truly an elegant (Fūga-) collection (-shū), a model of the sober insight, the acute and elegant ideology of its conceiver.

The ideological and poetic wisdom of Hanazono came too tardily to save waka from precipitous decline, and the remaining four royal collections show that the political situation was out of anyone's hand. The last two of the twenty-one were royally ordered, but at the request of the ambitious Ashikaga shoguns. The twentieth, the *Shingoshūishū*, was completed in 1383 or 1384. The twenty-first, the *Shinzokukokinshū*—a title appropriately enough recalling Daigo's first collection in the last—was completed in 1439. For these two, there is what appears to be a wholesome connection that unites the tennō ordering the collection, the shoguns requesting them, and the nobility writing prefaces. For the *Shingoshūishū*, Nijō Yoshimoto wrote a Japanese preface, and for the *Shinzokukokinshū* Ichijō Kanera (1402-1481) provided both a Japanese and a Chinese preface. Yoshimoto and Kanera held court titles (such as regent and chancellor) reserved to a restricted few Fujiwara families. Like Hanazono, they were genuinely learned, and they genuinely esteemed poetry. Moreover, they well understood the political realities to which an ideology must accommodate power. They knew that their institutions and culture could survive only by reaching out to a far wider world than any individual except Hanazono had conceived. But the problems were insuperable.

The court had become so demoralized that in poetry it could only cling to the hollow conventions of the past. And the wretched nation was so breaking into anarchy that the Ashikaga shoguns similarly sought after the forms of power to the extent that they could not realize them in actuality. No amount of wisdom could alter the fact that Japan was now less one country than many disputed territories. The best people at court were wiser than people in other possible positions of legitimacy and power. But the court was wise too late, and the other powerful groups were so dispersed, so anarchic that chaos followed. Yoshimoto had the remarkable insight to see, almost against the grain of so highborn a person, that renga offered new alternatives. But the vitality of any central ideology including waka and power was dead.

This account of the ideology implicit in the twenty-one royal collections may perhaps seem too detailed for a single essay on collections, or too brief to honor the many complexities.[20] Certainly the evidence available could begin with those collections that initiate Japanese literature and continue on throughout so-called classical literature into the modern times formally said to begin in 1867 or 1868. In view of the importance of Japanese collections as argued here, a little further may be said by way of comparison. When Wordsworth and Coleridge published *Lyrical Ballads* in 1798 (and again with Wordsworth's preface in 1800), there must have been ideological implications in the wake of the French Revolution, as there certainly were poetic implications in the so-to-speak inauguration of the Romantic age in English literature. But

[20] I have not troubled the reader with numerous citations in this discussion of the ideology of waka collections because, although I am unaware of any Japanese account that has brought these details together, each of the matters is very familiar to any person who has studied the nature and history of the twenty-one royal collections. To Konishi Jin'ichi I owe suggestions about the *Kin'yōshū* and *Shikashū*; his suggestions have helped me strengthen my argument.

no one has succeeded in establishing that important collection as the name of a literary period, as Japanese speak of the age of the *Kokinshū* and *Shinkokinshū*. If that is true of the most famous of English poetic collections, the reason must be that it lacks comparable ideological significance. If Japanese collections have greater ideological meaning, it can only be because collections are of so much greater importance to Japanese thinking. The politically ideological basis can only rest on other, more central grounds in Japanese ways of thought.

For ease in understanding those grounds, we must leave ideology as an explicit subject, although the discussion of the royal collections should show that in Japan collections are not merely bringings together of poems or prose works. They imply far more than do their Western counterparts and, in turning from ideology, we may well inquire into what the collections imply on other terms. Those can only involve conceptions of units, relations between them, and the wholes they constitute. These, too, are matters more readily recognized than explained. They involve relative rather than absolute matters, and danger lies equally in claiming too much and in discovering too little. In what follows, it may not be amiss to begin with the simple and proceed to larger, if relative, matters.

The Individual and the Collective

Every Western reader of Japanese poetry is struck by the relative brevity of poetic forms and by the tendency of those formal units to become briefer.[21] This simple fact implies that Japanese conceptions of literary integers differ from Western ones, and no doubt many people have drawn, or might draw, inferences about some Japanese inability to think in grand terms. It is a major purpose of this discussion to discourage such ready inferences, because the full evidence reveals that there is a conception of collective integers, of large, composite wholes that the very brevity of the poetic units

[21] See Konishi, *History of Japanese Literature*, vol. 1, 10-12, for discussion of the point and for a significant context.

either made possible or was in fact responsible for encouraging: that conception promoted, as it were, one kind of brevity so that another kind of extension would be feasible. To put matters differently, the brief unit is brief because it is not accorded the independent existence that Westerners assume formal poetic integers to possess. By being less discrete, independent, separate, a formal unit is considered to find its true function in a collective whole. Or, in complementary terms, because composite wholes of integrated elements are assumed, no single constituent example is allowed a Western scope. Although this discussion has dealt chiefly with poetic collections, the same features can be observed in numerous other kinds of literature, of art, and of Japanese social thought.

With the very necessary caveat that these are relative matters and open to important exceptions as, I believe, is shown by lengthy prose narratives, we may postulate certain distinctive features of the individual entities of Japanese literature. Such entities are presumed to be:

1. interdependent, not discrete;
2. varied, not equal in status;
3. defined by relation to other also unequal units and to a larger, composite whole;
4. defined by relation to each other and their composite whole rather than to some external principles (such as chronology of composition, single-author canons, etc.); and
5. "adhesive" in being relatable to elements not the same in nature (prose to verse, verse to pictures, pictures to prose, etc.).

The features of units imply counterpart features of the wholes they can constitute. Or we must infer that the counterpart of brief units is a tendency the reverse of brevity, a tendency to aggregating, relating—and, in a word, to collecting. Units highly integral in such Western schemes as epics or novels are at once more themselves, more discrete and independent, and yet more unified (than collective). Whether character, episode, or an entire novel, discreteness, independence, and unity tend to be characteristic of

Western literature in comparison with Japanese. To use an analogy, in Western literature there is, as in Western democracy, a unity of equals, or to speak perhaps more accurately, a fruitful tension between coexisting ideals of unity and of equal, separate individuals. By comparison, the constituents of Japanese literature are unequal, the connections between them are relational, and the relation between them and the whole is composite, collective (rather than uniform). We see this in the easy joining of prose and verse in the *Kojiki*, and thereafter in numerous other versions. Linked poetry—renga and haikai no renga—shows this most clearly. We must read serially: there is no Western-style subordinating unity, and therefore semantic sense goes stanza to stanza rather than being derived from a synchronically perceived entity. Moreover, the highest art is that of stanza relation (tsukeai), which involves joining a stanza to its predecessor by varying its formal impressiveness, degree of closeness of relation, topic, or motifs. In this sense stanzas are perhaps conventionally or prosodically alike, but they are *functionally* unequal, and the whole is a composite with an emphasis on radical sequence unusual even in Japanese collections outside of poetry. To use another analogy, in Japanese society there is far greater gradation in status of individual people and a far stronger sense of relation (when there is relation) of one to another, and more particularly of one to the group. Independence-unity is a dominant Western ontological concept. The individual-collective is the counterpart Japanese ontological concept. The Japanese concept does not depend on abstract concepts of independence and unity but rather on the relational, something so inherent to the coexistence of part and whole that we may fail to recognize it and have great difficulty in expressing it abstractly.

The preceding discussion will have made clear that Japanese ontological conceptions are not purely literary but are in fact founded on a whole system of values and assumptions. For example, the indigenous beliefs that we term Shinto are founded on a non-oppositional concept of graded, continuous relations among what in English we must term the natural, the human, and the divine. It is no accident that it was in Japan that there fully developed the Buddhist belief (nearly a heresy) that plants and trees might be considered sentient, have the Buddha nature (sōmoku jōbutsu is the Japanese term for this doctrine), and so be eligible for enlightenment. Other emphases in Buddhism that were found particularly congenial in Japan include the concept of kū: the void, emptiness, relativity, interdependence, etc. To explain impermanence in the phenomenal world, early Buddhists postulated that people and things arose and subsided in time by the principle of dependent origination (engi). The Mahāyāna Buddhism dominant in Japan held instead that dependent origination was not a principle of temporal sequence but of essential dependence of people and things on each other (kū). In turn, this dependence is not separate from the world but the same reality as phenomenal experience (rinne) which, when properly understood, is itself Nirvana. Thought of as arising interdependently, all people and things are empty of persistent, static form. And yet the provisional reality (ke) of this same world is not to be denied: "Form is no other than emptiness, emptiness no other than form" (*Heart Sutra*). This complex metaphysics of interdependence offers one philosophical basis among others less refined to explain the Japanese concept of the relation of the integer to the collective whole, just as (for example) it also has explanatory force for that unique Japanese poetic kind, linked poetry.[22]

The Japanese definitions of these matters obviously underlie the premises held about individual literary units and collections, for which concepts of relation are the most important. When differing ideas of relation cause too great stress or strife, a larger collective whole must be discovered or the system breaks down until a new collective conception can be created. A similar explanation has been offered for radical changes in scientific thought.[23] To the extent

[22] See Konishi, *Sōgi*, pp. 120-22, on Buddhist concepts of Existence dependent on relation (in the context of renga): "When we realize [in Buddhist terms] that all exists in dependence and interdependence, we understand that without the whole there can be no parts, and the parts are not distinct from the whole" (p. 121). With the principle of sequentiality (see the next chapter by Ueda), these presumptions seem equally fundamental for Japanese collections.

[23] See Thomas S. Kuhn's highly influential work, *The Structure of Scientific Revolutions* (Chicago: University of Chicago Press, 1962). His ideas of "paradigms" and "structure" are, however, ones of exclusion that differ from the relational, inclusive—collective—Japanese ideas.

that we can discover differences between patterns of Japanese thought and those of other cultures, the differences do not rule out change but do involve the persistence of what has been once established. Gagaku disappeared in China and is preserved in Japan. Waka is as old as the *Kojiki*, but there are still many tanka societies today. There was once a ritualized tennō as head of state, and there is one now.

The Social and the Individual

If what has been said to this point has validity, there must be implications for a wider range of phenomena in Japanese life. Those should include assumptions governing social organization, ideas of the family, the organization of political parties, and the nature of various other groups like the literary establishment (bundan) or a farmers' cooperative. Although this discussion is already lengthy, I should like to make some suggestions that are best introduced with a warning and a theoretical argument.

The warning is that the evidence I am giving derives chiefly from Japanese literature, particularly in its premodern phases. Corroboration, correction, or qualification will require attention to a variety of nonliterary evidence, and in particular from modern times. The key theoretical matter concerns the relation of individuals to their groups. I have been proposing that, over the centuries, Japanese have presumed a kind of relation between the individual and the collective that is distinct, different in its emphasis from that presumed in other highly developed societies—and also that, rather than assume pure hierarchy or pure equality, Japanese have assumed individual entities that are essentially relational. That is, that Japanese have postulated, not a unity of uniform, equal, or fully stratified and competing entities, but a collectiveness dynamic in its relations, both between one element and others, and between constituent elements and the collective whole.

In pursuing this theoretical formulation of Japanese assumptions, I should like to offer what seems a particularly telling example or two involving names. In matters concerning the relation between individuals and their society—or indeed the social status of individuals—few matters are more crucial than names. Just to have a name is to have a social existence, and since Japanese "names" so often involve titles, sobriquets, or pen names, the range of implication is yet larger. By common consent, the greatest work of Japanese literature is the *Genji Monogatari (The Tale of Genji)*. Leaving aside the rich subject of "names" of characters in that work, the author is said to be Murasaki Shikibu. The "Murasaki" is taken from the heroine of the novel, and the "Shikibu" derives from the court title of some male relative holding a position in the Bureau of Rites (Shikibu). This is as if we knew nothing of the name of William Shakespeare but spoke instead of Hamlet Globe (after the theater with which he is associated). A yet better (because actual) example is provided by three exact contemporaries (1769-1858): Santō Kyōden, who was a writer of prose fiction in the Edo period; Kitao Masanobu, who was an illustrator of such fiction and an artist of similar kinds of pictures; and Kyōya Denzō, an enterprising merchant. Kyōden will be found writing stories illustrated by his contemporaries, and Masanobu illustrated stories written by others. The fact is that all three—Kyōden, Masanobu, and Denzō—are guises of one and the same individual, a man named Iwase Sei. Hardly any Japanese has ever heard of Iwase Sei, and it is next to impossible to find out any information concerning *him* in the numerous biographical dictionaries. One must go instead to a literary or artistic reference book for Santō Kyōden or Kitao Masanobu. Or, for modern examples, when Ernest Hemingway committed suicide in 1961, Ernest Hemingway died. When Mishima Yukio committed suicide in 1970, it was Hiraoka Kimitake who died. I can think of no Western counterpart for this situation, and we may therefore consider what it seems to imply.

The names of the Edo-period story-writer, artist, and merchant are names of *persons* in the strict sense. Iwase Sei must also have been a person in social and other terms, but "Iwase Sei" differs in relating more directly to a *self*. Even without a name, without a person, an individual may have a self. A chattel slave is the readiest example. To paraphrase Shakespeare's Shylock, if you prick a self, it bleeds. That is not true of a person, which is an abstracted social concept. The Municipal Prefecture of Tokyo, the English House of Commons, and General Motors are all persons without selves, although there are many persons-selves implied by those entities. One can harm a slave or sentence the slave to death, but a slave cannot sue in court as can General Motors. The examples just given of Japanese names suggests that in Japan the concept of person is far more lively, more crucial than concepts of self.[24] It is no accident that in spoken and written usage, the Japanese language is relatively seldom drawn on for its rich variety of personal nouns (the equivalent of pronouns). When possible, a title is used instead. And when personal nouns are used, they designate in a way our pronouns do not certain social or status functions—relations—such as senior or junior, stranger or friend, female or male, etc.

Earlier (pp. 54-55) I attempted to specify five features "of the individual entities of Japanese literature." The social counterparts of those matters need no special discussion. But strong confirmation of my proposals is given by Konishi Jin'ichi when he describes the distinctive features of Japanese literature, among which he includes the lack of "clearcut oppositions." He sets forth such absences in another set of five:

1. the lack of an opponent in the organization [no heroic or tragic opponent];
2. the lack of distinction between the human and the natural;
3. the non-existence of class barriers in literary kinds;
4. the tendency to harmonize the individual with the group;
5. the relation of mutual dependence between author and audience.[25]

All five features relate to what is being discussed here, and particularly the last two points. Konishi's explanation of the fourth point offers, in his terms, confirmation of what I have been arguing

[24] In *Accomplices of Silence* (Berkeley and Los Angeles: University of California Press, 1974), Masao Miyoshi argues with great suggestiveness that modern Japanese prose fiction is weak in its conception of self. My counterpart argument involves stress by Japanese on concepts of personhood and relation.

[25] Konishi, *History of Japanese Literature*, 1, 12-16.

to be the social implications of the individual and the collective in literature. He emphasizes that literary groups consist of people who think in like ways and use a mutually valued linguistic code that enables Japanese to prize brevity: when so many assumptions are shared, lengthiness offers an unnecessary redundancy. Only when a writer seeks to appeal beyond the immediate group does length and "redundancy" become desirable.

Konishi also recognizes a kind of exception, or semi-exception. The groups themselves are usually dominated by a single individual. When "an individualistic person creates a new style, that author does not act alone but instead institutes a group of like-minded people, and the new group goes on self-sufficiently writing and appreciating what its members produce."[26] No one can deny the role of striking *individuals* in Japanese literature or other social enterprise. There are no better instances of this than in the practice of the two varieties of linked poetry, renga, and haikai, the former of which prospered most in a period of anarchy and the latter during a time of rigid social stratification and peace. When the renga master Sōgi died, and when the haikai masters Bashō and Buson died, the work of their associates dropped radically in quality. Charismatic individuals are perhaps all the more necessary in Japanese literature and society precisely because the practice is collective. Linked poetry in its two forms is doubly collective—in authorship and in poetic result. The readiest explanation of what may seem to be a paradox is that set of principles designated by Konishi or those others on pp. 54-55. That is, the striking individual and the subordinate individuals function collectively, relationally. Their persons are what matter, and their status is relational but unequal. The same holds throughout almost the whole of Japanese society.

I believe that there are at least two exceptions, and if they are highly prized by Japanese it is surely because they are rare. One is the tie of old schoolmates. To be sure, the sense of the collective is particularly strong in this instance, but there is a sense of equality in that relation that is unusual otherwise in Japanese life. The

[26] Ibid., pp. 15-16.

other exception is yet more radical, involving recluses. To be desired by society and to choose a reclusive life is to evoke enormous admiration from Japanese. The mystique of the poet-priest Saigyō depends on that combination. And the attractions of yet other figures in literary, religious, and other circles depends on much the same self-sufficiency. Moreover, if we look closely into the lives of Saigyō and his counterparts, we shall usually find that they alternated periods of reclusion with periods of participation in ordinary life. This is no paradox in Buddhist terms. A priest or nun is someone who has left the world—and yet (in earlier, restricted periods) had more freedom to move in all levels of society than a layperson. (One reason why Saigyō took orders was to be able to enter the court as a poet.) And in Zen Buddhism at least, one was to achieve, as an individual, a unique enlightenment and thereafter to "return" to the dust of this world to assist others. Such exceptions are, then, sufficiently partial to emphasize the rule.

As these various kinds of literary evidence are dealt with by students of other features of Japanese life, the postulates of this study can be collected and amplified. It does seem unlikely, however, that anyone will postulate purely Western conceptions to explain Japanese views of the individual and the collective, of self and person, and of relation. In conclusion, let us return to one of the most acute observers of Japanese life, Sei Shōnagon, whose words preceded this discussion. At one point in her *Pillow Book* she tells of an eavesdropper who takes pleasure in observing a human or social collection:

> The master of a private house takes special delight in overhearing ladies-in-waiting *collected* [atsumarite] on leave from the palace as they chat in praise of the noble persons they serve and as they share talk with each other.[27]

[27] *Makura no Sōshi, Murasaki Shikibu Nikki,* ed. Ikeda Kikan et al. (Iwanami Shoten, 1958; *Nihon Koten Bungaku Taikei*), p. 313. This is part (dan) 303 in the textual line Ikeda follows and part 283 in the Nōin line. The epigraph I have chosen quotes in its entirety dan 68 of Ikeda's edition. It is part 68 in the Nōin text, which adds a third collection, "*Gosen[shū].*"

This is from her conclusion:

> This book was made from *collected* jottings [kaki*atsumari-taru*] when I was at home at leisure, setting down things I had seen and thoughts that occurred to me, not expecting that they would ever be read by others.[28]

With her accustomed pithiness, Sei Shōnagon shows that to be or to write is to collect. In conjunction, her two remarks show that literature has a corresponding collective version in other features of human society, of human life as Japanese understand it, and as they illuminate it for us.

[28] Ibid., p. 331; dan 319. As the preceding note suggested, various editors (or the author in differing versions of her work) have combined or broken and reordered units. Each version reflects different notions of what makes the better or best collection, producing different collections in different sequences.

CHAPTER 2

THE TAXONOMY OF SEQUENCE: BASIC PATTERNS OF STRUCTURE IN PREMODERN JAPANESE LITERATURE

BY MAKOTO UEDA

To while away the idle hours, seated the livelong day before the inkslab, by jotting down without order or purpose whatever trifling thoughts pass through my mind, verily this is a queer and crazy thing to do!

—Yoshida Kenkō

Stanzas should be linked to each other through fragrance, reverberation, semblance, flow, fancy, or some such indefinable quality.

—Matsuo Bashō

I like to write with the flow of associations, which emerge one after another as I write on. Perhaps all writers are like that, but I suspect I am more addicted to the habit than most. I am probably lacking in ability to screen my associations.

—Kawabata Yasunari[1]

[1] The epigraphs are from the following. First, *Tsurezuregusa, Nihon Koten Bungaku Taikei*, 100 vols. (Iwanami Shoten, 1957-67. Abbreviated as *NKBT* hereafter), 30, 89; translated by George B. Sansom in *Transactions of the Asiatic Society of Japan*, 39 (1911), 9. Next, cited in Hattori Dohō, *Sanzōshi, NKBT*, 66, 418; finally, "Makura no Sōshi," *Kawabata Yasunari Zenshū*, 19 vols. (Shinchōsha, 1969-1974), 12, 277. Unless noted otherwise, translations are by me. [The connections between this chapter and Miner's hardly need stressing.—Ed.]

THESE THREE COMMENTS, made by a fourteenth-century essayist, a seventeenth-century poet, and a twentieth-century novelist, all point toward a structural principle that is characteristic of Japanese literature, a principle that may seem more incidental, associational, and irrational than its Western counterpart. The structure may appear to be "without order or purpose," to have an "indefinable quality," and to unfold "itself with the flow of associations." For lack of a better term, I shall give it the all-inclusive name "sequence." In my tentative definition, sequence is a succession of literary units that attains an overall artistic unity—or semblance of unity—by means other than logic. It is an antithesis of "plot," in which the law of causality unites all the parts into a whole. Kenkō, Bashō, and Kawabata were all speaking about the presence of sequence and the absence of plot in their respective works. Knowingly or unknowingly they were expressing a predilection shared by a large majority of fellow Japanese authors.

This chapter is a preliminary attempt to study sequential structure in premodern Japanese literature. It will also deal with plot to some extent, in order to clarify by contrast the nature of sequence. For materials I shall use classical poetry in the main, because the whole corpus of Japanese literature is obviously too large, and because classical literary criticism focused more on poetry than on other genres. Renga poets in particular had a serious concern for structural principles, and I shall be making frequent references to their ideas. I shall also cite titles of literary works outside of poetry, since I believe that concepts underlying the structural unity of poetry are, in the final analysis, little different from those that help attain the unity of a tale, a play, or an essay. However, these works will not be analyzed as extensively as the poems.

For methodology, I shall use a critical framework as well as terms and concepts developed in Western literary criticism. I shall be resorting especially to the works of Kenneth Burke, Yvor Winters, and Barbara Herrnstein Smith, all of whom have shown a special interest in structural problems of poetry.[2] On the basis of

[2] See Kenneth Burke, "Lexicon Rhetoricae," *Counter-Statement*, 2nd ed. (Los Altos, Calif.: Hermes, 1953), pp. 123-83; Yvor Winters, "The Experimental School

these studies, I propose to consider the basic structures of poetry under six general headings: (1) the method of repetition, (2) temporal sequence, (3) narrative method, (4) logical method, (5) double mood, and (6) qualitative progression. Inevitably, such a categorization will run the risk of oversimplification, as all generalizations do. Also, a poem—especially a long poem—is likely to make use of two or more of the six methods, and often with modifications. Yet literary criticism always requires a degree of simplification; it can be likened to an attempt to obtain the exact value of pi. The constant can never be translated into an exact number, but an approximation is helpful and has its merit. This account should be considered in the same light; it is an experimental attempt to study principles underlying various structural methods—methods that, in their manifestations, are never completely analyzable.

The Method of Repetition

By "the method of repetition" I refer to a structural form in which a single theme is restated in each of the parts that constitute the poem. Images, metaphors, and wording differ from part to part, but all the parts reiterate the same point. It is the simplest and one of the oldest of structural methods. Primitive songs, nursery rhymes, military marches, and traditional lullabies often have this structure. A long poem using this method can bore the reader, since it shows no forward progression of thought or feeling; as a matter of fact, some lullabies take advantage of this very feature, enticing little children to sleep. The structure also has its weakness in having no inherent principle of ending; it permits an endless repetition of the same theme. But it has one strength: simplicity. Especially when the writer wishes to cultivate such an effect as forthrightness, honesty, strength, or even naïveté, the method can be put to good use. Poets both in England and in Japan have indeed done so.

in American Poetry," *Primitivism and Decadence* (New York: Arrow, 1937), pp. 15-63; and Barbara Herrnstein Smith, *Poetic Closure* (Chicago: University of Chicago Press, 1968).

The English poem frequently quoted to illustrate this method is Sir Walter Raleigh's "The Lie." "The Happy Life" by Henry Howard, Earl of Surrey, has also been mentioned in this connection. But here I will quote a song by Thomas Nashe known as "In Time of Plague":

Adieu, farewell earth's bliss.
This world uncertain is;
Fond are life's lustful joys,
Death proves them all but toys.
None from his darts can fly;
I am sick, I must die.
Lord, have mercy on us!

Rich men, trust not in wealth,
Gold cannot buy you health;
Physic himself must fade.
All things to end are made;
The plague full swift goes by.
I am sick, I must die.
Lord, have mercy on us!

Beauty is but a flower,
Which wrinkles will devour;
Brightness falls from the air;
Queens have died young and fair;
Dust hath closed Helen's eye
I am sick, I must die.
Lord, have mercy on us!

Strength stoops unto the grave,
Worms feed on Hector brave;
Swords may not fight with fate.
Earth still holds ope her gate.
Come, come! the bells do cry.
I am sick, I must die.
Lord, have mercy on us!

Wit with his wantonness
Tasteth death's bitterness;

Hell's executioner
Hath no ears for to hear
What vain art can reply.
I am sick, I must die.
    Lord, have mercy on us!

Haste therefore each degree
To welcome destiny;
Heaven is our heritage,
Earth but a player's stage.
Mount we unto the sky.
I am sick, I must die.
    Lord, have mercy on us![3]

The theme of the poem is a familiar one in both English and Japanese literature: the mutability of human life. The first stanza presents the theme in a clear statement, and each of the following stanzas repeats it in a different guise. The second stanza deals with the transitory nature of wealth; the third, with that of beauty; the fourth, with that of strength; and the fifth, with that of intellectual power. The thrust of each stanza is the same: hence the refrain "I am sick, I must die. / Lord, have mercy on us!" The ending of the poem is beautifully achieved in the sixth stanza, which tells the reader what to do under the circumstances. Depending largely on the method of repetition, the poem succeeds in creating a distinct sense of beginning and ending, and thereby a clear sense of unity.

A good many Japanese poems have similar structure. One of the finest examples is Yamanoue Okura's elegy on the impermanence of human life. It is an appropriate counterpart to Nashe's poem, since it treats the same theme. The original poem has no stanzaic scheme, but for the convenience of our analysis I shall break it down into four units:

We are helpless before time
Which ever speeds away.

[3] Fred Inglis, ed., *English Poetry, 1550-1660* (London: Methuen, 1965), pp. 100-101.

And pains of a hundred kinds
Pursue us one after another.

Maidens joy in girlish pleasures,
With ship-borne gems on their wrists,
And hand in hand with their friends;
But the bloom of maidenhood,
As it cannot be stopped,
Too swiftly steals away.
When do their ample tresses
Black as mud-snail's bowels
Turn white with the frost of age?
Whence come those wrinkles
Which furrow their rosy cheeks?

The lusty young men, warrior-like,
Bearing their sword blades at their waists,
In their hands the hunting bows,
And mounting their bay horses,
With saddles dressed with twill,
Ride about in triumph;
But can their prime of youth
Favor them for ever?

Few are the nights they keep
When, sliding back the plank doors,
They reach their beloved ones
And sleep arms intertwined,
Before, with staffs at their waists,
They totter along the road,
Laughed at here, and hated there.
This is the way of the world;
And, cling as I may to life,
I know no help![4]

[4] *Man'yōshū*, 5, 804. Translated by the Japanese Classics Translation Committee in *The Manyoshu* (New York: Columbia University Press, 1965), pp. 201-202. [Makoto Ueda has specified that transliterations of Japanese poems be used only for shorter forms.—Ed.]

As in Nashe's poem, in this elegy the first and the last stanzas are general statements of the theme, and the middle stanzas reiterate the theme by presenting concrete evidence. The two pieces of evidence used, the fates of beauty and strength, parallel the third and fourth stanzas of the English poem. On the other hand, Okura's elegy includes more narrative elements, contrasting youth and old age in both men and women. Nashe's poem is more intellectual and makes a greater number of abstract statements. Overall implications are more pessimistic in the Japanese poem than in its English counterpart. "In Time of Plague" is a litany, allowing hope for salvation through religion. Okura's elegy offers no such hope. Its ending cry, "I know no help!," echoes the fifth line, "We are helpless before time." The poem has made no forward progression in its argument. In this sense the Japanese poem may be said to show the method of repetition in a purer form.

Another good example of a Japanese poem using the same method is a song found in *Ryōjin Hishō*:

> May the man who gained my trust yet did not come
> Turn to a devil, sprouting triple horns.
> Then he would find himself shunned by mankind.
>
> May he become a bird of the water paddy
> With frost and snow and hailstones raining down.
> Then he would find his feet were frozen fast.
>
> May he become the duckweed on the pond.
> Then he would sway and shiver as he walked.[5]

This is a curse written by an irate woman neglected by her lover. The curse is restated in three successive stanzas, each stanza using a different metaphor. Inasmuch as the three metaphors are unconventional, the poem makes a remarkably refreshing impact. With no formal beginning or ending, it has a simpler form than Okura's elegy, and that artlessness adds to its force. There seems to be no progression through the stanzas—if there is any, it would

[5] *Ryōjin Hishō*, no. 339. Translated by Geoffrey Bownas and Anthony Thwaite in *The Penguin Book of Japanese Verse* (Baltimore: Penguin Books, 1964), p. 89. The poem has been broken into units by the translators.

be in a reverse direction, for the duckweed is a more subdued image than a devil. One might argue that the poem would have been more effective if the image-order had been reversed, ending with the image of the devil. On the other hand, one might counterargue that the present sequence of images suggests the order in which the author's emotional state changed—namely, from intense anger to semi-resignation. At the end of the poem, the woman does not appear quite as angry as she was at the beginning.

In the renga tradition this type of structure does not seem to have fared well, probably because it is lacking in forward progression. Among various methods of stanza integration cited in books on renga, the one that comes closest to this structure is shakushi or explicative linking. Here is an example, followed by an explanation, as it appears in *Renga Shotai Hiden Shō*:

Hana chirite	Blossoms have fallen
kozue ni nokoru	and in the branches nothing
kaze mo nashi	is left of the wind
oiki no sakura	with an old cherry tree
haru kurenikeri.	spring has come to its close.

> Here the second stanza repeats the first, explaining its meaning. When a poet uses such an expression as "spring departs from an old tree" and "blossoms have fallen," or "it is near" after "not far away," or "I am alone" after "without company," no sense of freshness arises from the way in which his stanza is linked to the preceding one. Such is the technique of a mediocre renga poet.[6]

Renga critics admired a subtle interplay of two successive stanzas in terms of imagery, diction, and mood. Mere repetition minimizes such an interplay. The homogeneity of vocabulary and imagery makes the link between two stanzas look flat, stagnant, and redundant. Simplicity, the main virtue of the method, does not harmonize well with the poetics of renga.

Interestingly enough, another linking method, called yotsude-

[6] Ijichi Tetsuo, ed., *Rengaron Shinshū* (Koten Bunko, 1956), pp. 140-41.

zuke, or linking through four hands, is praised by the author of *Renga Shotai Hiden Shō* although it looks somewhat like shakushi at a glance. Below are his example and comment:

Fune hayaku yuku Yodo no kawamizu	The boat speeds away on the water of the Yodo River
yo fukaki ni isoganu michi mo aru mono o.	in the depth of night is there not a more leisurely way of traveling?

> The linking is done so thoroughly in this instance that one need not talk about tai ["primary subjects"] and yū ["auxiliary subjects"], but I would say the Yodo River is the tai of this verse. There is a connection between "the boat" and "way," between "speeds" and "not . . . leisurely," and between "the Yodo River" and "the depth of night." Such is a technique to be desired.[7]

This is a method of close linking. Two stanzas linked by it look like sumō wrestlers in cross grips. There is a close correlation of meaning between the stanzas. Yet, unlike shakushi, this method allows just enough novelty in the second stanza so as not to be redundant. In the example cited, the couplet is an objective observation of a bystander, with no time of day mentioned. The triplet sets the time in the depth of night and expresses a more subjective sentiment: pity for a person who has to hurry along his way on an emergency despite the poetic setting that surrounds him. For all the close connection in imagery and diction, there is a definite progression of mood.

These examples from renga point to a danger latent in the method of repetition. Unless handled with tact, the method can easily make the poem sound monotonous. The poet has to supply each stanza with a sense of novelty, and variety, so that the repetition will not be felt to be redundant. On the other hand, if he gives too much novelty and variety, the poem will lose simplicity, straightforwardness, and other strengths of the method. Nashe's litany, Okura's

[7] Ibid., p. 110.

elegy, and yotsudezuke are cases in which the poets have succeeded in keeping this perilous balance.

The method of repetition is sometimes observable in a section of a Japanese poetry anthology. The *Man'yōshū*, for instance, has such sections as "Love" and "Laments," and if each such section is considered an autonomous literary unit, its overall unity can be said to have been attained through topical similarity of the poems that are paratactically arranged. The same type of unity is present in each of the one hundred sections that constitute *Horikawa In Hyakushu*. It is true that some volumes of the *Shinkokinshū* and other imperial poetry anthologies show a more complex principle of unity.[8] But even in these collections such sections as "Parting" and "Laments" have a structure that is largely repetitive. The *Sankashū* of Priest Saigyō (1118-1190) includes several sequences of poems following such headnotes as "I have written many poems on the moon" or "I have written many poems on blossoms," and each sequence is a random collection of waka on the moon or blossoms or some other designated topic. Likewise, the Bashō-school haikai anthology *Arano* contains sections called "Thirty Hokku on Blossoms," "Thirty Hokku on the Moon," and so forth, each section showing no principle of unity except thematic similarity.

Sometimes a subsection within a section makes good use of repetitive structure. For example, the "Laments" section in volume two of *Man'yōshū* includes a subsection listing twenty-three waka written by servicemen at the palace of the late Prince Kusakabe. The arrangement of the poems shows no specific order, yet the lack of order itself helps to suggest the widespread grief among the servicemen regardless of their rank, age, or personality. To take another example, the *Kinkaishū* of Minamoto Sanetomo (1192-1219) contains a famous sequence of three waka that he composed upon receiving a secret message from Cloistered Sovereign Gotoba. The three poems are arranged through their common topic and

[8] The standard study on this topic in English is Konishi Jin'ichi, "Association and Progression: Principles of Integration in Anthologies and Sequences of Japanese Court Poetry, A.D. 900-1350," translated and adapted by Robert H. Brower and Earl Miner in *Harvard Journal of Asiatic Studies*, 21 (1958), 7-127.

nothing else, and yet each poem is so simple and straightforward in its expression of loyalty that the artless juxtaposition contributes to the powerful effect of the sequence. In general, the method of repetition seems most effective when the poems constituting a sequence are sequential composition (rensaku), and not an arbitrary collection of poems written on a common topic by different people at different times.

Some Japanese collections of tales can be said to have a similar structure in part or as a whole. *Jikkinshō* (or *Jikkunshō*), for example, consists of ten didactic sections as the title implies, each headed by a maxim like "Persevere in All Things" or "Be Careful in Selecting Your Companion," and the arrangement of tales within the section shows no specific order or progression. Each tale is like a stanza supporting the main theme of the poem of which it is a part. Saikaku's stories collected in *Buke Giri Monogatari* do not seem to be arranged by any deliberate scheme, except that they all point toward the image of an ideal samurai as conceived by the author. Likewise, his *Seken Munesan'yō* presents, with no discernible internal logic, a series of tales describing the struggling lives of merchants on the last day of the year.

The method of repetition is all too easy to use. One need only string together at random two or more stanzas, poems, or tales that share a common theme. That is why there are many instances of this method in classical Japanese literature. Yet one has to be wary of its two major weaknesses. A literary work using the method can become monotonous, since it does not by itself generate a sense of progression. The work can also become open-ended, with no sense of conclusion. Poets and compilers who overcame these weaknesses in one way or another have been the more successful users of the method.

Temporal Sequence

Temporal sequence emerges when a poet or a compiler uses the flow of time as the ordering principle. In its most typical case, the structure of a literary work will be based on the passage of time and no other principle of unity. The arrangements of units will be chronological: spring-summer-autumn-winter, or morning-midday-afternoon-evening-night, or birth-infancy-youth-manhood-old age-death, or some such order. It is another simple, natural method of structure, inasmuch as nature and human life alike progress with time, and it is therefore easy for the poet to use and for the reader to follow. As a consequence, instances of temporal sequence abound in both English, Japanese, and other literatures.

To start with an example of the simplest kind, here is a short poem by Tennyson entitled "The Oak":

> Live thy life,
>   Young and old,
> Like yon oak,
> Bright in spring,
>   Living gold:
>
> Summer-rich
>   Then; and then
> Autumn-changed,
> Soberer-hued
>   Gold again.
>
> All his leaves
>   Fallen at length,
> Look, he stands,
> Trunk and bough,
>   Naked strength.[9]

The sequential structure of the poem is largely temporal, beginning with a general statement followed by lines on spring, summer, autumn, and winter, in that natural order. Its unity has been made tighter by having a central image, an oak tree. The structure is simple—almost naive—as are the imagery and diction, but that simplicity helps to strike home the main message of the poem.

[9] Christopher Ricks, ed., *The Poems of Tennyson* (London: Longman, 1969), pp. 1425-26.

Equally simple is my first example from classical Japanese literature, a rice-planting song from present Aomori Prefecture:

When spring comes,
there's water in the paddy pools.
the mudloach and the singing frog
are happy, are happy,
thinking they're in the sea.

When summer comes,
the paddy pools grow warm.
the mudloach and the singing frog
are happy, are happy,
thinking they're in the bath.

When autumn comes,
the hills and dales turn red.
the mudloach and the singing frog
craning their necks above,
must think the hills on fire.

When winter comes,
the paddy pools are filmed with ice.
the mudloach and the singing frog
must think their heaven has stretched
has stretched and grown above.[10]

The poem has an orderly structure, with its four stanzas corresponding to the four seasons of the year. As in Tennyson's poem, the poet's eyes are focused on a specific aspect of nature, in this case the life of a mudloach and a frog. Unlike "The Oak," however, there is no overt didacticism; instead there is simple, earthy humor. Again the simplicity of the structure well matches the rusticity of the life and mind that pervades the poem.

Many poems on travel use temporal sequence, with a structure tending to follow the progress of the journey. The following poem

[10] Machida Kashō and Asano Kenji, eds., *Nihon Min'yōshū* (Iwanami Shoten, 1960), p. 25.

from the *Man'yōshū*, written by Ōtomo Yakamochi (d. 785) in the guise of a frontier guard, is one such example:

In obedience to the royal command,
Though sad is the parting from my wife,
I summon up the courage of a man,
And dressed for journey, take my leave.
My mother strokes me gently;
My young wife clings to me, saying,
"I will pray to the gods for your safekeeping.
Go unharmed and come back soon!"
As she speaks, she wipes with her sleeves
The tears that choke her.
Hard as it is, I start on my way,
Pausing and looking back time after time;
Ever farther I travel from my home,
Ever higher the mountains I climb and cross,
Till at least I arrive at Naniwa of wind-blown reeds.
Here I stop and wait for good weather,
To launch the ship upon the evening tide,
To set the prow seawards,
And to row out in the calm of morning.
The spring mists rise round the isles,
And the cranes cry in a plaintive tone,
Then I think of my far-off home—
So sorely do I grieve that with sobs
I shake the war arrows I carry
Till they rattle in my ears.[11]

Here the flow of the poem is identical with that of time: the young man receives a summons, bids farewell to his family, leaves home, travels through mountainous areas, and arrives at the port of Naniwa. The progression is temporally linear, and its setting changes with the advance of time, yet there is an overall thematic unity that remains throughout—the sorrow of parting. The poem itself is probably too neatly written to have the powerful appeal char-

[11] *Man'yōshū*, no. 4398. Translated by the Japanese Classics Translation Committee in *The Manyoshu*, pp. 175-76, slightly adapted.

acteristic of primitive poetry, but for that very reason it shows its temporal sequence well. What are known as michiyuki (travel pieces), so abundant in classical Japanese literature, employ this temporal flow, although they often incorporate other structural principles also.

Temporal sequence was not widely popular among Japanese poets. Writers of linked verse showed no great enthusiasm for it. In renga, the case of a stanza on an autumnal topic following a summer stanza is relatively rare because that would be too simple, too orderly, too artless. The interest in writing or reading renga lies precisely in seeing an autumn stanza following a spring stanza, a winter stanza, a love stanza—anything but a summer stanza. In most cases, a seasonal stanza or a succession of seasonal stanzas is preceded and followed by one or more stanzas on miscellaneous topics, so that two successive seasons of the year rarely follow one another. Also, the rules of renga say that a summer (or winter) stanza can follow another such stanza twice at most in any one stretch. Spring (or autumn) stanzas must form a succession of at least three and no more than five stanzas. Thus the seasonal scheme of the first twenty stanzas of the *Sōgi Dokugin Nanihito Hyakuin* by Sōgi (1421-1502) is: spring, spring, spring, miscellaneous, miscellaneous, miscellaneous, winter, winter, autumn, autumn, autumn, miscellaneous, miscellaneous, miscellaneous, spring, spring, spring, miscellaneous, autumn, and autumn.[12] It is as if time stopped and flowed with no regularity; in some cases, time seems to have flowed backwards. One might say that renga thrives on an atemporal sequence.

Interestingly enough, the most celebrated of renga anthologies, the *Tsukuba Shū*, follows seasonal sequence in its first six volumes, Part One beginning with stanzas on early spring and Part Six ending with those on late winter. The arrangement emulated the normal structural scheme of royal waka anthologies, all of which had made use of seasonal sequence. The practice was kept in haikai anthologies, too, although in many cases an additional section, "The New Year," preceded the section collecting spring poems.

[12] See Earl Miner, *Japanese Linked Poetry* (Princeton: Princeton University Press, 1979), pp. 234-43.

Even the fact that the most famous of haikai anthologies, *Sarumino* (1691), swerved from temporal sequence in its structure had little impact on this traditional practice. Temporal order is also maintained within the seasonal sections of waka anthologies. The section, "Spring," normally begins with poems on the first day of spring and concludes with those on the end of spring, and the same is true of sections on summer, autumn, and winter.

Some poetry collections follow another type of temporal sequence—the dates of composition. A large part of Book Six of the *Man'yōshū* consists of poems arranged by the years of composition. Book Ten of the *Shinkokinshū* (ca. 1206) seems to trace in a general way the historical development of waka from the earliest times to the thirteenth century. The *Jōjin Azari no Haha no Shū* presents the author's poems roughly in the order in which she wrote them, beginning in 1067 and ending in 1103. The *Kenrei Mon'in Ukyō no Daibu Shū* also follows chronological order, although in it a subtler, more psychological principle of structure seems to be at work simultaneously.[13] The second half of Bashō's *Nozarashi Kikō* is a sequence of hokku, with occasional headnotes, arranged in the order of composition, as is the first third of the *Shin Hanatsumi* of Yosa Buson (1716-1783). Many of the poetic works by Kobayashi Issa (1763-1827) surviving today are kunikki (hokku diaries) or kuchō (hokku notes), which can be considered collections of poems recorded in the order in which they were written.

In prose literature, diaries and travel journals as well as historical literature most obviously show temporal sequence. The main structural principle stringing together fifty-five segments that make up the *Tosa Nikki* of Ki no Tsurayuki (d. 945) is the passage of time, although recurring themes such as longing for home, fear of pirates, and grief over the death of a child add to the unity. The diary of Fujiwara Teika (1162-1241), *Meigetsuki*, is more massive, covering a span of over half a century, but its structural principle is similar. The structure of Bashō's *Oku no Hosomichi* is mainly

[13] See Phillip Tudor Harries's discussion of the topic in his introduction to *The Poetic Memoirs of Lady Daibu* (Stanford: Stanford University Press, 1980).

based on the flow of time, too, although the flow is expressed in terms of space by the traveling diarist. In historical literature, the *Nihongi* (720) most clearly shows temporal sequence, as befits an annals-like history chronicling events that happened in early Japan. The *Mizukagami* follows suit, although outwardly it is a tale or monogatari narrated by a young Buddhist monk. Temporal sequence also provides the basic principle unifying the some two hundred episodes that make up the *Heike Monogatari.*

Some works of prose fiction can be said to have temporal sequence. Several sections of *Kojidan* and all sections of *Kokon Chomonjū* contain tales arranged in chronological order. The *Kōshoku Ichidai Otoko* by Ihara Saikaku (1642-1693) is a single tale, but its constituent fifty-four sections are so loosely strung that they look like independent tales with a common hero. Its structure can be said to be founded on the method of repetition, since all the episodes illustrate Yonosuke's amorous nature; or it can be compared to the progression of a traditional linked poetic sequence, starting slowly with a preparatory part and ending with a sense of speed and liveliness. But its general framework is temporal sequence, as the episodes trace the hero's life chronologically. Another such example is *Dōchū Hizakurige* by Jippensha Ikku (1765-1831), which traces the fictional journey by its two principal characters. Although it was first published as a single piece of prose fiction, it is substantially a collection of hilarious episodes loosely strung together by temporal sequence, which in this instance has been translated into spatial progression. It is characteristic of this kind of fiction that the main character does not grow psychologically by experience. If he did, the connection between episodes would become plot rather than sequence, and the work would look more like a tale than a collection of tales. Thus the more plot-like structure of Saikaku's *Kōshoku Ichidai Onna* is less of a temporal sequence, because the heroine comes to repent her earlier behavior as she grows older.

As the foregoing examples make clear, few literary works depend exclusively on temporal structure. That is because, from a human view, time itself does not provide a sense of beginning or ending; it flows eternally, without a beginning or an end. For this reason, a piece of writing that exclusively relies on temporal sequence for its structural unity is often inferior as literature, as is the case with the *Nihongi* and *Meigetsuki*. Better literary works make use of an additional principle of structure and cut up the flow of time in some artful way. The principle may be the cycle of the seasons, the itinerary of a journey, the rise and fall of a clan, or the beginning and ending of an event. A more compelling structural unity will be attained when temporal sequence is assisted by one or another of such subsidiary principles, for the former provides a sense of natural progression, while the latter creates a sense of beginning and ending.

The Narrative Method

A poem may tell a story. In such a case, different parts of the poem will be integrated by the progress of the storyline, or what may be called narrative logic. The storyline may follow the chronological order of events, but when narrative logic rather than the passage of time plays the major role in providing the poem's unity, the technique will have to be called narrative method. What distinguishes this method from temporal sequence is the presence of causality. When an incident happens in real life, it always has a cause or causes, although that may not be immediately apparent. The cause may be traced to a natural phenomenon (a snowstorm, an earthquake), to a social condition (the generation gap, racial discrimination), or to a personality trait (reckless nature, too much pride), but when it leads to an event or a series of events in a chain reaction, there emerges a story. The structure created by the narrative method is, then, more "plot" than "sequence," if we understand "plot" as meaning a succession of events revealing a natural causative chain.

Poems using the narrative method go back to the beginning of literature, and they have been produced in great numbers in the Western world. Epic poems, such as *The Iliad* and *The Aeneid*, all rely on this method, and many shorter poems and ballads tell stories also. Early romances were written in verse, utilizing narrative method. And then there are latter-day imitations of all these traditional forms—Milton's *Paradise Lost*, Coleridge's *The Rime of the Ancient Mariner*, Tennyson's "The Lady of Shalott," and so forth. Also there are a great many other poems that do not clearly fall into any of these traditional categories and that nevertheless are narrative in structure, for example, Pope's *Rape of the Lock*, Wordsworth's "Michael," D. H. Lawrence's "Snake," T. S. Eliot's "Journey of the Magi," and any number of others. English literature is thick with narrative poems.

By contrast, Japan has produced only a small number of poems using narrative method. There has been no epic poem. The *Heike Monogatari* and parts of the *Kojiki* have some epic features, and both works include a number of shortish poems; but the stories they tell are written in prose. Most Japanese ballads such as those found in the *Kanginshū* are too short to tell a story. And there was no tradition of romance in Japanese poetry. Why Japanese literature is lacking in narrative—or plotted—poetry can be easily explained. Waka, the dominant verse form in classical Japanese literature, was too brief in form to present a narrative plot. It was more congenial to write a narrative in prose and use waka in a climax to enhance the emotional impact. One might say that uta monogatari such as the *Ise Monogatari* and *Heichū Monogatari* substituted for narrative poetry in Japan.

Some poems written before or outside of the waka tradition do show something of the narrative method. The poem of a frontier guard, written by Yakamochi and quoted earlier, attains its unity through temporal sequence in the main, yet it also has narrative elements as it tells, albeit fragmentarily, the guard's story. In the following short poem from the *Ryōjin Hishō*, narrative logic seems to prevail over temporal sequence:

> The young man come to manhood
> Came to claim his bride.
> The first night and the second
> They slept a deep sound sleep.
> Then, the third midnight,
> And long before the dawn,

He grabbed his trousers in his hand
And fled far out of sight.[14]

Temporal sequence is present, as the descriptions move from the first night to the third. Yet what gives the poem its unity is its storyline, cryptic though it is. A young man comes to his girlfriend's home, sleeps with her for two nights, and then escapes in a fluster during the third night. Konishi Jin'ichi once speculated that the young woman's indiscretion was found out by her parents on the third night.[15] Whatever reason there may have been for the young man's flustered exit, here is the genesis of a tragi-comic story that might have been expanded into a tale.

Among early Japanese poets, the one who had the greatest penchant for the narrative method was no doubt Takahashi Mushimaro. Several of his long poems are built around an ancient legend, and the plot of the legend supplies the main structure of the poem. For example:

In the land of Azuma
Where the cocks crow,
Still they tell today
A story of the past:
How the maiden of Mama
In Katsushika
Wove pure hemp
To make herself a skirt
And made a blue collar
For her hempen dress.
Her hair uncombed,
She went unshod, yet
No well guarded damsel,
Cocooned in brocade,
Was ever fair as she.
Her face full as full moon,
Her smile like a flower,

[14] *Ryōjin Hishō*, no. 340. Translated by Bownas and Thwaite in *The Penguin Book of Japanese Verse*, p. 91.

[15] Konishi Jin'ichi, *Ryōjin Hishō Kō* (Sanseidō, 1941), p. 453.

Men sought and crowded round her
As summer moths seek fire,
As boats hurry to port.
Why, when she knew full well,
That life is not lived long,
Did her body lie in death
By the sounding estuary
Where sea and river clash?
This happened long ago,
Yet I am made to think
I saw her yesterday.[16]

This has a more formal structure than the poem from *Ryōjin Hishō*. It has an introduction and a conclusion: in the *Ryōjin Hishō* the narrator introduces the poem as a true story, and in the latter he recapitulates the same point and tries to convince the reader of the story's authenticity. The bulk of the poem is a narrative, recounting how a pure, beautiful maiden met a tragic death; the law of causality is made unmistakably clear. Both the material and the methods are distinctly of narrative poetry. In Europe, the material might have been made into a ballad.

Renga poets sometimes made use of narrative method. They invariably refrained from following the storyline too far, however, because doing so would create rinne, an overlong succession of similar stanzas. Among the traditional methods, that of linking, the one called honzetsu (or linking by allusion to an old story) comes closest to the narrative method. Explaining the method, Nijō Yoshimoto said: "Do not use it more than three successive stanzas. The substance of a Chinese poem, a tale, or a popular story can be used for a link, too."[17] This influential renga poet did not cite examples, but the following stanzas included in his *Tsukuba Shū* would illustrate the method:

Kesa mezurashiku	This morning, a rare sight—
fureru shirayuki	white snow on the ground!

[16] *Man'yōshū*, no. 1807. Translated by Bownas and Thwaite in *The Penguin Book of Japanese Verse*, p. 44.

[17] "Renri Hishō," *NKBT*, 66, 51.

Ono to iu	to a village
sato made hito no	known as Ono, a visitor
tazunekite.	makes his way.[18]

This looks like a fragment of a story. The snow has fallen during the night and piled up on the ground. The story's hero is overjoyed to discover the rare sight in the morning. He wants to share the joy with his friend who, he knows, understands such poetic beauty; thereupon he pays a visit to a remote village where the friend lives. Because the village is identified as Ono, the hero must be someone like Ariwara Narihira who, as the *Ise Monogatari* tells us, visited his close friend, Prince Koretaka, in the latter's retreat in Ono one winter day.

A similar method was used in haikai, too, although it was called by a different name, omokage or semblance. At the outset of this essay, we saw Bashō using the term. Compared with honzetsu, allusion employed in this method seems more indirect and vague. Mukai Kyorai, Bashō's most faithful disciple, explained:

> In olden days poets often used direct allusion, but now we do the linking through omokage. For instance:

Sōan ni	For a little while
shibaraku ite wa	I remain at my hermitage
uchi-yaburi	and then am off again
inochi ureshiki	happy in old age that my poems
senjū no sata.	have won place in a collection.[19]

The first stanza was written by Bashō, and the second by Kyorai. According to Kyorai, however, the first draft of his stanza was:

waka no ōgi wa	Of the craft of waka
shirazu sōrō.	composition, I know nothing.

These two lines are almost identical with Saigyō's reply to Shōgun

[18] Fukui Kyūzō, ed., *Kōhon Tsukubashū Shinshaku*, 2 vols. (Waseda Daigaku Shuppanbu, 1936-1942), 2, 127.

[19] "Kyorai Shō," *NKBT*, 66, 371. The stanzas have been translated by Earl Miner in his *Japanese Linked Poetry*, p. 311.

Yoritomo, who had asked him about the craft of waka writing, as recounted in an episode in the *Azuma Kagami.* Apparently Bashō felt that such a clear identification restricted the reader's imagination; he wanted the reader to have room to think of other poet-recluses as well. The new stanza by Kyorai corrected the situation; the narrator "I" may be Saigyō, or may not be. There is an indistinct image of a wandering poet who is pleased with the honor in his old age, and it can be a fragment of any such older account.

Although the narrative method was seldom used as a unifying principle of a poetry anthology, the "Love" books in royal waka collections make some use of it. The poems are arranged roughly in the order in which a love affair proceeds, beginning with poems on first love and concluding with those on the end of a romantic affair. A shorter sequence of poems within a section sometimes shows narrative structure. In Book Thirteen of the *Man'yōshū,* for instance, a story of the man who came far to Hatsuse only to meet his love in vain is narrated in a sequence of four dialogue poems, the first two by the man and the last two by the woman.

In genres other than poetry, prose fiction most obviously shows the narrative method. Indeed, its distinguishing feature lies in this very method. In classical Japanese literature there is much prose narrative, starting with the *Taketori Monogatari.* It is characteristic of Japanese works in this genre that they tend to be short. When they are long, structural principles other than the narrative method are often involved. The *Taketori Monogatari,* for example, is unified more or less by a romantic plot built around suitors' rivalry for a beautiful woman's hand. Yet the plot is loose enough to allow for a subsidiary use of repetition. When, one after the other, the five competing princes tell their adventures, the plot slackens and looks as if it were a collection of five tales. The *Heike Monogatari* also has a central theme—the fall of the Heike clan. Yet the connecting link among the episodes involves temporal sequence more than narrative logic. As a matter of fact, medieval bards used to recite the episodes as though they were independent tales. I have already touched on *Kōshoku Ichidai Otoko* and *Kōshoku Ichidai Onna,* which are, especially in the former instance, less tales than collections of tales. Each episode has a plot, but the link connecting the episodes is sequence more than plot. Only in late Edo fiction—e.g. Bakin's *Hakkenden* and Shunsui's *Umegoyomi*—does narrative logic begin to emerge as a general unifying principle of a long work of fiction.

Some modern Japanese novelists have forwarded theories explaining why traditional Japanese narratives lack tightly knit plots. Tanizaki Jun'ichirō, for example, seemed to believe that Japanese writers lacked the physical strength to construct a long plot. Nagai Kafū emphasized the unpredictability of the Japanese climate and the resulting tendency among people to believe in coincidence and fate. In a famous literary controversy with Tanizaki, Akutagawa Ryūnosuke articulated his liking for a "lyrical plot," which is actually more sequence than plot, and in doing so he was unknowingly speaking for the lyrical impulse of many a premodern Japanese storyteller. Kawabata Yasunari felt that premodern Japanese writers refrained from constructing a tightly wrought plot because they viewed life as formless and structureless. Probably none of these theories is satisfactory by itself, but when these and other similar theories are combined, they go a long way to explain one of the distinguishing features of premodern Japanese fiction.

The Logical Method

When a poem is substantially a proposition or an argument, its structural unity is often attained through discursive reason. In using logical means, the poet tries to convince the reader of the rightness of an argument for which the best proof entails such tightly constructed logic as a syllogism. When the poet presents premises and then shows, step by step, how they force a conclusion, the reader can only be convinced of the validity of the argument. The method is an intellectual one, and the poem utilizing it appeals mainly to the reader's rational faculty.

The logical method has been common in the poetry of the West, where logic and rhetoric have been part of basic school education for many centuries. Scholars have shown, for instance, how familiar Shakespeare was with these school subjects and how he made use of them in his plays—in, say, Brutus' speech before the mob after the assassination of Caesar. English metaphysical poets often used logical progression in their works, too. The most famous example is "To His Coy Mistress" by Andrew Marvell. As T. S. Eliot noted, the three paragraphs that constitute the poem have something of the structure of a syllogism.[20]

Lacking the Graeco-Roman tradition, classical Japanese culture did not promote the arts of logic and rhetoric. Consequently, within the total corpus of classical Japanese verse the ratio of poems having logical structure is much smaller. Still, some Japanese poems do show syllogistic progression, or part of it. An early example is found in the *Kojiki*—in Princess Suseri's song addressed to her husband Yachihoko. The husband, who had many wives in different parts of the country, was about to go on a trip and leave her behind. As he mounted a horse, she called out to him:

> Divine prince of eight thousand spears,
>   great ruler of our land,
> because you are a man,
> at every island point you row around,
> at each and every shore point you row around
> you must have a young-grass wife.
> But look, because I am a woman,
> I have no man besides you,
> I have no husband besides you.
> Under fluffy painted curtains,
> under downy silken covers,
> under rustling mulberry covers,
> breasts youthful as soft snow,
> arms white as mulberry rope—
> hold them with your bare hands, caress them;
> and, your hand and my hand for a pillow,
> let us sleep, thighs outstretched.
> Drink this superb wine.[21]

[20] *Selected Essays, 1917-1932* (New York: Harcourt, Brace, 1932), pp. 254-55.

[21] *Kojiki, NKBT,* 1, 105. Translated by Hiroaki Sato in *From the Country of Eight Islands* (Garden City, N.Y.: Doubleday, 1981), p. 6.

The argument of the story progresses logically: a man can have many wives, but a woman is allowed to have only one husband; I am a woman; hence I have only one husband—you. The corollary of the conclusion is, of course, "I love you dearly since you are my only husband." The structure is logically rigorous, and the conclusion arrived at is forceful because of the strength of the logic. In this particular instance the forcefulness has been well proven: as the *Kojiki* tells us, upon hearing the song, Yachihoko had a change of heart and decided to stay home with the princess.

The *Kokinshū* is well known for its play with logical procedures. Because waka is such a short verse form, however, not all parts of the argument are verbalized. Some must be tacitly suggested. A poem by Ariwara Narihira will serve as an example:

Yo no naka ni	If there were no such thing
taete sakura no	as cherry blossoms
nakariseba	in this world,
haru no kokoro wa	in springtime how untroubled
nodokekaramashi.	our hearts would be![22]

What the poem states is a conditional proposition. It leaves unstated the middle and the conclusion of the syllogism, which are, of course, "But there is such a thing as cherry blossoms. Therefore, our hearts have to be troubled in springtime." The impact of the poem is more poignant because of the omission, since the reader has to make the deduction, thereby becoming more active.

The following waka by Lady Ise also uses the logical method, but in this instance the part omitted is the premise:

Harugasumi	Now when spring mists rise,
tatsu o misutete	the wild geese
yuku kari wa	turn and fly away!
hana naki sato ni	They must be used to living in villages
sumi ya naraeru.	where no cherries bloom.[23]

The missing premise is that all normal creatures love cherry blossoms. Again the reader is invited to identify with the poet's aes-

[22] *Kokinshū*, 1, 52. Translated by Burton Watson in *From the Country of Eight Islands*, p. 108.

[23] *Kokinshū*, 1, 31. Translated by Watson, p. 127.

theticism and induce the premise, which is the main point of the poem. One is expected to be amazed, along with the poet, at the insensitivity of the wild geese that do not appreciate the beauty of cherry blossoms. The logical method of the poem has resulted in a witty conceit.

The logical method was never very popular among renga poets, but they did make use of it in the same manner as waka poets. It manifests itself most often in what is called kokorozuke or linking through meaning. As the author of *Renga Hiden Shō* explains it,

> Kokorozuke is a method that precludes conventional associations, linking through words, or integration by describing or suggesting scenes. It depends solely on meaning.

Uma wa aredomo kachi nite zo yuku	Although a horse is available he chooses to travel on foot
asaborake yo no ma ni tsumoru yuki o mite.	at daybreak discovering the snow that has piled up during the night.[24]

The premise is omitted, but it must refer to the fact that anyone with a poetic mind enjoys a snow scene. Obviously the traveler in this verse is such a person; he would rather go on foot and leisurely enjoy the rare sight. The stanzas state the middle and the conclusion of a syllogism, inviting the reader to deduce the premise. Although not all the cases of kokorozuke rely on syllogism, most make some use of discursive logic. Of all the methods of linking used in renga, this is the one that comes closest to logical progression.

Outside poetry, the literary form that makes most use of discursive logic for its structure is a detective story. In the typical case, a victim is slain by someone at the outset, and the rest of the story is a process of ratiocination by a detective to discover who the murderer is. Outwardly the writer uses a narrative method, but the plot must be constructed by careful logic, so that all the premises given or hinted at in the narrative lead to a conclusion pointing toward the hitherto unknown killer. Sometimes the au-

[24] Ijichi Tetsuo, ed. *Rengaron Shū*, 2 vols. (Koten Bunko, 1953-1956), 2, 90.

thor may include a trial scene and present numerous logical arguments exchanged between the prosecutor and the defense attorney. In classical Japanese literature there is no story with this type of plot. The *Konjaku Monogatari* and other setsuwa collections include some murder stories, but the identity of the murderer is either revealed at the time of the crime or is not the point of the story. Some late Heian monogatari—the *Torikaebaya Monogatari,* for example—have a highly schematic, logical plot, but again their mystery is unraveled at the outset in most cases and leaves little scope for the reader's speculation. To read an authentic detective story, the Japanese had to wait until the Meiji period when Western literature began to be introduced. The Japanese term for a detective story, tantei shōsetsu, came into existence around 1890.

Another literary form that often shows logical structure is an essay. Dryden's *Essay of Dramatic Poesy,* Locke's *Essay Concerning Human Understanding,* and Berkeley's *Essay Towards a New Theory of Vision* all have a great deal of discursive logic in structure as well as in substance. Classical literature in Japanese includes no such elaborate essay. The important literary works now termed zuihitsu are more like stray notes, expressing random thoughts in a casual manner. Some zuihitsu do show a semblance of logical structure. For example, the general framework of Kamo no Chōmei's (1153-1216) *Hōjōki* is logical, the premise (the world of men is filled with disasters) forcing the conclusion (the best way to live in such a world is a hermitic life). The framework of the *Tsurezuregusa* by Yoshida Kenkō (1280-1350) is far from logical, but its sections intermittently show something of logical structure. In the famous section on the beauty of things perishable, the author first sets out the premise about the brevity of human life and then induces the conclusion: it is desirable to die before the age of forty. Some works of Edo fiction include many controversies and arguments; these might have been written in the form of an essay. Several tales in the *Ugetsu Monogatari* and *Harusame Monogatari* provide better-known examples.

Chikamatsu's plays, especially his sewamono (plays based on contemporary life), would seem to have logical structure, all the parts of the play pointing toward the suicide of the doomed lovers. In many of those plays, the hero's honor as a merchant is compromised by a villain through a trick or some dubious scheme. Proceeding from this premise, the play carefully unfolds a logical plot that inevitably reaches a tragic climax at its end. The logic used, however, is more emotional than discursive. In *Sonezaki Shinjū*, for instance, the hero Tokubei is cheated by the villain Kuheiji and robbed of an enormous amount of money. Yet it does not logically follow that he has to kill himself to "show to all of Osaka the purity of my heart," as he says he has to.[25] For example, he could have appealed to the authorities and tried to have his name cleared, especially if he had been an honorable merchant all his life. But Chikamatsu constructed the play in such a way as to convince the audience emotionally that suicide was the only way out. Tokubei is beaten up by Kuheiji and five other rascals in public view, so that his decision for suicide becomes the most natural course of conduct for him to take. He is also depicted as young and emotional, not cool and calculating. Thus the play's structure has to be said to depend more on narrative—not logical—method. The same can be said of other plays by Chikamatsu on contemporary subjects. In his jidaimono, or historical pieces, a temporal sequence is employed as well. It is difficult indeed to point to a major work of premodern Japanese literature that distinctly shows a logical structure dominating over the temporal and other kinds I have discussed.

The Double Mood

The double mood refers to a structure in which two different, often contrasting tones are used in successive or alternating literary units. A poem with a lyrical mood may suddenly take a sarcastic turn in midcourse, or an elegant love story featuring a nobleman and a court lady may be interspersed with bawdy scenes involving people of the lower classes. The effect of such a technique varies,

[25] *NKBT*, 49, 27. Translated by Donald Keene in his *Anthology of Japanese Literature* (New York: Grove, 1955), p. 399.

depending on the way in which the two tones relates to each other. The combinations may involve surprise, humor, irony, or a sense of indecision and insecurity. The method is a sophisticated one, providing a double set of voices and attitudes, intermingling them in complex ways.

Yvor Winters, who coined the term "double mood," noted that this method was most popular among European and American poets preceding and following Jules Laforgue. The names he mentioned included Tristan Corbière, Théophile Gautier, T. S. Eliot, Ezra Pound, Wallace Stevens—poets he did not highly esteem. Other examples he cited were Dryden's *Mac Flecknoe*, Pope's *Dunciad*, Voltaire's *La Pucella*, and Churchill's *Dedication to Warburton*—although in these instances he liked the poems. My example, however, is a stanza of a poem by Byron:

When a man hath no freedom to fight for at home,
Let him combat for that of his neighbours;
Let him think of the glories of Greece and of Rome,
And get knocked on the head for his labours.[26]

The first three lines of the stanza sustain a serious, almost heroic mood, and then—suddenly in the last line—that mood is mocked. The sudden change of mood is as effective as it is surprising.

Very similar methods have been exploited by Japanese poets for humorous effects. A good example is the following kyōka attributed to Hosokawa Yūsai (1534-1610). According to an episode related in *Seisuishō*, Yūsai was at the residence of Toyotomi Hideyoshi (1536-1598), the military ruler of Japan, when soybeans coated with shredded green seaweed were served for refreshments. When, on the spot, Hideyoshi asked Yūsai to compose a poem fitting the occasion, the poet responded with this kyōka:

Kimi ga yo wa
chiyo ni yachiyo ni
sazare ishi no

May my lord's reign
last for a thousand, ten thousand
generations hence

[26] From "Stanzas." Ernest Hartley Coleridge, ed., *The Poetical Works of Lord Byron* (London: John Murray, 1905), p. 1036.

iwao to narite	till the smallest pebbles become
koke no musu *mame.*	*soybeans* covered with moss.[27]

The tone of the first four lines is serious, even solemn; as a matter of fact, these lines are identical with those of an old poem which is now the national anthem of Japan:

Kimi ga yo wa	May my lord's reign
chiyo ni yachiyo ni	last for a thousand, ten thousand
sazare ishi no	generations hence
iwao to narite	till the smallest pebbles become
koke no musu *made.*	*boulders* covered with moss.

But that somber mood is suddenly broken in the last line: in place of the image of stately boulders greened with moss, there are small soybeans covered with moss-like seaweed! The surprise is greater in the original Japanese, which keeps the suspense intact until the very last syllable of the poem.

A similar technique is often used in senryū, which, however, cannot build up suspense as much because of its shorter form. The following example from *Yanagidaru* shows it well:

Zenshū wa	Zen priest,
zazen ga sumu to	meditation finished,
nomi o tori.	looking for fleas.[28]

The first two lines are serious in tone, portraying a glum-looking Zen priest in a monastery. The final line unexpectedly changes the mood from the sublime to the ridiculous: the priest, who has just been in search of spiritual enlightenment, is now in search of fleas. The humor is accompanied by moral implications here, for the poem points toward the difficulty of the Buddhist ideal of transcending humanity.

The effect of the double mood does not have to be humorous

[27] *Kindai Nihon Bungaku Taikei,* 25 vols. (Kokumin Tosho, 1928), 24, 40. Rocks were popularly believed to grow larger with the passage of time.

[28] Ibid., 22, 734. Translated by Bownas and Thwaite in *The Penguin Book of Japanese Verse,* p. 131, slightly modified.

or ironical. It can be doleful, as shown in this poem from the *Kokinshū*:

Momochidori	When large groups of plovers
saezuru haru wa	continue to cry out in spring,
monogoto ni	everything alive
aratamaredomo	finds itself renewed again,
ware zo furiyuku.	except that I alone grow old.[29]

The mood of the first four lines is a happy one, but that is suddenly reversed in the final line, creating an effective contrast. The same technique is used with similar effectiveness by Buson in the following hokku, although the nature of the impact created is markedly different:

Asakaze ni	In the morning breeze,
ke o fukare iru	letting the hair be blown—
kemushi kana.	a caterpillar.[30]

The first line immediately establishes a refreshing mood, and the second suggests a lovely young woman letting her hair be blown in the morning breeze. Then comes the shocking third line: instead of a woman, there is a hairy caterpillar. The poem produces a surprise, but the surprise leads not so much to humor as to a discovery of novel beauty. The image of a caterpillar, with sparkling dewdrops on its hair blown in the morning breeze, harmonizes beautifully with the rest of the verdant scene.

Buson was a master in utilizing the technique of the double mood, but the structure was generally common in hokku. It was only that other hokku poets seldom created as striking a contrast as he did. Indeed, one of the time-honored conventions of hokku composition was the kireji or cutting-word, a technique by which to create a caesura in the poem. A kireji semantically cuts the poem in two parts, one of which is related to the other by either a similar or a contrasting mood. When the two parts are contrasted, as in Buson's caterpillar poem, the technique can be said to be the double mood. Hattori Dohō (1657-1730) was apparently referring to the

[29] *Kokinshū*, 1, 28.

[30] Ebara Taizō, ed., *Yosa Buson Shū* (Asahi Shimbunsha, 1957), p. 197.

technique when he wrote in *Sanzōshi*, "A hokku has a certain movement of mind: it goes and then returns."[31] In other words, before the caesura the poem has the mood of going away, and after the caesura its mood is that of returning; there is an interplay of the two contrasting moods.

The double mood appears frequently in renga, too. This is natural, because in renga two successive stanzas that make a unit are composed by two different poets. The first stanza was often given a very different interpretation by the composer of the second stanza. In fact, one of the charms of writing renga must have lain in seeing how the author of the second stanza worked on the mood of the first and changed it. A method of linking called rakitai, or form that overpowers an ogre, provides an extreme case. Here is an example cited in the *Renga Shotai Hiden Shō*:

Aoku akaki mo onaji oni no na	Green or red, they are terrifying ogres alike
kawaraya no nokiba no matsu no shita momiji.	under a pine tree in the yard of a rooftile shop leaves have begun to color.[32]

The mood of the couplet is rough, crude, and even a bit grotesque, presenting ogres of all sizes and colors. The following triplet subdues that inelegant mood by changing ogres into gargoyles. What looked like ogres were really gargoyles piled up by a rooftile shop, and they looked red and green when seen through tinted autumn leaves.[33] The method of linking used here is clever, witty, and imaginative. The author of *Renga Shotai Hiden Shō* stressed that this kind of method had to be used when the previous stanza had a rough, inelegant mood. "If the second stanza should also go wild like the first," he said, "it will impair five, or even ten, stanzas that follow."[34]

The double mood is observed in another conventional method

[31] *NKBT*, 66, 430.

[32] Ijichi, ed., *Rengaron Shinshū*, p. 119.

[33] The pine tree is evergreen, but there are some deciduous plants growing under it.

[34] Ijichi, ed., *Rengaron Shinshū*, p. 120.

of linking renga stanzas. This one is called ibutsu no tai, or form with an alien object. To cite an example again from the *Renga Shotai Hiden Shō*:

Tsuki no wazuka ni kasumu yūgure	The moon looks a little hazy in the evening twilight
kuma no sumu utsubogi nagara hana sakite.	on a hollow tree where bears make their home, blossoms are in bloom.[35]

The couplet depicts an exquisitely beautiful scene of a spring evening, with a large moon hanging hazily in the sky. The triplet that follows, however, abruptly changes the tone by introducing "an alien object," the terrifying image of bears. Yet the elegant mood is restored in the last line of the stanza, which refers to cherry blossoms blooming on an old tree. The elegant and inelegant moods coexist in these two stanzas, and the method is distinctly that of the double mood.

Examples of the double mood can also be found in genres other than poetry. We may begin with a tale entitled "Haizumi" in the *Tsutsumi Chūnagon Monogatari*. This starts as a pathetic story of a submissive wife who voluntarily leaves her house when her husband asks her permission to bring a mistress to live with them. But toward the end of the story the tone suddenly changes to comic when the mistress, flustered at her paramour's unexpected visit, mistakes eyebrow paint for face powder and puts the black stuff all over her cheeks. One might say that the mood termed "aware" in Japanese is succeeded by the mood of okashi. In the first book of the *Uji Shūi Monogatari* there is a tale about a farmer's son visiting Mt. Hiei in Kyoto one gusty day in spring. Watching cherry blossoms scatter in the strong wind, the boy weeps bitterly. A passing observer speculates that the youngster must be a poet begrudging the destruction of nature's beauty. He is surprised to discover, however, that in reality the boy is worried not about the blossoms but about his father, whose wheat farm he thinks must have been devastated by the gusts. The poetic mood of the tale is

[35] Ibid., p. 134.

abruptly replaced by a materialistic concern. Again, Saikaku's *Budō Denraiki* is supposed to be a collection of revenge stories extolling traditional samurai valor. But not all the heroes succeed in revenge in the way a model samurai is expected to. In one tale, a young samurai eager to avenge his father's death finally meets the enemy he has long been looking for, but when he finds a certain young woman passionately in love with his enemy he gives up the revenge and lets the lovers be united. What should have been a thoroughgoing story of valor ends as a romantic love story.

Perhaps the most subtle use of the double mood in classical Japanese literature is observed in the alternation of the serious and the comic in the nō theater. As has often been pointed out, kyōgen are short interludes that provide "the other voice" for the nō. The nō *Utō* for example, narrates the gruesome story of a hunter who, because he has killed numerous birds during his lifetime, suffers dreadful torments in hell after his death. In contrast, the kyōgen play *Esashi Jūō*, which similarly portrays a hunter in the nether world, depicts the sinful man bribing the mighty king of Hades and eventually gaining three additional years of life on earth. The somber message of the nō is modified considerably by the lighthearted mood of the kyōgen. Of course, in actual performance *Esashi Jūō* does not necessarily follow *Utō*, but there is no doubt that the melancholy mood of the nō plays, with their emphasis on cosmic laws and deemphasis on the power of humanity, are mitigated by the interspersed kyōgen plays with their assertive attitude toward the human world. It is as if the contrasting voices of human and superhuman laws were speaking alternately.

In general, Japanese literary works that make use of the double-mood technique do not seem to reflect ambivalence and insecurity of mind, as Yvor Winters thought they did in Western poetry after Jules Laforgue. What they do show is the coexistence of two sets of values and attitudes—courtly aesthetics versus agrarian economics, or a Buddhist negation of passions versus a humanistic affirmation of them, or a samurai's idealism versus a merchant's realism. By and large, Japanese writers seem to have accepted these contrasting attitudes without trying to resolve them. They would use the technique for artistic purposes—for instance, to subdue an inelegant mood or bring about a happy ending—and did not care much about apparent inconsistency in moral attitude. The double mood does not always produce humor, but when it does so in Japanese literature it has tended to be happy, and not cynical, laughter. If this fact implies anything, it implies Japanese acceptance of experience rather than ambivalence or insecurity.

Qualitative Progression

"Qualitative progression," a term invented by Kenneth Burke,[36] refers to a structural method in which the quality of personal mental experience is the central principle unifying different parts of a literary work. It is similar to the double mood in its lack of logical coherence. But whereas the double mood deliberately builds up an expectation and then destroys it, qualitative progression does not even build up an expectation. It is more illogical and unpredictable. One might call it "associative sequence," as Barbara Herrnstein Smith did, since it integrates different parts of a literary work through the association of the author or a main character.[37] One might also relate it to the stream-of-consciousness technique, as Yvor Winters did, since the mind in its normal state shows a flow of associations that are personal and whimsical.[38]

In Western literature, qualitative progression has most often been utilized in the twentieth century. Burke mentioned T. S. Eliot's *The Waste Land* and Malcolm Cowley's sonnet "Mine No. 6" as examples. Winters, who disliked the method, saw it in such works as Ezra Pound's *Cantos*, Rimbaud's "Larme," and James Joyce's *Finnegan's Wake*. One can go on citing any number of works showing qualitative progression because, in spite of Winter's protest, Eliot and Joyce became highly influential figures in their time and enjoyed a great number of followers emulating their technique. Modern poetry devoid of Eliot, Pound, and Wallace

[36] *Counter-Statement*, pp. 124-25.

[37] *Poetic Closure*, pp. 139-50.

[38] *Primitivism and Decadence*, p. 51.

Stevens, or the modern novel devoid of Joyce, Proust and Virginia Woolf, would be poorer indeed.

Japanese literature is rich in qualitative progression, and before modern times, too. The comments by Kenkō, Bashō, and Kawabata, quoted at the outset of this chapter, are testimonies to its pervasiveness. But the genre that makes most frequent use of qualitative progression is renga, in which stanzas are linked largely by association. Many of its codified linking methods fall in this category. The simplest of these is called keiki, or linking through the mood of the scene. *Kyōchūshō* gives an example:

Kasuka ni tsuzuku nobe no furumichi	Barely continuing onwards, an old trail across the fields
hitomura no take no ha kashige ume sakite.	amid a cluster of slanting bamboo leaves, plum blossoms in bloom.[39]

The couplet describes a country scene. The author of the subsequent triplet caught the spirit of the scene, which was that of lonely beauty. Then, dipping himself deep into that lonely mood, he came up with a stanza that creates the same impression: plum blossoms blooming amid a bamboo bush. He did not say, but the blossoms are sparse, for the tree is wild and has to compete with the vigorous root system of the bamboos for its nourishment. The progression from the couplet to the triplet works subtly, using a mental quality that is the core of qualitative progression.

The connection between two stanzas is more remote and personal in the method called uzumizuke, or linking through a hidden allusion. The method is somewhat akin to honzetsu, except that in this instance allusion is less obvious and need not be to an old story. Indeed, the allusion may be so vague that the reader may miss it; even so, no great damage will be done to the poem. The *Renga Hiden Shō* has an example:

Kogiyuku fune ni samuki urakaze	A boat rowing out to the sea in the chilly coastal wind

[39] *Zoku Gunsho Ruijū*, 19 vols. (Keizai Zasshisha, 1902-12), 17, 1238.

matsu tōki shiohi no yuki no asaborake.	far away, a pine grove: on the beach covered with snow the day begins to dawn.[40]

At first glance these two stanzas may look as if they were connected by keiki, since a beach scene follows the image of a boat. Fukui Kyūzō, one of the modern authorities on renga, in fact has said this is an instance of keiki.[41] But the author of *Renga Hiden Shō* notes that the connection has been made through a waka by Priest Mansei:

Yo no naka o nani ni tatoen asaborake kogiyuku fune no ato no shiranami.	To what shall I compare this life? the way a boat rowed out from the morning harbor leaves no traces on the sea.[42]

Upon reading the couplet, the poet next in turn was reminded of this poem by Mansei and came up with the image of snow-white waves pounding the beach. The allusion is vague: it is so well hidden that even the most knowledgeable reader may miss it. In an extreme case of uzumizuke, only the author of the verse may know the allusion, because the association is too personal.

In another technique used in renga, the link between stanzas is obvious but nevertheless whimsical and has to be included in the category of qualitative progression. Called kotobazuke or linking through diction, the technique is common in renga and uncommon in modern Western poetry. Basically it is play on words. The author of the second stanza picks out a word from the first stanza and builds his own stanza around its homonym or homophone. The two stanzas thus joined have no ostensible relation to each other except by coincidence in pronunciation. The *Shoshin Kyūeishū* has an example:

[40] Ijichi, ed., *Rengaron Shū*, 2, 90.

[41] See Fukui, ed., *Kōhon Tsukubashū Shinshaku*, 2, 108.

[42] *Man'yōshū*, no. 351. Translated by Ian Hideo Levy in *The Ten Thousand Leaves*, 1 (Princeton: Princeton University Press, 1981), 189.

Uramite mo nao nagusaminikeri	I tried to hate her, and that consoled my heart a little
matsubara no shiohi ni kakaru tabi no michi.	extending toward a pine grove on the beach, this traveler's road.[43]

The English translation does not make much sense. The subject of the couplet is love: a man rejected by a woman is trying to console himself by hating her. The triplet, on the other hand, is about a traveler who is enjoying scenic beauty. The connecting link is a Japanese word "urami," which means at once "to hate" and "to see a bay." The author of the couplet intended the word to mean "to hate," but the writer of the triplet took it for the other meaning. According to the second author's interpretation, the couplet would mean something like:

> I saw a bay, and that
> consoled my heart a little.

Here is a traveler whose loneliness is mitigated a little by the beautiful sight of a coast. Kotobazuke, then, is quite a complex and subtle technique. On the surface, two stanzas are linked by a coincidence in pronunciation, yet underneath they create an interesting interplay of meaning. To put it simply, the stanzas just cited seem to imply: "Man has to face many hateful things in this life, but fortunately there is a consoling element in the very act of hating, just as a traveler who meets many sorrowful events along the road may come upon a beautiful scene of nature once in a while." The two stanzas, first brought together by the whimsical association of the word, "urami," have been made to convey an interesting message about human life.

There are many more methods of linking stanzas in renga that can be considered variations of qualitative progression. Yosei (linking through surplus meaning), sōtai (linking through contrast), honka (linking by allusion to a well known poem), nadokoro (linking by allusion to a famous place)—they all utilize associations for

[43] Ijichi, ed., *Rengaron Shū*, 1, 235.

connecting stanzas. It is no wonder that renga should be called a poetry of associations. The main pleasure of writing renga lies precisely in seeing the stanzas progress in an unpredictable way through the associations of different individuals participating in the writing.

The methods of renga composition were taken over and refined further by haikai poets. The names by which the methods came to be called were different, but by and large they were varieties of associational sequence. Nioi (fragrance), hibiki (reverberation), utsuri (reflection), and omokage (semblance) are all impressionistic terms that suggest the ways in which the mood of one stanza is transmitted to that of the next. It is as if the fragrance of a flower were drifting in the air, or the sound coming from an object were causing some other object to reverberate with it. I will cite just one example from *Kuzu no Matsubara*:

Ine no hanobi no chikara naki kaze	Rice plants in their growing season feeble in the feeble wind
hosshin no hajime ni koyuru Suzukayama.	starting a new life as a monk, he travels through the Suzuka Pass.[44]

On the surface it is difficult to see what integrates the second stanza with the first. The couplet is a description of rice plants in summer, whereas the triplet presents a man who has recently had a religious awakening and who is leaving the capital for the remote eastern provinces. A closer examination reveals, however, that there is a common quality of mind implied in both stanzas. In the couplet, rice plants are not growing vigorously because of bad weather. There is something stagnant, feeble, and indecisive in the picture described. That mood is reflected in the image of a man who, although having renounced the world, still finds himself attracted to the capital even as he travels through the Suzuka Pass. The subtle connection between the two stanzas has been termed

[44] Miyamoto Saburō et al., eds., *Kōhon Bashō Zenshū*, 10 vols. (Kadokawa Shoten, 1962-1969), 7, 258. The Suzuka Pass is located to the east of Kyoto on the main highway to the eastern provinces.

nioi in *Kuzu no Matsubara*. It is like keiki, only more remote in connection.

There are instances in which a similar principle seems to be at work in collecting and arranging poems on the same subject. For example, the well-known group of thirteen waka written by Ōtomo Tabito in praise of wine might appear to use the method of repetition, since all the poems reiterate a single theme—the merit of drinking.[45] But there is a subtle, renga-like progression of mood through the poems, their tone growing more emphatic and high-pitched as they proceed. It is as though the poet became more intoxicated and his voice grew louder. In the *Shinkokinshū* and some other royal anthologies, the seasonal sections generally show temporal sequence in their arrangement of individual poems. But, as Konishi Jin'ichi has shown, associational progression plays an important role within that general framework.[46] To a lesser degree the same can be said of private waka anthologies such as the *Sankashū* and the *Kinkaishū*, as well as of renga anthologies like the *Tsukubashū*. Hokku collections have either repetitive, temporal, or associational structure.

There are many instances of qualitative progression in genres other than poetry, too. As admitted by its author, Kenkō, the *Tsurezuregusa* has no logical structure as a whole; its different sections are put together by the whim of his mind. Ostensibly, Bashō's *Oku no Hosomichi* has a temporal sequence. But, as many scholars have pointed out, there is something like a progression of renga or haikai stanzas at work throughout its different segments, too. Scholars have also discovered haikai-like structure in some of Saikaku's works in prose fiction and attributed it to this training as a haikai poet in his youth. But probably the most radical type of qualitative progression is observed in the texts of nō, especially in the concluding lyrical part where the shite vents emotions while performing a climactic dance.[47] The play progresses less through narrative or discursive logic than through images, associations, and allusions. In those scenes, we find many examples

[45] [*Man'yōshū*, 3, 338-50. Ed.]

[46] See Konishi, as in note 36.

[47] [The shite (something like "the doer") is the principal role in nō. Ed.]

equivalent to keiki, uzumizuke, kotobazuke, and other similarly irrational methods of structure, so much so that there may be little or no normal syntax. The reader is induced to suspend reason and enter a strange world of differing moods where reason cannot reach. If qualitative progression implies an attempt to go beyond reason, nō playwrights knew it all along and made use of the technique with remarkable success.

In conclusion, then, it may be said that what I have called "sequence" is either the method of repetition, temporal sequence, double mood, qualitative progression, or a combination of two or more of these. Classical Japanese poets and writers were not greatly interested in narrative or logical method: hence the relative lack of "plot" in Japanese literature. To analyze a Japanese literary work, especially a poem, it seems more profitable to apply the concepts we have been discussing than to try a logical analysis. We have considered simpler examples of poems in classical Japanese literature and, I hope, have shed some new light on them. For each structural principle, prose works have been mentioned for examples without analysis.

Where do we go from here? I see at least two possible directions. First, we might probe into the reason or reasons why classical Japanese poets and writers were so fond of repetitive method, of temporal sequence, and especially of qualitative progression. Clearly the question is related to the identity of Japanese literature, indeed of Japanese culture as a whole. Ultimately the answer or answers will have to come from extraliterary areas of study, such as anthropology, psychology, or religious studies. But before seeking help from these areas, literary scholars need to do more explorations on their own.

Second, our methodology may be used as one means of analyzing literary works. My examples have been relatively simple. But we should be able to apply the same criteria to more complex and complete works combining two or more structural methods. For example, the *Minase Sangin Hyakuin* may be analyzed by reference to methods of repetition, narrative, qualitative progression, and so on, as well as to more traditional concepts like kuzai (topic), ji-mon (ground-design), and shin-so (close-distant). Buson's

"Shunpū Batei Kyoku," for which no traditional method of analysis exists, may be studied in the same way. The utmost challenge for a literary critic would be the *Genji Monogatari,* which seems to combine various methods of structure in a complex way. Of course there is a serious—and perhaps extraliterary—question of whether the present order of chapters of that work was the one intended by the author. But putting that unanswerable question aside, one can say that the existing story uses both temporal sequence and narrative method for its general framework. Within the story, the sequence of "Hahakigi," "Utsusemi" and "Yūgao" chapters does show something like the method of repetition, the latter two chapters supporting the generalizations made in the former chapter. The progression from "Waka Murasaki" to "Suetsumuhana," on the other hand, seems to be that of double mood, since the mood of romantic (and illicit) love is followed by a comic episode. One may go on and analyze this and other tales in a similar way. I have no intention of claiming that this is the best or the most effective way to do a structural study. But this kind of analysis has seldom been attempted in the context of Japanese literature, and in that sense it can be said to be new. When applied with discretion, it might lead to some interesting discoveries in classical Japanese literature.

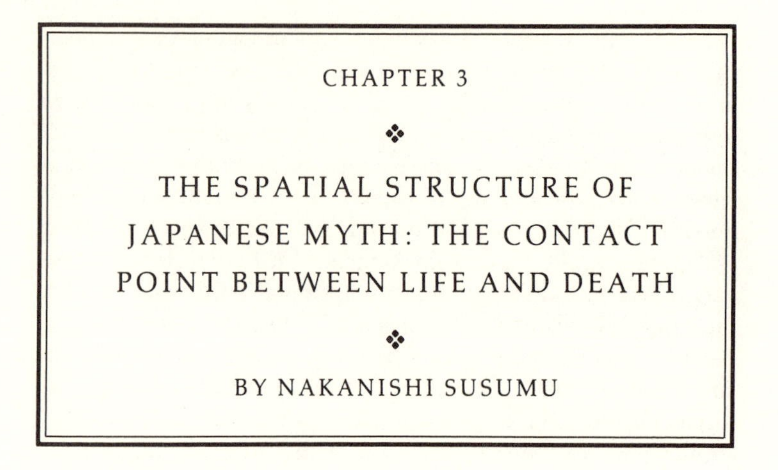

CHAPTER 3

THE SPATIAL STRUCTURE OF JAPANESE MYTH: THE CONTACT POINT BETWEEN LIFE AND DEATH

BY NAKANISHI SUSUMU

Death and Time as Spatial Matters

The *Nihon Shoki* (*Chronicles of Japan to A.D. 697*) narrates the story of Izanagi's visit to the Land of Yomi.[1] He longs to be reunited with his deceased wife, Izanami, and so travels to the Land of Yomi. Upon seeing her hideously foul appearance, however, he flees the scene. He narrowly escapes his wife's pursuit by declaring a divorce at Yomotsu Hirasaka, "the Level Pass of Yomi" (Aston, pp. 24-25). The *Nihon Shoki* continues: "Some say that the Level Pass of Yomi is not any place in particular, but means only the space of time when the breath fails on the approach of death" (p. 26). But "the Level Pass of Yomi" is most commonly believed today to have been thought a place that divided the world of the dead from that of the living, and more specifically, a slope that

Translated by Yoshiko Yokochi Samuel.

[1] The *Nihon Shoki*, also called *Nihongi*, is cited from vols. 67 and 68 of *Nihon Koten Bungaku Taikei* (hereafter *NKBT*) (Iwanami Shoten, 1967), 67, 90-96: Section 5, paragraph 6 of the chapter "Kami no Yo: 1" ("The Age of the Gods: 1"). The translation used is that by W. G. Aston, *Nihongi: Chronicles of Japan from the Earliest Times to A.D. 697* (Rutland, Vt.: Charles E. Tuttle, 1972 repr.). [All citations of Aston refer to page numbers in the first series of numbers. The translator has enlarged on the author's notes and has transferred some material from the text to the notes, a double practice I have further augmented—Ed.]

descends from the mouth of the tomb into an inner chamber. The "hira" in Hirasaka is believed to have been derived from an Ainu word, "pira," meaning slope. A "thousand-men-pull-rock," with which Izanagi obstructs the Pass before forsaking Izanami (p. 25), is believed to have been a stone slab that was used to shield a sarcophagus in ancient times.

This interpretation is not without legitimate bases. The *Kojiki (A Record of Ancient Matters)* explains that the "Pass" is "now called the pass Ipuya (Ifuya)-zaka in the land of Idumo (Izumo)" (Philippi, p. 67).[2] Furthermore, we find "Ifuya Shrine" registered in both "Jimmyōchō" ("A List of Shrines")[3] and *Izumo Fudoki (The Topography of the Province of Izumo).*[4] *The Topography* tells us that Ifuya Shrine is located in the county of Iu in Izumo and that there was another place, Ifuya, in the hamlet of Uka in the county of Izumo. The latter place is said to have a cave with a hollow inside, which was called "since olden days to the present . . . 'the Pass of Yomi' (Yomi no saka) and 'the Hollow of Yomi' (Yomi no ana)" (p. 182). Both the *Kojiki* and *The Topography* lead us to believe that Ifuya not only is an actual place but is also the very border between death and life, that is, "the Level Pass of Yomi."

What, then, does the *Nihon Shoki* explanation for "the Level Pass of Yomi" mean? It is indeed difficult to imagine that any *place* is designated as the world of the dead. Death is a state one reaches after life; it has little to do with space. The border, or entrance into the state of death, is the threshold into unconsciousness and not into any particular place. The exact location of "the Level Pass of Yomi," therefore, seems entirely irrelevant. Nonetheless, a question remains: if death is a matter of a transition in time and not in space, why is it given a specific place name and location in mythology?

[2] *Kojiki,* as in *NKBT,* vol. 1 (1957). The translation used is by Donald L. Philippi, *Kojiki* (University of Tokyo Press, 1968), which is cited by page number in the text.

[3] "Jimmyōchō," in "Jingi 9" in vol. 9 of *Engi Shiki Mokuroku.*

[4] *Izumo Fudoki (The Izumo Topography)* in *Fudoki, NKBT,* 2 (1957), citations given in the text.

It appears that ancient Japanese believed death to be the beginning of a long journey into the other world, and the first place to cross on this journey to be "the Level Pass of Yomi." Time and space were undifferentiated in their minds: they conceived of death as both a spatial and a temporal transition. In the lives of ancient people, time and space often blended with each other to the point of fusion. Following his flight from Yomi, for instance, Izanagi gives birth to the so-called three noble children—the Sun Goddess, the Moon Deity, and Susanō. There are five versions of this episode, including the two in the *Nihon Shoki* (Aston, pp. 27-28, 32). But the one in the *Kojiki* differs from all others. It tells us that, at the time of the Moon Deity's birth, Izanagi commanded him to rule "the realms of the night" (p. 71). But where are the "realms of the night," the place where the night "rules"? Such a place, needless to say, does not exist. Since the night denotes a time, the "realms of the night" is, therefore, a creation of ancient people who perceived time as place, the temporal night as a place that could be named. In other words, these people conceptualized the passing of time as a perpetual process of two worlds, the night and day, replacing each other. The night, moreover, "rules" these realms: it is a "doer," an animated entity. A song compiled in the *Kojiki* demonstrates this view. In response to Yachihoko's marriage proposal, Numakawa Hime recites:

> As soon as the sun
> hides behind the verdant mountains,
> the jet-black
> night will come.
> (pp. 106-107)

The dark night in this song is a being capable of taking action; it will "come" and "rule" the land. Night, which we conceive of temporally, is presented here as a ruler, or is even presented as a space that is ruled. This synthesis of time and space is an outstanding characteristic of mythology. In myth there is no difficulty in perceiving the point of contact between life and death as a spatial point, since to ancient peoples time and space were simply the obverse of each other.

The syllable "yo" in "Yomi" was originally a word meaning a

duration of time. Consider, for instance, the following poem from the *Man'yōshū (The Ten Thousand Leaves)*.[5]

Kimi ga yo mo	The span of your life,
waga yo mo shiru ya	and my life too,
iwashiro no	is determined by the grass
oka no kusane o	on Iwashiro Hill.
iza musubite na.	Come, let us bind it together.
	(1, 10; Levy, p. 43)

Using the word "yo" for both her life and her lover's, the author of this poem hopes to "bind the grass together," that is, prays for happiness in life. This "yo" gradually evolved and became a compound word, yononaka, meaning society, the world, and the public. Yononaka is an indigenous Japanese word that is conceptually derived from a Buddhist term, seken, a certain area of space. Here again, we find an example of time and space overlapping with each other, rather than being dichotomized. Mythology captures the very final stage of life in a concrete spatial image. It is important to keep in mind, however, that this same image is a temporal image as well.

The mythic view of time and space is an intriguing one in itself. But I should like to sharpen the focus by examining some place names in Japanese mythology. These are metaphors that suggest a variety of meanings, including time, by visual images of places. The specifity of the metaphors give the impression that these places actually existed.

Deities and Place Names

The story of Izanagi's ordeal is delivered in the *Nihon Shoki* as follows:

> [Izanagi says to Izanami] "Come no further," and threw down his staff, which was called Funado no Kami. [Akami is

[5] *Man'yōshū, NKBT*, 4-7 (1957). [The translation used for poems in the first five books is by Ian Hideo Levy, *The Ten Thousand Leaves*, 1 (Princeton: Princeton University Press, 1981). Citations by scroll or book number and poem, as also of

> a deity. See the Introduction.] Moreover, he threw down his girdle, which was called Nagachiha no Kami. Moreover, he threw down his upper garment, which was called Wazurai no Kami. Moreover, he threw down his trousers, which were called Akigui no Kami. Moreover, he threw down his shoes, which were called Chishiki no Kami (pp. 24-25).
>
> The rock with which the Level Pass of Yomi was blocked is called Yomido ni Fusagaru Ōkami. Another name for it is Chigayeshi no Ōkami (p. 26).[6]

The passage that explains "the Level Pass of Yomi," quoted at the beginning of this essay, occurs between the two paragraphs above. The present framing passages do depict the births of deities on the path from the world of Yomi. The point is to show the connection between these deities and time. Some of the names appearing here share a character, "michi," meaning a path or a road. Such usage demonstrates that a path or a road connotes a flow of time, that is, a lifetime. The "chi" in "michi" denotes a soul or a spirit; it is the same "chi" we find in "inochi," life. It seems reasonable to define this chi as the fundamental force that controls one's life. Consequently, Nagachiha no Kami is a deity that insures a continuation of the resolving cycles of life, and Chigaeshi no Ōkami is responsible for the resurrection of life. Living in the realms between life and death, these deities are those of immortality. The deity of resurrection, appropriately ranked as Ōkami, a Great Deity, is particularly important. He is the boulder that obstructs the path to the world of the dead.

Funado no Kami is indispensable for guarding the cross-section of life and death. The association between this deity and a staff probably developed from a folk custom of erecting a decorated

---

Levy, are given in the text. When Levy is not mentioned, the translations from the collection are the work of the translator and myself.—Ed.]

[6] [The spelling of proper names has been normalized. Names ending "no Kami," "no Mikoto," and "Ōmikami" designate deities, the second and third designating superior ones. After a first mention of a deity, the deity designation is dropped here. On these deities, see the discussion of this chapter in the introduction.—Ed.]

spear alongside a road in order to prevent evil spirits from entering a village. Ancient Japanese wished to keep the spirits of the dead at as remote a distance as possible. Wazurai no Kami is perhaps the deity of misfortunes, including diseases, and Akigui no Kami can be interpreted as the god of provision in the world of the dead, for this deity represents the widespread motif of initiation into the underworld by sharing its foods.

These deities were born of objects that were "thrown." As Izanagi's staff traverses time and space, for instance, it communicates freely with the spirit of Funado no Kami and becomes the deity himself. Ancient Japanese saw in the movement of a hurled object the metamorphosis of substances in life.

Such an interpretation of ancient Japanese thinking assists our understanding of the story of Izanagi and Izanami. Yet, may not mythology name actual places as well? How are we to understand how specific place names such as Ifuyazaka in the *Kojiki* came into being? Let us consider the following passages from *The Izumo Topography*:

> There is a sandy beach along the shore facing north. . . . There is a cave to the west of the beach. It is approximately six feet high and six feet wide. There is a hollow inside. No one is able to enter this cave. The distance inside is unknown. If one approaches this cave in his dream, he is sure to die. Because of this, the native inhabitants, since olden days to the present, call [this place] the Pass of Yomi and the Hollow of Yomi (p. 182).

This describes Ifuya in the hamlet of Uka, not the Ifuya Shrine that is located in the county of Iu. But I assume that there was a similar legend about Ifuyazaka, where the shrine must have been located. In any event, the mention of a dream is a factor crucial to the theory that this place is "the Level Pass of Yomi." A specific, actual place is directly linked with one's dreams, with that mysterious state of simulated death or pseudo-death. This cave probably would not have suggested any association with the "Level Pass of Yomi," if folk belief did not include a dream.

PLACE AS A FINAL STAGE OF LIFE

Another mythological episode deserves attention. The Sun Goddess Amaterasu Ōmikami commands Ame no Torifune no Kami to accompany Takemikazuchi no Mikoto, who will descend to the Central Land of Reed Plains and govern it. These two deities are received by Ōkuninushi no Mikoto, who remains quite uncertain about whether he should resist the new ruler or to submit to him. For a decision, he relies on his children, Yaekotoshironushi no Kami and Takeminakata no Kami. The children choose to cooperate with the new commander, and Ōkuninushi decides to retire to a life of seclusion (pp. 39-43).

According to the *Kojiki*, the place to which the heavenly ruler descends is "the beach of Inasa," and Ōkuninushi's home in retirement is on "the beach of Tagishi." *The Izumo Topography* tells us that "the beach of Inasa" is located near the Inasa Shrine. There has been no convincing theory concerning the location of Tagishi, but this name, too, should be considered in the same manner as others. "Inasa" is registered as "Izasa" in the *Bettō Kojiki.*[7] Moreover, a similar name, "the beach of Isasa" appears in the *Nihon Shoki* as the name of the place to which Sukunahiko no Mikoto returns from the sea (p. 62). Similarly, Section nine of "Kami no yo: 2" (The Age of the Gods: 2) in the *Nihon Shoki* claims that the place where the new ruler, Takemigatsuchi (or Takemikazuchi), reaches is "the beach of Itasa" (pp. 64-68). Here, we have a series of similar names, Inasa, Izasa, Isasa, and Itasa. Among them, Itasa and Isasa are actually one name, pronounced differently in local dialects.[8]

Inasa can be divided into two parts: "Ina," meaning "refusal" and "sa," meaning "consent." "The beach of Inasa," then, is indeed an appropriate name for a place of confrontation between the new ruler and Ōkuninushi no Mikoto. Furthermore, at the time of this confrontation, Kotoshironushi—one of Ōkuninushi no Mikoto's children—happens to be away in Miho. Ōkuninushi

[7] Watarai Enkei, *Bettō Kojiki* (1687), 3 vols., s.v. "izasa."

[8] Matsuoka Shizuo, *Nihon Kogo Daijiten* (Tōkō Shoin, 1962), p. 152. See also *Nihon Shoki*, 1, 130, n. 14.

subsequently dispatches a messenger, Inasahagi, to Miho. With "hagi" meaning a messenger, his "Inasa" is a suitable one for a person whose mission is to ask whether his master should refuse or consent to obey.[9] Because of the common meaning of these place names, we can assume that Inasa and Inase are versions of each other.

Izasa and Isasa are more difficult to deal with. This is due, at least in part, to the possibility that the "za" in Izasa may simply be a miswriting of the "sa" in Isasa. These two characters are strikingly similar. In any event, "Iza" itself is a word for urging oneself or someone else to take an action. "Isa," on the other hand, means "unknowing." Izanagi and Izanami, for instance, are the creators of the nation. We can interpret the "Iza" in their names as an expression of their determination, their mutual encouragement for creation of a new land. Matsuoka Shizuo asserts that "Isa" in Isasa means "sacred," but "unknowing" seems more accurate. Consider the following verse, for instance, from the *Man'yōshū*:

Ōmiji no	Shall I spend these days in longing,
Toko no yama naru	uncertain, like the Isaya River—
Isayagawa	"the unknowing"—
ke no korogoro wa	that flows by Toko Mountain
koishitsutsu mo aran.	on the road to Ōmi?
	(4, 487; Levy, p. 246)

Moriya Toshihiko speculates that there were originally two stories of heavenly descent: one of Ninigi no Mikoto's descent to Hyūga, and the other of Amenooshiho no Mikoto's journey to Izumo.[10] "Iza" in Izasa, where he descended, also captures the resolution of this deity as he descends.

There is, however, something special about Takemikazuchi's descent. It is only in this case that the deity urges obedience by demanding a response, refusal or consent. Both the *Nihon Shoki* and the *Kojiki*, and particularly the latter, describe the new com-

[9] See *Nihon Shoki*, 1, 139, n. 22.

[10] Moriya Toshihiko, *Kiki Shinwa Ronkō* (Yūzankaku, 1973), p. 304.

mander's intimidating attitude toward Ōkuninushi no Mikoto. The first deity to receive this heavenly deity is the god of words, and the second, Takeminakata no Kami, is the deity of strength. Through the submission of these deities and of Ōkuninushi as well, the Heavenly Realm wins the control of the Reed Plains. "The beach of Inasa" is, therefore, one of the most significant places in Japanese mythology. This is not the kind of name attributable to any ordinary place.

Miho is another important place. In the *Kojiki*, Ōkuninushi himself is in Miho (an honorific "mi" with "ho," splendor or excellence). He receives Sukunaiko in this place (p. 115). Miho is the center for the governing of the nation, and Ōkuninushi resides there, not as a deity who amuses himself with "bird-shooting and fishing," but as a god who is to give official responses to visitors. It is important that Miho is recorded in the *Nihon Shoki* as "the beach of Isasa" (p. 62), the same place where, in the *Kojiki*, the heavenly deity descends. This means that Ōkuninushi encounters both Takemikazuchi and Sukunaiko in the same place. Since there is no indication in the *Nihon Shoki* that Ōkuninushi's son is away, he must be with them as well. This is perhaps the original version of the story of Ōkuninushi. The *Kojiki* version, in which only the son is in Miho, appears to have been developed in order to give him autonomy and the role of a decision maker. Moreover, this version is later incorporated back into the *Nihon Shoki*, and we learn that a messenger is sent to Miho to inquire whether his father should refuse or consent.

As I have suggested earlier, Ōkuninushi builds a heavenly temple on "the beach of Tagishi" and retires. The whereabouts of this place is as yet undetermined. But, again, the place is not of a nature that can be defined by its location. Tagishi also appears in another part of the *Kojiki*. Yamatotakeru no Mikoto laments, "now my legs cannot walk; they have become wobbly" ("tagitagishiku narinu"; p. 274). Saigō Nobutsuna defines "tagishi" as objects that are curved or bent. "Tagishi" appears in yet another place in the *Kojiki*, in the chapter that describes the death of Jimmu Tennō.[11]

[11] [Jimmu is the legendary first sovereign of Japan, and his supposed reign was said to have lasted from 660-585 B.C.—Ed.]

In this episode, a deity by the name of Tagishimimi no Mikoto fails in his attempt to murder his three brothers, all of them potential heirs to the throne, and he is killed for his effort (p. 183). "Tagishi," thus, is a name for a betrayer in this story. It also appears to be a word that describes matters that can be judged as just or unjust.

Furthermore, "tagishi" is a metaphor for the defeated and for the cruelty found in some mythological figures, as the following examples from the *Kojiki* illustrate. Ōkuninushi's son, Takeminakata, flees after he is "grasped, crushed, and thrown aside" by Takemikazuchi and begs for his life when he is subdued (p. 133). This story has some resemblance to the story of Yamatotakeru no Mikoto, who not only murders and mutilates Ōusu no Mikoto, but also kills Kumaso no Takeru, taking over the responsibility of his elder brother who had been commanded to do so (pp. 232-35). Similarly, Tagishimimi's half-brothers plot to murder him. The eldest of the three half-brothers fails, and in his stead his younger brother kills Tagishimimi (pp. 234-35). Etymologically, the "tagi" in "tagishi" shares the same roots with "tagiru" (to sprout) and "tagichi" (to sprout out). "Tagi," therefore, connotes an active and aggravated state or condition. In the case of Yamatotakeru, "tagishi" communicates with sympathy the aggravated movements of his limping, but also with a severe criticism of his cruel deeds. Similarly, "the beach of Tagishi," on which Ōkuninushi retires, is a metaphor for the cruelty he experiences.

"The beach of Tagishi" appears to have the following meanings as well. According to the *Kojiki*, Ōkuninushi builds his heavenly temple, saying "I will conceal myself and wait [upon you] in the fewer-than-one-hundred eighty road-bendings" (p. 134). The "eighty road-bendings" (yasokumade) means the world of the dead as the following poem from the *Man'yōshū* suggests:

Momo tarazu	If I offer prayers
yasokumasaka ni	to the god of this winding slope
tamukeseba	with eighty bends
suginishi hito ni	might I meet the one
kedashi awan ka mo.	who has passed beyond?
	(3, 427; Levy, p. 218)

The "eighty bends" ("yasokumasaka") is a road to the other world. The "de" of "kumade" is the same as the "te" of "Nagate," a long path. According to the *Nihongi*, Ōkuninushi (Ōanamuchi no Mikoto) dwells in "the palace of Ama no Hisumi" (p. 80). "Ama" is a complementary prefix for a sacred and awesome object or being, and "sumi" is from "sumu," to dwell, according to the note offered for this passage in the text followed. But I would interpret this word by the character with which it is written, that is, "sumi" meaning "recess" or "corner." "A Palace of Ame no Hisumi" is a place in the corner of the world, that is, a palace situated at the furthest end of the "eighty road bendings."

In this palace, Ōkuninushi wishes to "let the August Grandchild direct the public affairs of which I have charge. I will retire and direct secret matters" (p. 81). Whereas the "public affairs," the governing of the land, is to be directed by a living person, religious rites that are "secret matters" are to be conducted by the spirit of the dead. By suggesting that he will journey to the place at the end of the "eighty road bendings" and perform his responsibility, Ōkuninushi pronounces a separation of his spirit from his body. His body will be in the world of the dead, but his spirit will be enshrined in the heavenly temple and will continue to exert its influence. Ōkuninushi intends to make

> my dwelling-place like the plentiful heavenly dwelling where rules the heavenly sunlineage of the offspring of the heavenly deities, firmly rooting the posts of the palace in the bedrock below, and raising high the crossbeams unto Takamanohara itself, then I will conceal myself and wait [upon you] in the fewer-than-one-hundred eighty road bendings (p. 134).

In the *Nihon Shoki* version, Ōkuninushi proposes that he will withdraw into the "concealment of the short-of-a-hundred-eighty road windings," if the Heavenly Grandchild will govern the land with the spear that he himself has used to pacify the land (p. 69). This passage also relates that Ōkuninushi is withdrawing into the world of the dead and that his spirit will reside on "the beach of Tagishi."

This part of mythology, commonly known as Ōkuninushi's surrendering of his land, has three major place names: Inasa, Miho, and Tagishi. Their significance lies in their illumination for us of the thinking of ancient Japanese. In life, when one's existence is challenged by outside forces, one faces a crisis demanding commitment, either an acceptance or refusal of these forces. It is natural to react in a crisis by resorting to words and power. Yet there is a discrepancy between the two: one may accommodate the forces by words, but one can only resist them with power. As a result, one's body may be subjugated and destroyed, but the spirit continues to struggle. This spirit, therefore, must be revered and pacified. In the view of ancient Japanese, this observation applies not only to people but also to objects.

The summary just given is abstract and general—intentionally so, because I do not wish to philosophize at length. After all, the perception of ancient Japanese was persistently concrete and immediately visual. They must have developed their view on the basis of experiences of various events and incidents, recording them in what we regarded as myth. In the examples I have given, they conveyed their sense of life's dynamism in terms of conflicts, using place names to connote the final stage of a hero's life.

The Michiyuki

Not only does Ōkuninushi's ordeal take place within a limited area, but the place names do not appear in any apparently significant sequence. Yet the sequence of the names—Inasa, Miho and Tagishi—reminds us of the structure of a michiyuki, a travel passage. A michiyuki is a technique used to depict characters' movements, typically their approach toward imminent death, by stringing together a series of place names. The most widely known examples of this kind are the michiyuki in the jōruri narratives by the Edo-period writer, Chikamatsu Monzaemon.[12] By his association with the place names, Ōkuninushi shares his destiny with the heroes

[12] [Jōruri are the performances of the puppet theater, termed "bunraku" today. In Chikamatsu's handling, lovers going off to double suicide usually have their progress marked by a michiyuki. It is a radical suggestion by the author that the michiyuki typically involve approach to death and related actions. He will enlarge on this later.—Ed.]

of michiyuki. Similarly, Izanagi's visit to Yomi and his flight from it are described in place-name symbolism. But why is it that place names, among all other types of names, have this special significance?

I believe that, since the age of the myths, michiyuki have offered a form of delineation of the progress toward death.[13] I shall elaborate this theory with some examples. According to the *Kojiki*, Yamatotakeru is wounded in a battle but, after soothing himself in "the spring of Isame," he walks again until his legs become "wobbly" when he reaches "Tagi." The hill he climbs with the aid of a cane comes to be called "Tsuetsuki Pass," and the place where his legs finally become a "threefold curve" is called "Mie" (pp. 246-47). This story depicts the declining process of a human life, from its beginning to a temporary recovery, then a regression to a state where one must rely on an aid and, finally, to a state of immobility and death, all expressed by place names [having the meanings of the translations here; e.g. "Tsuetsuki Pass" is "Cane Using Pass]. We can well imagine the deities of Isame, Tagi, Tsuetsuki, and Mie springing out of these places as the hero approaches his death. The story tells us that Yamatotakeru eventually dies in Nobono, the Field of Nobo.

The story explains the origins of the place names involved. The Field of Nobo is one exception, but this name must also have a symbolic meaning. It is not clear what "nobo" denotes, but it seems to share the same root with nohogiri—an object that "resembles a serrated blade," according to the *Wamyōshō*.[14] Taking "Nobo" as a prefix for serrated objects, the Field of Nobo suggests a visual image resembling that of the "eighty road bendings" leading to Ōkuninushi's resting place.

Another michiyuki is found in the chapter on Suinin Tennō in the *Kojiki* (pp. 224-25).[15] He summons four maidens from the

[13] Nakanishi, *Kodai Jūisshō* (Mainichi Shimbunsha, 1974), pp. 22-24.

[14] [*Wamyōshō* is an abbreviation for *Wamyō Ruijūshō*. It was compiled ca. 931-937, and is what might be termed the first Japanese encyclopedia or dictionary.—Ed.]

[15] [Suinin is the traditional eleventh sovereign, and the legendary dates of his reign are 29 B.C.-A.D. 70—Ed.]

province of Tamba. But two among them, Utagori Hime and Matono Hime, are sent home because they are extremely unattractive. Humiliated, as well as fearful of the rumor of this dishonor spreading to neighboring villages, Matono attempts to hang herself when she reaches Sagaraka in the land of Yamato on her return journey. This attempt fails, but she does commit suicide by throwing herself into a deep pool at Otokuni in Yamashiro.[16] The *Kojiki* explains that Sagaraka was originally called Sagariki, a hanging tree, and that Otokuni was Ochikuni, a falling place. This michiyuki, recorded for the purpose of explaining the etymology of place names, depicts the process of the maiden's journey toward her death.

The episode of Takehaniyasu no Mikoto's tragedy in the *Kojiki* is another example of a michiyuki. Failing in his revolt, the hero flees from the scene of a battle. The battle takes place in "Idomi," meaning "a challenge," where two armies have "challenged" each other from the opposite banks of a river. Takehaniyasu succumbs to an arrow that pierces his body, and his army retreats in the confusion of defeat. When the army arrives at the ford of Kusuba, the soldiers are so tightly pressed that their bowels loosen, soiling their trousers. Kusuba, therefore, was originally called Kusubakama, Beshitted Trousers. The fleeing soldiers are cut down, and their bodies float down the river like cormorants. This is the reason, the *Kojiki* claims, that the river is called Ugawa, the Cormorant River. The victorious enemy continues to pursue a few surviving soldiers and eventually slaughters them at a place called Hafurisonoi, "the place of completed action." This story, like the one about Matono Hime, explains the origins of place names. It appears that ancient people pondered over the meaning of familiar place names and presented their theories in the form of mythic michiyuki, well according with my earlier discussion of mythic place names.

A michiyuki constitutes, then, a technique that captures a flow of time by depicting the movements of characters who pass significantly named places. It is a form of expression that has been derived from the narrative structure of mythology. Michiyuki

[16] [Matono Hime's tragic story is told in the *Kojiki*, Book 2, Chapter 75.—Ed.]

enabled ancient Japanese to capture "the time when the breath fails on an approach of death" and express it with a single place name, "the Level Pass of Yomi."

One of the best michiyuki is the following song compiled in the *Nihon Shoki* (no. 94):

Iso no kami	Passing Furu
Furu o sugite	that is in Iso no Kami and
komomakura	passing Takahashi
Takahashi sugi	famous for high pillows,
monosawa ni	passing Ōyake
Ōyake sugi	where things are in abundance,
haruhi	passing Kasuga
Kasuga o sugi	casting the spring sun in haze,
tsumagomoro	passing Osao
Osao o sugi . . .	where couples live secretly . . .

Kage Hime captures here the final moments of the life of her beloved husband, Shibi, by means of a sequence of space. Furthermore, all the place names appearing in this song are preceded by pillow words [makurakotoba]. As I have discussed the matter elsewhere, pillow words reflect the mythological experiences of ancient people.[17] Each pillow word developed as a crystallization of mythology and came to be applied to place names. Its function is identical with a mythic explanation for a specific place name, for instance, Miho or Tagishi in the story of Ōkuninushi.

The most important characteristic of a michiyuki is that it describes an approach toward death. But does this apply to the story of Izanami's flight away from the world of the dead, which has led to my discussion of michiyuki in the first place? I believe that

[17] Nakanishi, "*Man'yōshū* no Shizen: Gengo to Shite no Shizen: 2," in *Man'yōshū Kenkyū*, vol. 7 (Takama Shobō, 1979), 33-47. [Pillow words—makurakotoba—are expressions preceding and in some way amplifying one or more words, including place names, natural phenomena, etc. Although once dismissed as meaningless decorations, in recent years they have been studied positively from many points of view. Both in their function and in the fruitfulness of scholarly inquiry into them, they somewhat resemble the Homeric epithets. Pillow words are, however, not always distinguishable, and they do not belong solely to oral poetry, some having been coined as late as this century.—Ed.]

it is possible to consider this case as a derivative of michiyuki. It is difficult to find examples for this reversed michiyuki in the *Kojiki* and the *Nihon Shoki*, but there are some in the *Man'yōshū*, particularly in Book 13. Among them, there are three poems (3236, 3237, and 3240) that trace the path from Yamato to Ōsakayama through Yamashiro. There is also one (3230) that proceeds from Nara to Mt. Kannabi. The first three are more representative of michiyuki than the last. The following is one of the first three:

Sora mitsu	In the land of Yamato
Yamato no kuni	that spreads beneath the sky
aoniyoshi	I crossed the hills of Nara
Narayama koete	rich in colored earth,
Yamashiro no	and at the Tsutsuki field
Tsutsuki no hara	in Yamashiro
chihayaburu	I crossed the Uji ford
Uji no watari	mighty in its flow;
Tagitsuya no	and came to the Agone field
Agone no hara o	at Tagitsuya,
chitose ni	where if I spent a thousand years
kakuru koto naku	I would not be sated,
yorozuyo ni	where if I lived countless lives
arikayowan to	I would always visit—
Yamashina no	yes, I have made offerings
Iwata no mori no	to the great divinity
sumegami ni	at the Iwata Shrine
nusa torimukete	in Yamashina,
ware wa koeyuku	where I crossed the hill—
Ōsakayama o.	the Ōsaka Hill.
	(13, 3236)

Here the michiyuki moves toward life. The symbolic meaning of Ōsaka Hill (or Mountain) is explicit in the following poem.

Ōsaka o	Past Ōsaka Hill
uchidete mireba	I emerge to look
Ōmi no umi	upon Lake Ōmi,

shirayūhana ni	its waves shining white
nami tachiwataru.	like mulberry in full bloom.
	(13, 3238)

The Province of Ōmi, a lake country at the foot of Ōsaka, is the destination for the traveler in "dark loneliness" (13: 3237). With its lake waters, however, Ōmi will lift the traveler's spirit and enable him to find a new life. There is no lack of evidence that people went to Ōmi for aquatic lustration. The author of the *Kagerō Nikki (The Gossamer Years)*, for example, traveled to Karasaki near Ōmi for just such a purpose—lustration in the waters of Lake Biwa.[18]

Another example is also found in the *Man'yōshū*:

Kimi ni yori	Because of you, my Lord,
koto no shigeki o	the talk flies thick about me.
furusato no	I am going to the Asuka River,
Asuka no kawa ni	in my native village,
misogo shi ni yuku.	there to wash away the stains.
	(4, 626; Levy, p. 292)

"Going to the river to wash the stains" shows that the land of the waters was one of purification, and, as the second half of the poem reveals, one reached this land by going over a mountain.

We ought now recall that there was such a place for Izanagi as well—the shore of Ahagi by the river mouth of Tachibana in Hyūga in Tsukushi—after he returned from the world of the dead. If the Suka River was a place of purification, the mountain that stood before it would be Mt. Kannabi, as the following poem reveals:

Mitegura o	Leaving the capital at Nara,
Nara yori idete	holy with votive cloth,
mizutade	reaching Hozumi

[18] [The author of the *Kagerō Nikki* is known as the Mother of Fujiwara Michitsuna. Although her dates are uncertain, she is known to have married Fujiwara Kaneie in 954. Her *Diary* is one of the most important examples of Heian diary literature. Nakanishi's point is that so much later people were still going for lustration to the Ōmi (Lake Biwa) area. His Ōsaka is that of the barrier near the later capital site at Heiankyō, not modern Osaka, then called Naniwa.—Ed.]

Hozumi ni itari	where water peppers grow,
tonami haru	then going beyond Sakate
Sakate o sugi	where bird nets are spread,
iwabashiru	at holy Mount Kannabi
Kannabiyama ni	we present our offerings
asamiya ni	in the morning at the shrine;
tsukaematsurite	and discovering that our Lord
Yoshino e to	has set forth to Yoshino,
irimasu mireba	we ponder times long past.
inishie obōyu.	(13, 3230)

The envoy to this poem describes Yoshino, but the michiyuki ends in Kannabi.

The river undoubtedly was a convenient place for purification rites. Yet unlike a beach like that of Ahagi, the river had an important symbolic meaning as well—it was also a border dividing this world from that of the dead. Although anciently few in number, bridges were the paths that joined these two worlds. A particular type of a party called ozume was held occasionally, as we learn from a poem (16, 3803) in the *Man'yōshū* and a song compiled in the *Nihon Shoki* (the ninth year of Tenji's reign).[19] The party, actually a gathering for an exchange of poems, always took place by a bridge. It was a form of utagaki, a celebration held by a body of water to celebrate revival through the pleasure of marriage or sexual union. A revival was possible only in a place where the world of the living bordered the realm of the dead. A bridge with its princess, Hashihime, was such a place. This princess appears as an important symbol in the *Genji Monogatari*.[20] Chikamatsu's *Shinjū Ten no Amijima (The Double Suicides at Amijima)*

[19] [The year is 670. There are various ways of calculating dates and naming eras in these years. The author follows one used by most scholars of the *Nihon Shoki*.—Ed.]

[20] ["Hashihime" is the title of the 45th chapter of *The Tale of Genji*, the first of the "ten Uji chapters" that close the work. In it the hero of those chapters applies the name to the eldest of the sisters at Uji, Ōigimi, whom he woos in vain. Earlier usage had treated the Uji no Hashihime as a female divinity of the bridge. After the treatment in *The Tale of Genji*, usage is mixed, and the Hashihime may be a mortal. The author has in mind here the earlier usage.—Ed.]

has a series of bridge names: Tenjin Bridge, Umeda Bridge, and Midori Bridge. These names are seemingly unrelated to the theme of this story, but they do have crucial roles in suggesting the tragic death, as well as the eventual rebirth, of the protagonist and his lover. The concept of time and space that is crystallized in the term, "the Level Pass of Yomi," thus continues to survive in michiyuki.

As this shows, the michiyuki, a literary technique for capturing the process of death and rebirth in the imagery of space, has its roots in myth. This space will continue to exist and function as long as we inherit the imagination of the creators of myth. Just as "the Level Pass of Yomi" is not limited to any specific place, this space is an abstract one, assuming its importance only within mythological imagination. Kakinomoto Hitomaro (fl. ca. 680-700) was undoubtedly a poet who inherited this way of thought. As many of his poems reveal, Hitomaro was well versed in mythology and cherished the thoughts of ancient people. Let us now examine one of his poems from the *Man'yōshū*.

"A poem written by Kakinomoto Hitomaro
when Crown Prince Karu sojourned on the
field of Aki"

Yasumishishi	Our lord, sovereign
wago ōkimi	of the earth's eight corners,
takaterasu	child of the high-shining sun,
hi no Miko	a very god,
kamu nagara	manifests his divine will
kamu sabi sesu to	and leaves behind
futoshi kasu	the firmly-pillared capital.
miyako o okite	He pushes through the mountains
komoriku no	of Hatsuse, the hidden land,
Hatsuse no yama wa	and bids yield to him
maki tatsu	the rough mountain road,
arayamamichi o	lined with thick black pines,
iwagane	and the cliffs and the trees
saeki oshinabe	that block his path.

sakatori no	In the morning, like a bird,
asa koemashite	he crosses the hills.
tama kagiru	As evening falls
yū sarikureba	faint as jewel's light,
miyuki furu	he pushes aside
Aki no ōno ni	the pampas grass
hatasusuki	that waves in banners
shino o oshinabe	and the dwarf bamboo
kusamakura	on the broad
tabiyadori sesu	and snow-fallen
inishie omoite.	fields of Aki.
	Grass for pillow,
	he sojourns the night,
	thinking of the past.
	(1, 45; Levy, p. 61)

In this chōka ["long poem"], Crown Prince Karu, "Our lord sovereign," "child of the high-shining sun," travels as a god from Kyoto on a rugged mountain path through Hatsuse, the land of death, and eventually to Akino, the fields of fulfillment. But why was it necessary to compose this long poem in the form of michiyuki? And what does the michiyuki signify? The purpose of Crown Prince Karu's journey was to complete his life as Crown Prince and to be reborn as a new person, the new sovereign. A similar initiation process is also described in the *Kojiki.* Led by Takeshiuchi no Sukune, Ōjin, then the Crown Prince, travels to Ōmi and Wakasa in order to take purification.[21] He eventually receives "a new name" and a blessing from the deity of Kai. This story, too, is told in the form of an explanation of place names.

Examining the following four tanka ["short poems"] by Hitomaro and Crown Prince Karu, the critic Mori Asao points out the significance of the hours of dawn.[22] He asserts that Hitomaro places

[21] [The legendary Ōjin was regarded as fifteenth sovereign and his supposed rule was from 270 to 310.—Ed.]

[22] [In the *Man'yōshū,* the short poems (tanka) that follow the long poems (chōka) are designated either as short poems or envoys (hanka). The former are poems more or less independent of the longer poems to which they are attached, whereas the envoys are integrated into a single expression with the longer poems.—Trans.]

an emphasis on these hours in order to establish an association between the Crown Prince's journey and the daijōsai, an important part of a rite of coronation, in which the sovereign dedicates new crops to the deities.[23] These poems (1, 46-49; Levy, p. 62) that follow the long poem, are as follows:

Aki no no ni yadoru tabibito uchinabiki i mo nu rame ya mo inishie omou ni.	The traveler sojourning on the fields of Aki stretches as in sleep, yet he cannot sleep, thinking of the past.
Makusa karu arano ni wa aredo momijiba no suginishi kimi ga katami to so koshi.	A wild field where they cut the splendid grass, but we have come to remember our Lord, gone like the yellowed leaves of autumn.
Himukashi no no ni kagiroi no tatsu miete kaerimisureba tsuki katabukinu.	On the eastern fields I can see the flames of morning rise. Turning around, I see the moon sink in the west.
Hinamishi no miko no mikoto no uma namete mikari tatashishi toki wa kimukau.	The time— When the Crown Prince, Peer of the Sun, lined his horses and set out on the imperial hunt— comes and faces me.

Mori claims that, like the story of the Ōjin's journey, these poems suggest Prince Karu's succession to the throne. They were com-

For a discussion, see Nakanishi, *Kakinomoto Hitomaro* (Chikuma Shobō, 1976), pp. 54-55.

[23] Mori Asao, "Kakinomoto Hitomaro no Jikan to Saishiki," in *Kanshō Nihon Bungaku: Man'yōshū*, ed. Nakanishi Susumu (Kadokawa Shoten, 1976), pp. 357-65.

posed in 693, however, a date not coincident with the time of his coronation. I therefore maintain that the theme of these poems is that of death and rebirth. The daijōsai does symbolize the beginning of a new life, but it appears that the element of michiyuki is much more explicit in these poems than the suggestion of daijōsai.

Because the third poem differs considerably from the others in both content and diction, we ought to concentrate our attention on the other two.[24] The first poem is a descriptive one—soldiers find it difficult to sleep, confined within the temporal space of the past. The second tells us that this space is a reminder of a person who has died. A reminder, katami, links the past with the present, obscuring their differences. In both poems, past and present realities are captured in the form of an action. In other words, an action in the past is projected into another action in the present, in spite of these actions that involve two separate individuals. The soldiers accompanying Prince Karu are reminded of the past because where they sleep now is precisely the place where the Prince's father, Prince Kusakabe, had once visited. In the last poem, therefore, "the Crown Prince" is not Prince Karu, but his father, Kusakabe (Hitameshi no Mikoto), who died four years before. In the soldiers' minds, he appears as a living person on a horse, ready for a royal hunt. This field is, then, a symbolic space where a past reality becomes the present reality.

As Mori has conceived the rite of coronation in these poems, this rebirth symbolizes a union of the Crown Prince Karu with the spirits of his predecessors. By this rite, the former sovereigns continue to live as spiritual immortals. This concept is the imaginative basis for "the Level Pass of Yomi" and, later, for the michiyuki. Hitomaro was one of the artists who inherited this concept from myth. Whether his intention was deliberate is an irrelevant question. The question here is how he gave a poetic form to his inherited view of life.

The concept of space in myth is not a concept held only by ancient Japanese. It is natural that it should be manifest in those nō plays in which the souls of the dead play key roles. The well-

[24] See Nakanishi, *Man'yōshū*, 1 (Kōdansha, 1978), 73.

known story, *Sumidagawa,* is about a mother who comes to the river looking for her lost child, Azume, with whose spirit she is reunited. Her journey represents a search for that union. *Unrin'in* is also a travel story about search for a spirit. The protagonist is led by a dream that appears in the *Ise Monogatari (Tales of Ise).* Moreover, the traveling monks who invariably appear in nō can be seen as travelers in search of souls. The michiyuki, which they recite near the beginning of a play, unites the living with the spirits of the dead and is a crucial element to nō. Just as, long after its devising, myth possessed vitality in the medieval nō, so "the Level Pass of Yomi" is the Ur-type of all literary forms that deal with the concept of death expressed in time and space.

Mythic Space

In addition to the examples I have given here, there are a number of episodes in both the *Kojiki* and the *Nihon Shoki* that demonstrate the mythic concept of space. Myth not only captures time in the language of space but also expresses other concepts spatially. In fact this spatial conception of narrative is the predominant characteristic of Japanese myth. Some may argue that the space or place described in myth designates a scene that was actually observed. Their argument is that "the beach of Tagishi," for instance, was an actual place and that expressions such as "tagitagishii," or "wobbly," were derived from this place name. But the word, "tagishi," was originally "tagiishi," rugged boulders. "Tagishi no hama," therefore, can mean a shore with many rocks, but such a shore is usually called "iso," rather than "hama." Therefore, "Taginishi no hama" was probably a beach with uneven coastlines, and this unevenness reminded people of evil deeds. The legend that explains the origins of this and other names seems to attest to the proposition. As I have explained before, the name "Otokuni" came into existence because a maiden, stigmatized for her unattractive appearance, threw herself into deep water. It was not that a place called Otokuni existed first and a story later developed in association with the place name. I do not disagree that there probably were cases in which place names were derived from existing stories. But what requires explanation here is why a story about a maiden annihilating herself in deep water came to be created. And, if there was a place called Otokuni, can we assume that a story of this sort would have developed naturally? Similarly, can we automatically expect a story similar to that of Ōkuninushi to emerge, just because Japan has beaches with rugged rocks or a curved shoreline?

The imagination that created these Japanese myths was a manifestation of literary energies—not of an individual, but of a group of people living in an ancient community. Another factor we must bear in mind is that myth came into existence as a consequence of these energies absorbing the many connotations of words. Put differently, myth was, first and foremost, a transferring of matters and events into spatial concepts and expressions. In myth, all things may be grasped spatially and visually. "The moment when one's breath expires," which no living person had yet actually experienced, could be explained only in the words, "the Level Pass of Yomi." This pattern of thinking, seemingly reversed from modern Japanese, was a fundamental force in the creation of Japanese myth.

Moreover, by bestowing a place name on a time, ancient Japanese offered a form of evaluation or criticism of their experiences. When the narrator of the myth tells us that Kotoshironushi was in Miho, rather than that he was in a verdant mountain enjoying bird songs; or that a maiden died in Otokuni, rather than that she threw herself into deep water; then, truly we are being told that these characters were at crucial points in their lives. Tagishi is no exception.

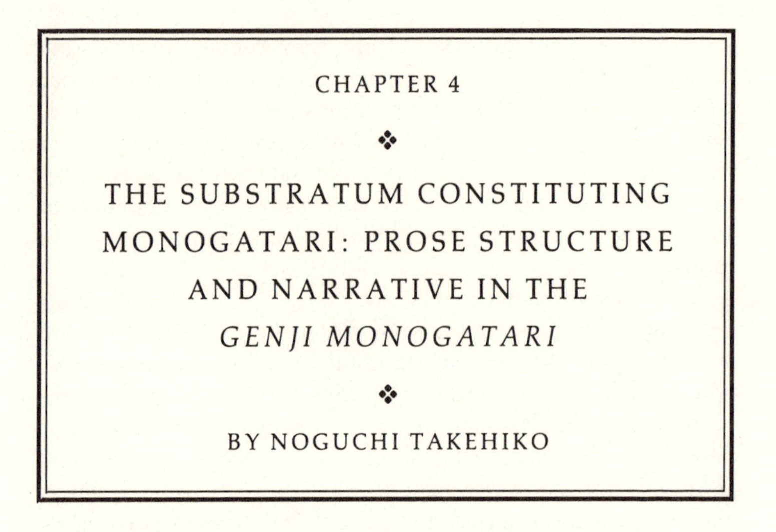

CHAPTER 4

THE SUBSTRATUM CONSTITUTING MONOGATARI: PROSE STRUCTURE AND NARRATIVE IN THE *GENJI MONOGATARI*

BY NOGUCHI TAKEHIKO

IN 1832, Kyokutei (or Takizawa) Bakin (1767-1848) made the following observation in his *Kyōkyakuden*:

> Japan has always produced stories (haishi) which are known as sōshi monogatari. *Taketori, Utsubo, Ise,* and *Genji* are examples from antiquity. Readers in later ages found these tales endlessly entertaining. However, they merely compiled commentaries; none has done a critical study of them. [Looking for a critical study] is like trying to find a man who really understands me.

Almost as if in response to Bakin's disgruntlement, a late Edo scholar, Hagiwara Hiromichi (d. 1863), undertook this formidable task—not just textual exegesis of, but critical discussion of, Japan's foremost piece of monogatari literature, the *Genji Monogatari (The Tale of Genji)*. His work, entitled *Genji Monogatari Hyōshaku,* contained both critical interpretation (hyō) and textual annotation (shaku), through which he sought to enhance our understanding of the world of *Genji*.

Hagiwara Hiromichi was a kokugakusha [scholar of Japanese

Translated by Bob Tadashi Wakabayashi.

studies] in the tradition of Kamo no Mabuchi (1697-1769) and Motoori Norinaga (1730-1801), but at the same time, he was an avid reader of prose fiction and had a thorough grasp of Bakin's stories. It was Hiromichi who completed *Kyōkyakuden* for Bakin after his death, and in doing this, he benefited greatly from the concepts of hōsoku (rules of composition) and bumpō found in Bakin's literary criticism. By "bumpō," Bakin meant "structural principles," and that is how that term will be used throughout this chapter.

As early as Mabuchi's *Genji Monogatari Shinshaku*, Japanese students of literature recognized that a particular style of writing accompanied monogatari structure.[1] Hiromichi revised and expanded these categories of structural principles. He did find inspiration for this task in Bakin's "Seven Rules of Stories" (*Haishi Nana Hōsoku*),[2] but it was Hiromichi's own originality that led him to apply those seven rules to analysis of the structure of the *Genji*. In the prefatory remarks to the "General Outline" of his *Genji Monogatari Hyōshaku*, Hiromichi listed a glossary of terms and categories employed in his analysis. Let me cite some that correspond to those used by Bakin in *Haishi Nana Hōsoku*.

(1.) PAIRING (shukaku)—The protagonist and his counterpart. For example, the PARALLEL PAIRING (seitai) of Genji and Fujitsubo; the ODD PAIRING (kitai) of Genji and Murasaki; or the PRINCIPAL AND AUXILIARY (seifuku) of Genji and Tō no Chūjō.

(2.) FORESHADOWING (fukusen, fukuan)—For example, the

[1] In the "General Outline" of his *Genji Monogatari Shinshaku*, Kamo no Mabuchi introduced the categories of *fukuan, shōō, tonza,* and *kisha no kotoba* (or *sōshiji*). [Of these terms only sōshiji survives in usage today, as the author will show. He also pairs some of these terms with current ones.—Ed.]

[2] In *Nansō Satomi Hakkenden*, Kyokutei Bakin noted, "In the stories of the Yüan and Ming eras, literary talents in China employed 'structural principles' such as 'shukaku,' 'fukusen,' 'shinsen,' 'shōō,' 'hantai,' 'shōhitsu,' and 'imbi.' " [None of these terms survives in modern usage. But, again, the author pairs some with terms more or less current.—Ed.] We should note that Bakin is thought to have obtained these "structural principles" from the Ch'ing writer, Mao Sheng-shan's work, *Tu San-kuo-chieh Fa*.

casual allusion to Lady Rokujō's presence in the story prior to presenting her in the "Aoi" chapter.

(3.) COHERENCE OF CAUSE AND OUTCOME (shubi)—For example, Genji's affair with Oborozukuyo in "Hana no En" leading to his self-imposed exile in "Suma" and "Akashi."

(4.) CORRESPONDENCE (shōtai)—For example, the "misdeed" (mono no magire) between Kashiwagi and Onna San no Miya, which is traced back to that between Genji and Fujitsubo earlier. Correspondence denotes a similar parallel development occurring between two different pairs of characters in succeeding generations.

(5.) CONTRAST (hantai)—Between, for example, the ideal woman, Murasaki, and the unattractive, dull-witted Suetsumu no Hana. Another example of contrast, as I shall relate below, is between Utsusemi and Yūgao in "Hahakigi."

(6.) ELLIPSIS (shōhitsu)—For example, the conscious omission of an actual account of the adultery between Genji and Fujitsubo in any of the existing chapters; or the nonexistent "Kumogakure" chapter in which Genji's death might have been described.

Hiromichi argues that the magnificence of the *Genji* as an example of monogatari literature lies in the fact that its development and organization adhere to structural principles such as those listed above. Of course, these structural elements are not themselves the source of Murasaki Shikibu's powers of imagination. That source can be found only in her inwardly felt concern for human beings, a concern that she constantly seeks to transform into fiction and which is unrelated to literary devices such as allegory or parable that are sometimes said to have motivated her writing. At any rate, it is the structured nature of monogatari, achieved through the use of this bundle of structural principles that permits Murasaki Shikibu to develop far beyond the limitations inherent in the stereotyped theme of "a young noble who suffers exile and is reinstated in his former position and achieves honor and riches."[3] By "bun-

[3] [The quotation refers to a folkloristic motif distinguished by Araki Hiroyuki and others.—Ed.]

dle" of structural principles, I mean that the categories of pairing, foreshadowing, coherence of cause and outcome, etc., do not appear singly in *Genji*. Instead, it was by skillfully combining them that Murasaki Shikibu integrated her powers of organization with her powers of thought and imagination. For example, according to Hiromichi, the relationship between Genji and Fujitsubo was one of principal and auxiliary, but he held that "because the affair with Fujitsubo was kept hidden," Murasaki no Ue could "be likened to a substitute for her," which in effect would make this latter relationship one of "odd pairing." Such an acute analysis accurately describes one aspect of Murasaki Shikibu's powers of thought and imagination that propel the development of the monogatari.

In the same fashion, Hiromichi noted with regard to the two misdeeds (mono no magire—those between Genji and Fujitsubo and Kashiwagi and Onna San no Miya) that "this naturally indicates 'cause and retribution' within the category of 'correspondence of cause and outcome.' " Thus, the concept of cause and retribution, which belongs to the dimension of plot, must be distinguished from the structural principle of correspondence. Hiromichi then goes on to point out a major convergence between Murasaki Shikibu's powers of organization and of thought and imagination: Genji's adultery with Fujitsubo could occur only in light of his longing for Kiritsubo, his deceased mother. His earlier emotions toward Kiritsubo, then, foreshadowed his love affair with Fujitsubo, and in turn caused him to marry Murasaki no Ue. The term "Murasaki-related incidents" refers to this double foreshadowing, which is the author's power of thought and imagination and which propels the monogatari's development.[4] Indeed, Genji's adultery with Fujitsubo was the cause in the "coherence of cause and outcome" that led to the happy ending in the first part of *Genji Monogatari*—his appointment to the rank of Jun Daijō Tennō (surrogate or acting retired sovereign). And needless to say, this adultery was "an affair kept hidden."

[4] [The "Murasaki-related incidents" is a widely accepted and complex concept relating three principal women in Genji's life: the mother lost (Kiritsubo), Fujitsubo, and Murasaki. Various parallelisms, images, and associations are given to sustain the relation of the three women in Genji's mind.—Ed.]

In what follows, I shall make use of Hagiwara Hiromichi's linguistic-theoretical approach in an attempt to identify the characteristic linguistic structure that makes the *Genji* a work of monogatari literature and that distinguishes it from the genres of setsuwa (brief narratives) and of Tokugawa or modern shōsetsu (usually rendered "novel").

We must first determine what analytical use can be made of the abstract structural rules and categories that Hagiwara has provided, for although they are an aid in thinking about monogatari in general terms, they themselves contain no specific plot elements. In other words, they are the joints in a skeletal framework that holds monogatari fiction together, and must be distinguished from monogatari flesh—the specific characters and incidents of the plot. For example, when Hiromichi speaks of "coherence of cause and outcome," he has in mind an abstract principle of organization devoid of proper names and specific situations. This is his concept of structural principles (bumpō). On the other hand, when he applies the structural principle of coherence of cause and outcome by stating, for example, that Genji's love affair with X in Chapter Y will later lead to outcome Z, he is operating on the level of thought and imagination (kōsō), which involves proper names and concrete incidents in the plot.

But what precisely is "structure"? We can take Hiromichi's principle of pairing (shukaku)—the relationship between protagonist and counterpart—as a point of departure for discussing all monogatari. Through means of a narrative, some proposition comes into being as a relationship between the protagonist and any group of named counterparts with whom he interacts. This proposition may be termed a plot component of the monogatari. But disparate plot components by themselves, of course, do not make a monogatari. Only when plot component A creates some change to produce or to become plot component B, does an actual plot come into existence. If we consider plot component A to be the cause in Hiromichi's structural principle of coherence between cause and outcome, it naturally anticipates the outcome of plot component B. But in *Genji*, the "outcome" very often is *not* anticipated by the cause; the cause produces an unexpected outcome. In this fashion, the internal structure provided by plot development both sustains thought and imagination (kōsō) in monogatari and is an organizing device that gives it the power to move along.

Thus, Hiromichi's structural principles can be seen as providing the monogatari with organization by determining the mutual relationships that connect various plot components. Armed with this understanding of his structural principles, we can reintroduce the proper names and specific incidents that we just a moment ago abstracted out of our discussion in an attempt to differentiate organization from plot and structure from thought.

When applied to the two misdeeds committed in *Genji*, we find that (A) Genji commits adultery with Fujitsubo, the wife of his father, and in turn (B) suffers adultery committed by his wife, Onna San no Miya. This is a "correspondence!" Hagiwara explains the relationship between these plot components A and B as one of correspondence of cause and outcome, which "naturally indicates 'cause and retribution.' " The concept of cause and retribution has to do with plot; only when it assumes structured form through the principle of correspondence does the series of chapters from the chapters "Kiritsubo" to "Wakana" [chapters 1-34] acquire continuity as plot. At the same time, this structural principle of correspondence bridges the happy ending in the first part of the *Genji* and the *Weltanschauung* of human decline characterizing the second part.[5] Herein lies the Janus-faced nature of structure and thought for Hiromichi.

The principles of structure and organization are also skillfully employed by him to shed light on the opening passage of the second chapter, "Hahakigi," and on a small portion of that chapter's famous "appraisal of women on a rainy night." As is well known, "Hahakigi" has the following narrative sequence of elements: (1) The opening passage by the narrator in the authorial voice (jigoe). (2) Recent events in Genji's life. (3) The dialogue between Genji

[5] [Japanese scholars accept, in one version or another, Ikeda Kikan's division of the chapters of the *Genji Monogatari* into three parts: the first (1-33) running up to the "Wakana Jō" ("Young Shoots," Part One) chapters; the second (34-41) through "Maboroshi" ("The Sorcerers"); and the third ([42] 45-54) the remaining chapters.—Ed.]

and Tō no Chūjō. (4) The appearance of Uma No Kami and Shikibu no Jō, which finally leads to the "appraisal of women on a rainy night." (5) Discussions about women in general come to be focused on "women from middle-ranking families." (6) Each speaks of his personal experiences; Uma no Kami, on the "woman who bit his finger" and the "woman of the wintry wind"; Tō no Chūjō, on the "woman of the wild carnation" (who turns out to be Yūgao); and Shikibu no Jō, on the "woman smelling of garlic"; which leads to the end of the "appraisal." (7) Genji unsuccessfully attempts to make love to Utsusemi on the following day.

Hiromichi uses his structural principles to demonstrate the brilliant organization of the three Hahakigi-related chapters—"Hahakigi" and the two following chapters, "Utsusemi" and "Yūgao." He is at his best when stressing Murasaki Shikibu's emphasis on "women of middle-ranking families" during the discussion of women as a psychological foreshadowing for the author's ensuing introduction of Utsusemi and Yūgao. Hiromichi's insight into the foreshadowing of Yūgao as Tō no Chūjō's "woman of the wild carnation" is also superb, as is his principle of contrast to elucidate the differing characters of Utsusemi and Yūgao. Furthermore, the little girl later left behind by Yūgao, of whom Tō no Chūjō speaks in "Hahakigi," will emerge as a beautiful, full-grown woman in "Tamakazura." We will not go into the issue of whether or not this was Murasaki Shikibu's original intention, an issue that belongs to the realm of thought and imagination; but from Hiromichi's point of view, this Yūgao-Tamakazura transition clearly accords with his structural principle of foreshadowing.

As these examples show, the structural principles that Hiromichi observed in the *Genji Monogatari* provide a qualitative length that connects separate plot components. Needless to say, every monogatari develops in linear fashion. But this does not mean that it is simply a string of one event after another. It is the qualitative organization, or length provided by these structural principles, that gives coherent outline to the events being related in the text. Qualitative length, then, is the structured totality of relationships connecting the various plot components. This takes the monogatari beyond a series of sentences to quantitative length.

What is the fundamental, defining characteristic of monogatari literature? I believe that it is this: although monogatari are written texts, the narrator's spoken words are in that text; the written text is, paradoxically enough, always a documentation of actual tales recited. The very word "monogatari," which we tend to use unthinkingly, has a double meaning. First, it is the written relation of "tales told," and second, it is the actual reciting of those tales. Throughout the remainder of this essay, I shall refer to the first meaning as "monogatari" or "monogatari text," and to the second as "tale-recitation," or "the reciting of tales."

Monogatari are not found only in the literature of the court at its prime. Works continued to be written in this genre in later centuries, important works such as the *Heike Monogatari (The Story of the Heike), Usuyuki Monogatari (A Story of Light Snow),* and *Ugetsu Monogatari (Stories of Moonlight and Rain).* The reciting of tales also continued to flourish. Examples can be found in jōruri and kabuki of the Edo period: "The Tale of Sanemori" in the *Gempei Nunobiki no Taki,* or "The Tale of Kumagai" in *Ichinotani Futaba Gunki* come to mind immediately. Thus, "The Story of So-and-So"—usually a battle motif—recited in a theatrical performance was the principal medium through which tale-telling was conducted in later eras. However, it was only in court literature that these two aspects of monogatari—its text and the act of its reciting—were combined in a single literary work to form its content and technique of presentation. This combination would never again take place in the history of Japanese literature; and needless to say, it finds its greatest achievement in the *Genji Monogatari.*

Clearly, Hagiwara Hiromichi's structural principles have to do mainly with monogatari in the former sense, monogatari texts; they are the rules of internal organization according to which monogatari in the latter sense, the tales recited, are arranged. Thus, the presence of *structural* principles is a necessary, but insufficient, condition that must be met for a piece of writing to qualify as monogatari. In addition, tales must actually be *recited*: *narrative* principles must also be present. Hiromichi did not overlook this second point in his *Genji Monogatari Hyōshaku*; he was concerned not only with the *arrangement* of tales recited in monogatari but also with the *act* of reciting them. He also addressed the problem of the author's speech-in-the-text. His narrative principles come into play at those points in the text where the author has decided to break off its linear development and recite a particular tale. These tales within the text constitute the monogatari's depth as opposed to its length. Monogatari depth is plumbed with his narrative principles; its length is measured by his "structural principles."

Hiromichi obtained various interpretive categories from commentaries on the *Genji* compiled by scholars such as Sanjōnishi Kin'eda in his *Sairyūshō*.[6] These categories, such as ordinary, plain narrative (ji no bun), narrator's comment (sōshiji), authorial intrusion (sakusha no kotoba), dialogue (kaiwabun), and character's inner thought (shinnaigo), are noted in his own *Hyōshaku*, and in this essay, I shall refer to them collectively as "narrative categories." These categories are determined on the basis of who is saying the words in question at present in the text. The best illustration of how Hiromichi employed his narrative categories is found in his treatment of the "Hahakigi" chapter. Although a long one, the opening section in his annotated text of this chapter is quoted below. I have followed his divisions in the text to break it up into five sections.

"Hahakigi," Section I—Authorial Intrusion
(Sakusha Kotoba).

> The Radiant Genji. The name itself was indeed grand, but he committed many blunders that would lead others to question its aptness. *[Genji's thought] "People may well find out about these wanton affairs in the future and I will earn a reputation for indiscretion,"* so thinking, he tried to keep such affairs secret, but even the most embarrassing of them leaked out. Ah, people are such busybodies. What I mean is, because Genji was so worried about their rumors, he did his utmost to appear straitlaced, and this reduced his amorous affairs to the point where he would earn the derision of a Captain Katano.

[6] See Takahashi Tōru, " 'Hahakigi' Sanjō no Jobatsu," in *Kōza Genji Monogatari no Sekai* (Tokyo: Yūikaku, 1975), p. 99.

"Hahakigi," Section II—Narrative (Ji).

Moreover, when Genji was a Chūjō [nominal guards officer], he liked to spend his time at court and went home to Aoi's residence less and less frequently. Many lady-servants there suspected, "is he harboring a clandestine love?" But he had no disposition for indulging in such run-of-the-mill escapades. Unfortunately, however, he tended on occasion to become involved in emotionally wrenching affairs even in spite of himself, and thereby caused trouble.

"Hahakigi," Section III—Narrative (Ji).

It was during the ceaseless drizzle of the rainy season when the court was in recess. He was staying away from his wife's home for even longer periods than usual. Though Aoi's parents and relatives were concerned and perturbed over this, they went out of their way to prepare festivities and do other things on his behalf. The minister's sons, Aoi's brothers, strove to serve him rather than the sovereign.

"Hahakigi," Section IV—Narrative (Ji).

Among the minister's sons, there was one, Tō no Chūjō, to whom he was especially close. Whether it was music or gaieties, Genji always felt intimate and at ease with him. Being an amorous man, Tō no Chūjō was displeased with the home provided for him by his father-in-law, the Minister of the Right. [On the contrary,] even when staying in the house of his birth [into which Genji had married,] he kept up his rooms beautifully. Whenever Genji came and went, Tō no Chūjō accompanied him. Their studies and pastimes were always undertaken together, and Genji was never much outperformed by his friend, if at all. Being together so much, any reserve between them naturally disappeared; they were such good friends that neither would conceal his innermost feelings from the other.

"Hahakigi," Section V—Narrative (Ji).

The day-long drizzles brought boredom, and late one wet evening when the court was virtually deserted, it seemed more peaceful than usual in Genji's room, so he pulled up a lamp and began reading a few works in Chinese. Tō no Chūjō picked up some of the several love letters written on pieces of colored paper that were lying about on a nearby shelf and displayed a keen interest in them. Genji would not permit this, saying, *[Genji's words] "I don't mind showing you some of them, but others, . . ."* Then Tō no Chūjō retorted with a touch of annoyance, *[Tō no Chūjō's words] "It's precisely those 'others,' the ones you'd rather not show, that I wish to see. I'm hardly adept in the ways of courtship, but even I am party to ordinary everyday love letters. It's the special ones—those written by women whose feelings you've hurt, or women who sit up nights waiting for you to come—those are the ones worth looking at."* Thus, Genji had no choice. Since he would not be so indiscreet as to lay a letter from a noble woman about in plain sight on any old shelf, no letters that really ought not be shown to Tō no Chūjō were in that bunch: showing them to him might even be rather amusing. Tō no Chūjō began reading this one and that one, saying *[Tō no Chūjō's words] "You have quite a collection of them, don't you?"* He then guessed that this was from one woman and that from another. Sometimes he was right, sometimes wrong, and sometimes when he was wrong, he suspected Genji of refusing to admit his having been right. Genji thought this great fun, but he said as little as possible, and hid the letters away. Then, when he said, *[Genji's words] "You're the one with the really sterling collection. Let me see a few of yours. Then I'll be happy to show you my whole batch."* Tō no Chūjō replied, *[Tō no Chūjō's words] "Mine would seem pretty unimpressive to you."*

As we can see, Hiromichi marked his narrative categories with the guide words, "Genji's thought," "Genji's words," and "Tō no Chūjō's words" next to the italicized passages. At the beginning of Section I, which reads, " 'The Radiant Genji.' The name itself was grand indeed," the narrator is actually reciting part of a tale in her direct voice. This Section I corresponds to authorial intrusion (sakusha no kotoba). Whether the narrator of the *Genji Monoga-*

tari is the author herself or some nyōbo (lady serving at court) appointed for that purpose is a problem that I will not take up here. Let us assume that the narrator is an extension of the author who serves as the medium through which the world of the monogatari and that of the reader are linked. The italicized portion in Section I marked "Genji's thought" is known as the character's inner thought (shinnaigo). The author imagines that, if Genji were to suffer having these affairs brought out in the open, he would be highly displeased; and having so imagined what Genji's thoughts would be, she inserts these in the narrative as her own words. The narrator then moves on to the next setting in the story.

Sections II, III, and IV tell about recent events in Genji's life; they represent the limited expanse of time "just passed." Section V begins the famous "appraisal of women on a rainy night." In this section the reader gets the impression that the narrator's "voice" has disappeared and been replaced by a form of written narrative (ji no bun) that characterizes modern novels. But this is not really the case. Even in such sections of the monogatari, the narrator's presence is indicated by her use of honorific forms of speech in telling of Genji and Tō no Chūgō. The narrator has not disappeared; she is merely operating in the shadow of the text. There is a voice, but it is not her direct voice. However, in the latter half of Section V, we reach a point where even this indirect voice seems to be missing—the italicized portions labeled characters' words. Yet even at this point, the narrator's voice can be detected, albeit at a minimal level. By relating the speech of these two characters, the narrator employs the technique of narrative polyphony. This technique of employing voice on top of another voice can be understood as a paradox of character's inner thought (shinnaigo).

In the following "Utsusemi" chapter, Genji again unsuccessfully attempts to make love to Utsusemi. He steals into her sleeping quarters but discovers that the object of his ardor has slipped away, leaving her daughter-in-law, Nokiba no Ogi, behind. Here, a variety of layered narrative principles are employed in a refracted manner. Hiromichi did not note interpretive categories in this part of his text, but I have supplied these after consulting other textual annotations such as those in *Sairyūshō* and *Mingō Nisso*.

"Utsusemi," VI—Narrative (ji).

> The young Nokiba no Ogi went to sleep innocently. Then Utsusemi heard the rustling of robes, smelled the scent of a fine perfume, and raising her head, she detected something moving toward her in the darkness where the curtain had been opened. Startled and not knowing what to do, she stood up, draped a singlet of raw silk over herself, and slipped away. Genji entered and was relieved to find only one person lying there. Two nyōbo were sleeping on the veranda outside. He pushed aside her bedclothes and moved closer only to find that she appeared larger than before. But never did he imagine. . . . He noticed other differences in the sleeping figure, and it gradually dawned upon him who she was. What a fool he had been, but then, *[Genji's thought] "I would be even more of a fool if she found out that I made this mistake. In addition, she would think me peculiar. If the woman I came for dislikes me to the point of sneaking away like this, there's no use pursuing her further. What's more, she would take me for a dimwit."* Then he thought that there was nothing at all wrong with this other woman who had looked so beautiful in the torchlight. WASN'T THIS AN ACT OF SHAMELESS INDISCRETION?

Section VI is a narrative (ji no bun) of Genji's entrance into Utsusemi's sleeping quarters and of her escape. The emotions racing through Genji's head when he discovers his mistake are related to the reader as the character's inner thought (shinnaigo). The very last line of the section, given in upper case, is known as sōshiji; here the author confronts her reader with a direct comment. She could not remain silent after Genji's amorous thought on realizing his mistake; "There was nothing at all wrong with this other woman who had looked so beautiful in the torchlight."

The narrative categories dealt with thus far cannot be classified in parallel fashion on the same dimension. Instead, they should be seen as part of a stratified structure, as in Figure 1.

The narrative categories in Section VI, as well, reverberate in tale recitation conducted through the characters' refracted thought and speech. The narrator's voice is at its maximum in the portion of sōshiji, when directly confronting the reader with a comment; it is at its minimum in the character's inner thought (shinnaigo), which lies at the deepest, innermost layer of the stratified structure that informs narrative categories. This is to be expected, for the charcter's inner thought is just that—the innermost, secret ideas and feelings embraced by characters that remain unspoken. Thus, they are not the words (kotoba) actually uttered by a Genji or a Tō no Chūjō in the monogatari; the narrator must enter into the character's innermost feelings and present these at the shallowest level of the stratified structure—the "narrative" (ji) or authorial intrusion (sakusha kotoba). Logically speaking, then, the character's inner thought is ultimately little different from the presumed standard narrative (ji) itself. However, a distinction has been drawn between these two literary concepts in traditional commentaries on the *Genji* for good reason. No doubt it is true that the character's inner thought is a voiceless voice. But to hear it, the author had to approach the characters' innermost feelings in the most intimate fashion. Thus, the paradox of character's inner thought comes into being: that which is furthest removed from the narrator in terms of the narrative structure is psychologically closest to the characters' emotions.

The originality of the narrative principles employed in the *Genji Monogatari* becomes all the more evident when we compare it to other works of monogatari literature containing less-developed techniques of "tale-recitation." In the work, *Ochikubo Monogatari (The Story of Ochikubo)*, which was written before the *Genji* and is famous for its theme of a cruel stepmother, there is a passage where the protagonist, Shōshō, enters the sleeping quarters of Ochikubo no Hime and tries to force his affections upon her. This scene is analogous to the one in *Genji Monogatari* where Genji first attempts making love to a disinclined Utsusemi, but despite the similar circumstances involved, there is a clear difference in the way that *Ochikubo*'s author "tells his tale."

Ochikubo, Section I.

Shōshō took hold of her, removed her costume and lay down

> beside her. She trembled with fear and cried with sorrow. Shōshō said, "Since you lament the sorrows of the world so bitterly, I want you to experience all the tenderness that love between a man and woman can bring. I wish I could take you away to some secluded spot, away from the sorrows of this world." Before she could think (omou), "Can it be he?" she thought (omou) of her coarse, shabby garments. The figure of her sobbing, "I wish I could die right here and now," was so pathetic that he was at a loss for what to do; he simply lay down and embraced her.

There is a narrative (ji) which describes Shōshō's actions, and there are words (kotoba). The narration is so clear that "thumb markings" are unneeded. The two uses of "think" (omou) that connect us with the Princess's mental state merely explain what she was thinking—these hardly constitute a character's inner thoughts (shinnaigo). Passages of sōshiji are also lacking. In sum, because the author is unconcerned with his characters' inner thoughts, he has no need to sympathize with, or comment upon, what goes on in their hearts. The prose is straightforward, not refracted. No doubt all this is related to the fact that *Ochikubo*'s author is thought to be a man.[7] In the similar passage found in the *Genji*, Murasaki Shikibu identified herself psychologically with Utsusemi, a fellow woman whose circumstances in life resembled her own. Precisely because they were of the same sex and were troubled by similar problems, the author was capable of imagining what Utsusemi must have felt like, and was capable of endowing this character with inner thought. From there, Murasaki Shikibu could then imagine Genji's psychological reaction to being spurned by Utsusemi—*his* inner thought—and could comment critically upon it in a sōshiji. All this enabled her to employ narrative techniques that contained a greater emotional intensity, a greater refraction of thought and speech in the *Genji* than could be expected from the *Ochikubo* author. This is more than a problem of technical writing skill; it is the dynamics of authorial self-identification with,

[7] [It is usually presumed that the monogatari before the *Genji* were written by men for women.—Ed.]

FIGURE 1

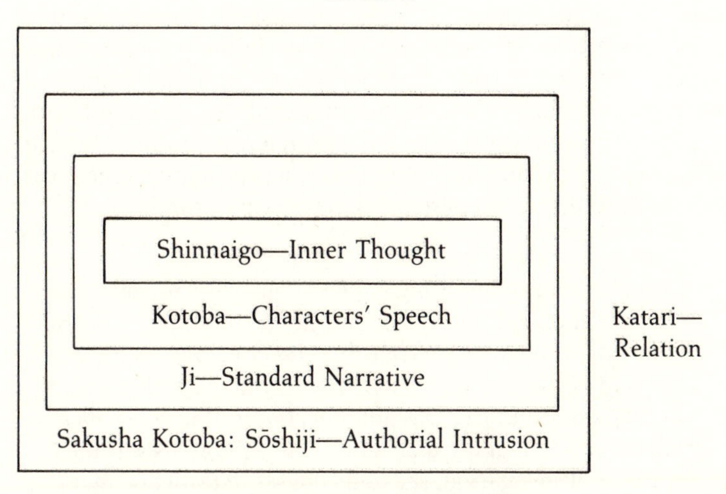

THE WORLD OF THE READER

and the creation of critical distance from, characters in the story; or in other words, the extent to which the monogatari writer can utilize narrative principles effectively.

There is one more occurrence in the *Genji* where a man enters the sleeping quarters of a certain woman only to end up finding someone else there. It takes place in the "Agemaki" chapter of the third, or "Uji," section of the story, and it concerns Kaoru and the sisters Ōigimi and Naka no Kimi.[8] This passage shows us the tenacity—for want of a better term—with which Murasaki Shikibu displayed her powers of thought and imagination throughout the work. Though similar or identical conditions are repeated in the story, they produce divergent lines of development for different characters. Truly, this "Agemaki" passage is an example of Hiromichi's narrative principle of correspondence (shōtai). Yet it is not simply a matter of identical conditions that produce certain effects in different characters of a later generation: the feelings of a woman who spurns an untoward suitor are plumbed at far greater

[8] [On the "third" section of the work, see n. 5.—Ed.]

depth in "Agemaki" than in "Utsusemi." In short, the later incident is no mere replay of the former. Earlier, I wrote that any point at which length and depth converge in the monogatari text appears as a breakoff point. The scene from "Agemaki" in question here is not brought about simply in accordance with the length supplied by Hiromichi's structural principles; but rather, through the author's desire to uncover even further the human consciousness conveyed through narrative principles of "length."

"Agemaki," Section VII.

> As evening turned into night, the winds blew roughly and made the ill-crafted shutters rattle. The waiting-lady led Kaoru in secretly, thinking to herself that the Princesses would not hear him because of the clatter. *[Ben's thought] "It worries me that the Princesses' sleeping together in the same room may prevent his telling them apart,"* but since this was their invariable sleeping habit, she could not separate them tonight. *[Ben's thought] "His Lordship probably knows enough to tell which is which."* However, Ōigimi, who was still awake, chanced to hear them approach, and slipped out of the room. As she crawled into hiding swiftly, ever so swiftly, her heart was wrenched by the sight of Naka no Kimi sleeping there so unsuspectingly, which made her think, *[Ōigimi's thought] "Oh what shall I do? I wish we could hide together,"* but her trembling prevented her from turning back; and then, when a brazen-faced man's figure in the torchlight pulled up the drape and came into the room, she was pained to wonder, [Ōigimi's *thought*] *"Oh, how would she feel?"*—yet she remained huddled in her cramped space between the screen and the shabby wall.

In this scene, all that can be heard is the howling wind at a mountain retreat in Uji. It is a silent drama that highlights a comical male and a sorrowful heroine. Kaoru is led to Ōigimi's bedchamber by Ben and is about to enter. Their approach is detected by Ōigimi, and she departs from the room, leaving the unsuspecting Naka no Kimi in her sleep. This is virtually a replay of the earlier "Utsusemi" scene. Since no one utters a sound, there are no words; the scene is propelled along by the use of narrative (ji) and thoughts. We should note that the lines beginning, "As she crawled into hiding swiftly . . ." constitute one sentence that runs to the end of the passage quoted. What is more, within this single sentence, three different subjects (Ōigimi, Naka no Kimi, and Kaoru) appear one after another; and the narrative and characters' thoughts come and go in rapid succession. In one breath, the author must describe the three characters and their different situations. A close look at this one sentence reveals that it is written in a particular syntax—from the viewpoint of Ōigimi looking out at Naka no Kimi and Kaoru—and is propelled by the alternating insertion of narrative and characters' thoughts. One critic has described the nature of Murasaki Shikibu's prose as follows:

> While treating her characters in combination and positioning them creatively in the story, she enters into their minds, grasps objective external conditions from the standpoint of their subjective observations, and then returns to their position in the scene.[9]

She is enabled to do this by deftly adjusting the various depths among the layered narrative principles and effectively manipulating them into a structure. In this manner, she is able to create monogatari scenes, to attain a level of psychological description, and even more important, to relate imagined psychological experiences better than any other Japanese author (See Figure 2.) Here we see that because of Murasaki Shikibu's self-identification with her character, that character's inner thought (shinnaigo) paradoxically is brought closer to her own innermost voice.

There is no sōshiji, which the author recites in her actual voice, to be found in this passage—there is no external comment on the intruding male's thoughts or feelings made by the narrator as was the case earlier in the "Utsusemi" passage. Or does this only appear to be so? The key to this problem lies in the long sentence beginning, "As she crawled into hiding swiftly . . . ," which describes Kaoru's actions. It succeeds in getting across an objective portrait

[9] Watanabe Minoru, *Heianchō Bunshōshi* (Tokyo Daigaku Shuppankai, 1976), p. 184.

of him—conceited, affected, tedious, gawky, knowing only enough about a woman's emotions to alienate her and, on top of that, downright comical. This may indeed be narrative (ji) according to Hiromichi's narrative categories, but at the same time, Kaoru's character is grasped from Ōigimi's subjective viewpoint, through the filter of her psyche. It is still more important that Murasaki Shikibu has included an implicitly scathing indictment of Kaoru in this passage that might be termed an internalized sōshiji. Here there are no smiles similar to those directed at Genji in "Utsusemi." The narrator as well has receded from the layer of voice to the substratum of the text, taking with her the sōshiji type of expression.

All the categories that compose the various depths in the monogatari's narrative structure—the narrator's direct comment or sōshiji, the words put into the mouths of characters in the story, the characters' inner thoughts so paradoxically most intimate to the author—form a separate layer on top of the author's own voice. (Of course, this author's voice is conveyed through the narrator, who, by being in the world of the story, does not expose herself as the author.) This is what I meant earlier by the term "polyphony," the layering of one voice upon another voice in the reciting of tales. These voices run the whole gamut from maximum to minimum in the monogatari text; but the layer of the narrator's voice is always present. This substratum, this fundamental narrative, itself exists below the surface of the text; when it emerges, it does so at various different parts of the narrative structure, from sōshiji, where it is at its maximum, to characters' inner thought, where it is at its minimum. This substratum of the narrator's voice can clash with other levels of voice in the monogatari, or it can be placed on top of these. However, I believe that this substratum—the narrator's voice—which lies at the deepest level of the monogatari, constitutes that genre's defining characteristic.

As we all supposedly know, in monogatari, people (mono) recite (kataru). But today, unless one affirms the beliefs adopted by Origuchi Shinobu based on a folklore approach to understanding Japanese classical literature, such clichés about monogatari are little more than figures of speech. This is because even the earliest of

FIGURE 2

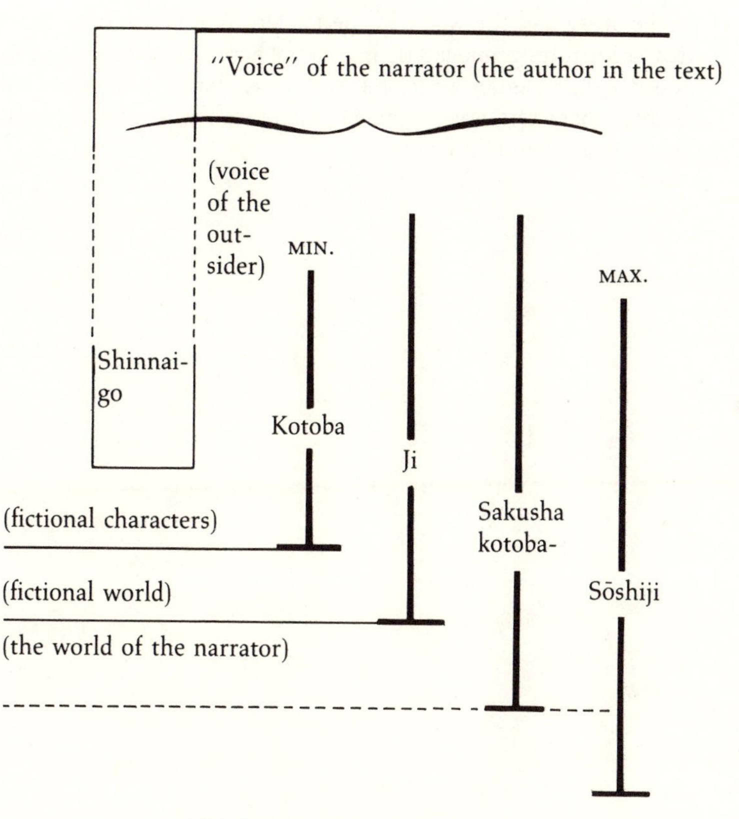

THE WORLD OF THE READER

the monogatari that have come down to us were produced in an era when tales (mono) were recited. The *Genji Monogatari* is no exception. Yet with the appearance of the *Genji*, we see a comeback staged by people as the agents of recitation—but in a new dimension. The characters in the story, created by Murasaki Shikibu, begin to recite on their own, apart from her. In other words, on the one hand she has them perform the act of recitation, but in order not to become totally preoccupied in their reciting, she has to place the narrator in a position to control both the fictive world of the story and the world of the reader. This is the substratum that constitutes monogatari. It is from here that the voice of an outsider becomes an actual human voice, that the voices of the fictional characters, accompanied by a physicality of presence, speak out to us in manifold layerings.

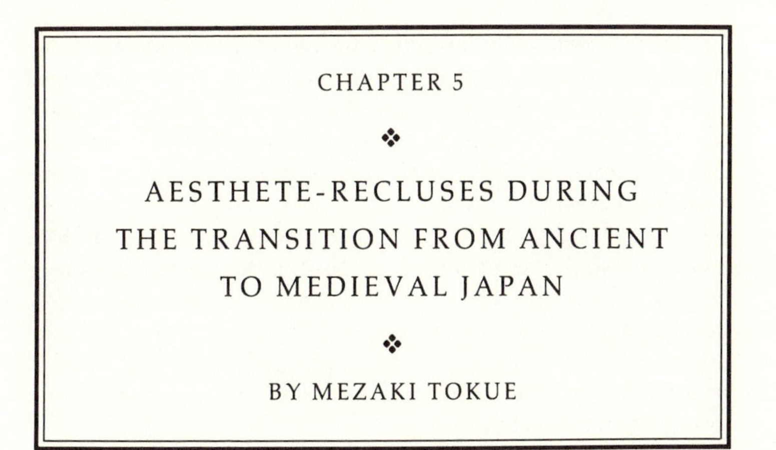

CHAPTER 5

AESTHETE-RECLUSES DURING THE TRANSITION FROM ANCIENT TO MEDIEVAL JAPAN

BY MEZAKI TOKUE

Renunciation and Aestheticism

From the tenth to the fifteenth centuries, reclusive poets appeared in great number, playing a strong and influential role in the literary world. This essay will trace their lineage in broad outline while considering their lives, works, and historical significance.

Although not only literature but almost all Japanese culture long existed under the dominance of Chinese norms, there were differences between the two traditions. For example, Chinese literature was invested with a highly sophisticated political character, and the littérateurs were mainly gentry, that is, government officials. In Japan, on the other hand, there was a flourishing of literature written by women in the eleventh century. And from the twelfth century on, the role of recluses in the literary scene grew conspicuously.[1] The contrast is complex and very revealing.

Translated by Matthew Mizenko.

[1] Twenty women poets and more than ten recluses appear in the *Ogura Hyakunin Isshū* (1235?), an anthology compiled by the poet Fujiwara Teika, representing by a single waka each of one hundred representative poets of the eighth through twelfth centuries. [As stated in the Introduction, this chapter fits closely with the next, by Konishi.—Ed.]

For comparative study, it would be valuable to explore similar contrasts in other nations or cultures, including those of Europe.

The terms "tonsei" (escaping the world) and "shukke" (leaving the family) have similar meanings and have often been used in the compound "shukke tonsei." There is a difference in nuance between the words, however, since shukke implies leaving one's home and family, and tonsei escaping from society as a whole. Moreover, shukke is an old concept basic to Buddhism throughout history, whereas the usage of tonsei is more limited, having been favored in society during the transition between ancient and medieval Japan. In other words, the tonsei recluses possess characteristics rather different from those who left home and became priests in traditional fashion.[2]

The intellectual historian Ōsumi Kazuo has written that "investigation of the usage of the term tonsei shows that shukke and tonsei were not identical, but that recluses [tonseisha] and those who formally entered the priesthood actually led distinct lives.[3] Professor Ōsumi shows that those who would enter formally into the priesthood during the Heian and Kamakura periods typically lived in a temple from childhood, used writing as an aid to study of Buddhist scriptures, and took the tonsure on reaching adulthood. In contrast, terms such as "nyūdō" ("entering the Way") were applied to those who entered the Buddhist world after having already lived in the secular world. In this way the latter were distinguished from those who had been destined for the clergy from the start. Recluses, or tonseisha—who were often called by the titles nyūdō, shōnin (superior man) and hijiri (saint)—did not enter into temple organization or concern themselves with matters of administrative operation. Nor did they study minute and complex aspects of religion or write works of doctrine. In effect, what the recluses sought was a life of belief, rather than one immured in organized religion. As Ōsumi puts it, the act of renouncing the world (tonsei) was a "step toward acquiring peace and freedom."

[2] Mezaki Tokue, *Shukke Tonsei* (Chūō Kōronsha, 1976), pp. 6-9.

[3] Ōsumi Kazuo, "Tonsei to Bukkyō," in a pamphlet appended to Mezaki, *Saigyō* (Yoshikawa Kōbunkan, 1980).

In conclusion, Ōsumi writes that "the tonsei constituted an approach to Buddhism unique to the Japanese in that it was based on life and its conduct, in the absence of a cosmology." Tonseisha may be called amateur practitioners of religion, rather than professional priests. They wished to break, to shed, the bonds of secular society, and to achieve a religious life with spiritual liberty. This desire can be ascribed to the fact that, under the social circumstances of the time, it was impossible for many people to live in peace and freedom except by formally or nominally entering Buddhist orders. Accordingly, although most of the recluses were naturally those who fervently pursued religious discipline, there were many others who devoted themselves to the arts they loved—whether literature or other aesthetic accomplishments—rather than religious practice. This latter group can be given the general name "suki no tonseisha," or "aesthete-recluses."[4] These aesthete-recluses were the main sustainers of literature, in particular of waka (Japanese poetry; tanka), during the Japanese middle ages.

The word "suki," a nominalization of the verb "suku," originally meant "irogonomi," which can mean a man aggressively desirous of relations with women. The word betokens deep desire for something. By extension, it came to embrace a deep love for literature and the arts.[5] Defined as hekiai (warped love) in the fifteenth-century dictionary *Kagakushū* (1444), its passion was viewed as something intense that veered from its proper course. Among those who felt such strong inclinations, some naturally thought onerous the task of serving the court and those in power. Such people experienced a religious awakening, discarded their identities as officials, and took Buddhist vows. By placing themselves outside secular society, they obtained the freedom to live in their grass-thatched huts in the mountains or along the coast, to wander about the countryside, or to pursue the art of poetry.

We should not view negatively decisions to renounce the world

[4] Mezaki, *Saigyō no Shisōshiteki Kenkyū* (Yoshikawa Kōbunkan, 1978), pp. 100-132.

[5] [That is, with a basic meaning of strong desire, "suki" came to convey a strong wish or dedication involving the aesthetic-reclusive life detailed in the following pages.—Ed.]

in order to pursue a life of refinement, thinking that it was merely an escape from the increasingly harsh realities of politics and society. With the waning of the Heian era and with the increase in social and political unease and instability, the act of becoming a tonseisha provided a basis for cultural creativity and the sustaining of spiritual liberty. This positive element requires emphasis. Those who discarded the privileged status of the nobility had to recognize that they would have to renounce decisively all worldly desires and resign themselves to lives of honorable poverty. Of course, we may assume that most noble hermits were blessed with estates or other economic resources to support their secluded lives. At the least, they shared a temperament that clearly valued spiritual nobility over material happiness. So it was that the aesthete-recluses came to define the type of life characteristic of the free and cultured people of medieval Japan.

What were the features of the aesthetic life of refinement that proved so attractive to the recluses? Two representative definitions can be cited here. The first appears in the *Hosshinshū* (ca. 1215), an anthology of exemplary Buddhist tales compiled by Kamo no Chōmei (1155-1216):

> aestheticism [suki] means taking no pleasure in social intercourse, refusing to grieve over misfortune, feeling touched by the bloom and fall of flowers, and longing for the rise and set of the moon. In this way we constantly keep our hearts clear of blemish and, before we realize it, we come to understand how it is that things appear and vanish, and we cease to have attachment to fame and profit. This is to enter the path of deliverance, of freedom from illusion.[6]

Kamo no Chōmei was born into a family that had acted as the priests of the Shimogamo Shrine in Kyoto. He devoted himself, however, to the art of poetry, and, after participating in the compilation of the *Shinkokinshū* (1205), he entered the life of a recluse. His famous *Hōjōki* (*An Account of My Hut*, 1212) describes his grass-thatched hut in the mountains. In his definition, Chōmei

[6] Miki Sumito, ed., *Hōjōki, Hosshinshū* (Shinchōsha, 1976), p. 278.

emphasizes that suki, or, in his case, a passion for literature, is born of a life marked by the cutting of ties to the secular world and a merging with nature, marking a starting point toward religious enlightenment.

A second discussion of suki is found in a passage from *Myōe Shōnin Ikun* (*The Posthumous Teachings of the Priest Myōe,* ca. 1235-1238).

> From times long past, there has been no one noteworthy in Buddhism who does not have suki as an intention and who has failed to give devotion to matters of the heart. . . . Then and now there have appeared praiseworthy Buddhists who are devoted to the spirit of suki. Although the creation of poems of praise [shōshi] and devotion to poetry [waka] and linked verse [renga] is not necessarily a matter of Buddhism, those who demonstrate in these pursuits a heart of suki will, in due course, turn to Buddhism. They acquire wisdom, and their gentle hearts are noble.[7]

Myōe (1163-1222), a slightly younger contemporary of Chōmei's, possessed a religiosity that was passionate to the point of madness. He was a learned clergyman who argued in defense of the old, traditional Buddhism against the popular Pure Land Buddhism (Jōdokyō) of the priest Hōnen (1133-1212). Although he did not fit the category of the recluse, he liked to compose waka and held a deep understanding of the spirit of suki. In the passage quoted, Myōe indicates that suki and Buddhism hold in common an opposition to spiritual degradation. He stressed that if he were one "who does not have suki as an intention," there would have been small possibility of teaching him the Buddhist truths. As a youth, he received instruction in the art of poetry from Saigyō (1118-1190), a principal *Shinkokinshū* poet.[8] Myōe's words may be said to reflect these teachings.

[7] Kubota Jun and Yamaguchi Akio, ed., *Myōe Shōnin Shū* (Iwanami Shoten, 1981), p. 213.

[8] According to the *Myōe Shōnin Denki* (Kamakura period), Saigyō said the following about one of Myōe's waka: "This lyric is essentially the true form of

Both passages share the recognition that suki is a way of life in which one cuts oneself off from the secular world and comes closer to nature, and that this alternative life constitutes a gateway to religion. Full realization of the recognition assumes the characteristic medieval concept of the oneness of religion and literature. A long philosophical search would be necessary before this point of identity between them could be reached, for as long as one's attitude was based on a religion that earnestly aspired to enlightenment for the next world, literature, being involved in worldly aestheticism, was fundamentally contradictory to religion. The T'ang poet Po Chü-i made a strong impression on the Heian nobility with a maxim that helped overcome the contradiction:

> I have long cherished one desire, that my deeds on this earth and the faults occasioned by my wild words and fancy language will be transformed, for worlds to come, into a factor extolling the Law and a link to the preaching of the Buddha's Word. May the myriad Buddhas of the Three Worlds take heed.[9]

The phrase, "wild words and fancy language" [J., "kyōgen kigo"] was used as a kind of slogan for waka from the Heian period onward. The phrase is said to have been constantly intoned, for example, by members of the Kangakue, a group composed of literati and priests of the Tendai sect that held meetings in the late tenth century.[10] They heard lectures on sutras, recited Buddhist prayers, and composed Chinese and Japanese poetry. Their leader was Yoshishige Yasutane (931?-1002), who later became a recluse under

the Buddha. Indeed, composing a poem involves the same way of thinking as carving a holy statue. Constantly keeping a verse in mind is the same as chanting the secret true word [shingon]. By means of this poem I can attain the Holy Dharma."

[9] [*Po-shih Wen-chi*; vol. 71, "Hsiang-shan Ssu Po-shih Lo-chung Chi-chi." See the chapter by Konishi, pp. 192-193, for fuller explanation of this matter.—Ed.]

[10] According to *Sambō Ekotoba*, a collection of Buddhist tales compiled in 984. [Here, and frequently in this chapter there is much that relates to Konishi's on the ideal of poetic vocation (michi), and much there that relates to this chapter.—Ed.]

the name Jakushin. In the early eleventh century, the slogan was further popularized by the cultural arbiter, Fujiwara Kintō (966-1041), who included Po Chü-i's poetic version of it in his anthology of Japanese and Chinese poetry, *Wakan Rōeishū* (1011-1012).

There is a close association between those "wild words and fancy language" and the Jōdo [Pure Land] sect that emerged from Tendai Buddhism. Even while literature was recognized as a powerful service to religious ends, its autonomy was conceived of solely in negative terms. The concept of waka based on esoteric Buddhism and Shinto-Buddhist syncretism transcended that conception. In esoteric Buddhism, waka was recognized as possessing a magical power similar to that of the true words (shingon) and incantations (darani) of esoteric practice. Also, from the belief that the native Japanese deities found pleasure in waka, there arose in syncretic practice a tendency to offer waka as entertainment for the gods (hōraku).

The development of ideas of the religious uses of literature was the result of the court nobility's earnest pursuit of a solution to a difficult question. Given the rapid decline and collapse of their society, how could the cult of aestheticism (suki)—which had been the elegant cultural accomplishment of the court's period of flowering—be conveyed to the medieval age, in which religion and a new social order were ascendant? For the aesthete-recluses, who emerged as the influential sustainers of literature, the assimilation of religion and poetry was a tactical means more than anything else. When the assimilation was expressed in literary works, a contradictory effect was, understandably, unavoidable. A variety of waka (called shakkyōka [or Buddhist poems]), which had themes related to the Buddhist scriptures, was excessively religious. And from our modern aesthetic perspective the effort can only be thought to involve a certain sacrifice of literary quality. Those seasonal poems infused with the Buddhist sense of impermanence (mujō) exhibited, however, a discovery of the subdued and monochromatic beauty of late autumn and winter, while poems of sorrow, parting, travel, and reminiscence showed a remarkable deepening of insight into human life. The greatest realization of these trends can be found in the *Shinkokinshū* and the works of its leading poet, the priest Saigyō.

The Lineage of the Aesthete-Recluse

We can define three distinct stages in the lineage of the aesthete-recluse in the history of Japanese literature, particularly in relation to waka. In the first period, the ninth century, the ritsuryō system of government, which had been constructed in imitation of Chinese law, was, in essence, still functioning soundly.[11] There appeared few nobles or officials who wished to escape the system, aside from a few exceptions such as the *Kokinshū* poets Priest Kisen (810-824) and Priest Sosei (fl. ca. 859-923). There are also two poets in the *Hyakunin Isshu* who manifest a latent desire for reclusion. They are, first, Sarumaru Dayu (eighth or ninth century) whose following poem is well known:

Okuyama ni	Deep in the hills
Momiji fumiwake	I walk my way through colored leaves
Naku shika no	And a deer cries out—
Koe kiku toki zo	It is when I hear that sound
Aki wa kanashiki.	That autumn really is so sad.
	(*Kokinshū*, 3, 215)

The second is Semimaru (fl. ca. 900?), whose poem is yet more often encountered:

Kore ya kono	Here, yes, it is here—
Yuku mo kaeru mo	Some who go, some who return,
Wakaretsutsu	Others who are parting,
Shiru mo shiranu mo	Those who are known and those unknown
Ōsaka no seki.	At the Ōsaka Barrier.[12]
	(*Gosenshū*, 15, 1090)

[11] [The "ritsuryō system" was the codified system of ranks and offices for the Nara and Heian courts, formally in operation from the Taika Reform in the seventh century to the end of the Heian period late in the twelfth century.—Ed.]

[12] [The *Hyakunin Isshu* was compiled by Fujiwara Teika and has remained the

During the second period, which lasted from the tenth to the eleventh century, court society became increasingly rigid as a result of the monopolizing of political power by the Fujiwara magnates. The middle- and low-ranking noble groups grew increasingly aware of their misfortune and obscurity. More and more they desired to escape that fate. Priests such as Ampō (mid-Heian period), a descendant of a sovereign; Nōin (988-1058?) of the Tachibana family, and Ryōzen (died ca. 1058-1064?), whose family origin is unknown, offer a range of examples of poets who became recluses under the influence of these attitudes.

In the third period, the twelfth century, court government as it had been known was in danger of collapse. Rule was marked by a newly complicating system [insei] in which great political authority and power was held by sovereigns who had officially abdicated in order to become Buddhist priests. The growing power of the warrior groups based in outlying regions led to a succession of militant disorders, with social unrest growing to a high pitch. The Buddhist idea of mappō (the final phase of the Law, marking a final degeneracy in which the Law could not be understood) provided a theoretical support for this social unease, which became so serious that for the first time in their history the Japanese became possessed by a deep pessimism. The aesthete-recluses who appeared during this time are too numerous to be discussed here except for some of the most outstanding of their number: the priest Shun'e (1113-?), a third-generation poet in the footsteps of his grandfather, the Major Councilor (Dainagon) Minamoto Tsunenobu (1016-1097), and his father Minamoto Toshiyori (Shunrai, 1055-1129?); the brothers who took on the religious names of Jakunen (Fujiwara Tamenari, ca. 1113-ca. 1181), Jakuchō (Fujiwara Tametsune, ca. 1114-after 1180), and Jakuzen (also sometimes pronounced Jakunen; Fujiwara Yorinari, ca. 1119-after 1173); the priest Saigyō, the most famous of all in art and legend; and Kamo no Chōmei. In the remainder of this essay I shall trace the back-

most popular waka collection. On Semimaru's poem, see Susan Matisoff, *The Legend of Semimaru Blind Musician of Japan* (New York: Columbia University Press, 1978), pp. 55-62. Mezaki Tokue put the two poems and other matter in this note. In this translation they have been made part of his main text.—Ed.]

grounds of these men while devoting a separate section to the life and works of Saigyō.

Waga io wa	Here is my hut
Miyako no tatsumi	Southeast of the capital—
Shika zo sumu	And so I dwell
Yo o Ujiyama to	In the Uji hills of suffering
Hito wa iu nari.	That people say we must escape.
	(*Kokinshū*, 18, 983)

This poem, practically the only legacy of Kisen, tells that he was a recluse who built a hut in the Uji area southeast of Kyoto. The phrase "yo o Ujiyama" uses a pivot-word (kakekotoba). The sense of seeing the world (yo) as a place of gloom and sadness (Uji-ushi) is hidden within the place name. We can surmise that the poet grew weary of the secular world and left the capital to lead a life close to nature in the hills. In fact, however, there exist no concrete historical records of Kisen's family background, personal history, character, etc. Even the Japanese preface to the *Kokinshū* can only report that little is known about him. Nevertheless, the name of this recluse, whose existence can scarcely be confirmed, appears among the six early illustrious poetic sages (rokkasen), and this must indicate that the author of the preface, Ki no Tsurayuki (ca. 872-945), was deeply impressed by the manner of life described in the poem. Although aesthete-recluses were still rare during this period, there was certainly aspiration to such a life.

Sosei deserves to be recognized as the pioneer in realizing the way of life of the suki no tonseisha. Like Kisen, Sosei's father, Bishop (Sōjō) Henjō (816-890), was numbered among the six poetic sages. Henjō, a grandchild of Kammu Tennō, held the important court position of kurōdo no tō, a position similar to that of secretary to the sovereign. Overcome by grief over the sudden death of the sovereign who had had such faith in him, Henjō entered the priesthood, and his son Sosei, although still a child, followed him into orders. The two, together with the rest of the group of discouraged and demoralized people, became deeply involved in waka gatherings at the temple Urin'in, which was located in a beautiful setting on the outskirts of Kyoto. The father, Henjō, was highly praised for his ability as a priest of the Tendai sect, and he later attained a position of leadership in Buddhist circles. He enjoyed the steadfast confidence of the court and was honored with fame and distinction. By contrast, Sosei lived in seclusion in a mountain temple in Yamato, much farther from the capital, where he pursued a life of refined taste and elegance. Uda Tennō (867-931, r. 887-897), who was a driving force behind the compilation of the *Kokinshū*, had deep affection for Sosei. Uda enlisted his services when he traveled to Yamato, having him accompany him on horseback (a distinct honor at the time).

Sosei's life as a recluse liberated him from the bonds that constricted the laymen who were engaged in day-to-day court affairs. This does not mean, however, that he was fully immersed in religious practice and totally isolated from secular matters. Rather, his life permitted him to enjoy himself in freedom while remaining at the fringes of the secular world. The lighthearted mood that emerged from this liberty is the distinctive characteristic of his waka.

On gazing at the capital with trees in full flower.

Miwataseba	I gaze at the sight
Yanagi sakura o	Of willows and flowering cherries
Kokimazete	Woven together—
Miyako zo haru no	Now the capital has become
Nishiki narikeru.	A bright brocade of spring!
	(*Kokinshū*, 1, 56)

With a tranquil heart, Sosei, who lives in hills brocaded (in the usual conception) with colorful leaves in autumn, gazes now at the capital's other "brocade," the interweaving of the green of the willows and the faint pink of the cherry blossoms. Sosei would not have created this unusually relaxed tone if his manner of life were different. Although he was a priest, in most of his poems it is almost impossible to discern the variety of religious suffering that typically accompanied the mujō idea of this world as one of transience and mutability.

The serene, springlike mood found in Sosei's waka changes dramatically in the next phase of the history of the aesthete-recluse. A kind of gloom emerges in both their lives and their art. One poet of this period, Ampō, was a descendant of Minamoto Tōru (822-895), the famous Sadaijin (Minister of the Left), who was the son of Saga Tennō (786-842, r. 809-823) and one who was noted for his extravagance. Tōru built a detached villa called the Kawara no In, where he constructed a large and beautiful pond by channeling water from the Kamo River. Legend has it that he even transported seawater from the distant port of Naniwa so that he could enjoy cultivating ocean fish and shellfish. Yet in one generation after he died, the villa had become so dilapidated, as a result of flooding and other factors, that it was rumored to be haunted by his restless ghost.[13]

It is not known when and why Priest Ampō became a recluse. In any event, he came to live in a section of his ancestor's ruined estate as his temple. Literati and poets who loved the old estate gathered around him, spontaneously forming a circle of suki devotees. Such major poets of the *Gosenshū* [the second court anthology, compiled in 951] as Minamoto Shitagō (911-983), Taira Kanemori (?-990), and Minamoto Shigeyuki (?-1000) were members of this group. It should be noted that all three were descendants of Heian-period sovereigns. Although they all boasted noble pedigrees and had confidence in their talent, their position was such that they could only lament their ill fortune in not belonging to the Fujiwara family, which held political power.[14] It was at the Kawara no In of recluse Ampō that they could console themselves.

Since there remain no particularly well-known poems by Ampō, I will cite one by the priest Egyō (also Ekyō; dates unknown), who belonged to this circle.

Yaemugura	The wild vines
Shigereru yado no	Overspread my hermitage—
Sabishiki ni	In this loneliness

[13] The "Yūgao" chapter of *The Tale of Genji* is believed to have been based on this historical situation, which was also the source of the nō, *Tōru*, by Zeami.

[14] [This bears in an important way on the ideology section of Miner's chapter.—Ed.]

Hito koso miene	Not a single person can be seen,
Aki wa kinikeri.	And only autumn visits here.
	(*Shūishū*, 3, 140)

This poem expresses the mood of autumn at Kawara no In. What is described here is not merely a seasonal sentiment, however. It also concerns the loneliness of the human world. We can discover from the headnote to the poem that Egyō sometimes journeyed to the capital region, perhaps to assuage his isolation and loneliness. Unfortunately, his personal history is virtually unknown. At the very least we can surmise that he was able to live a life of leisurely retreat in a grass-thatched hut and wander around Japan. These two elements, solitary reclusive life and itinerant motion, paradoxically coordinate the life of the aesthete-recluse.

Such characteristics are displayed most typically in the life of Priest Nōin, who followed Ampō and Egyō by one generation. Born into the learned Tachibana family, Nōin was famous for his extraordinary talent in literature, but about the age of thirty he entered the life of a recluse. He set up his hut in Kosobe, near Kyoto's seaport, Naniwa [the location of present Osaka], where it seems he lived a half-religious, half-secular life. His economic support may have come from a horse-breeding farm he owned.[15] There are few historical sources for his life aside from the more than two hundred poems that comprise his personal anthology, *Nōin Hōshi Shū*. In their stead we have many legends that recount his extremely unconventional activities. Here is one of his most famous poems.

> Upon spending the night at the Shirakawa Barrier during a short trip to Michinoku [or Mutsu] in 1025:

Miyako o ba	From the capital,
Kasumi to tomo ni	Together with spring haze
Tachishikado	I took my way,
Akikaze zo fuku	But the autumn wind now blows
Shirakawa no Seki.	At the Shirakawa Barrier.
	(*Goshūishū*, 9, 518)

[15] Mezaki, *Heian Bunkashi Ron* (Ōfūsha, 1968), pp. 332-34.

A long-standing legend has it that Nōin never actually visited Michinoku Province, the setting of the poem, but that he merely pretended he had gone just in order to make the poem more effective.[16]

Although many still believe this legend, it is a fiction, since it is clearly stated in Nōin's personal anthology that he made several trips to Michinoku. For his era, Nōin was in fact unusually given to travel. His tracks led not only to Michinoku in the most distant north but also to eastern and western Japan, areas where he resided for long stretches of time. It is thought that the motivation leading to such frequent travel was the one revealed by the seventeenth-century haikai poet Matsuo Bashō, who was a great admirer of Nōin.[17] In *Oku no Hosomichi (The Narrow Road Through the Provinces)*, Bashō ascribed his own journey to the spirit of suki, which, he said, is like a demon whose true form is unknowable.[18] What Nōin longed for most of all were the utamakura, the famous places named in poetry from the *Kokinshū* and later poetry. The Shirakawa Barrier was one of these places more familiar in poetry than experience. It was the privilege of the liberated recluses to journey great distances to visit utamakura that could only be dimly imagined by the secular nobility of the capital.

Not only did Nōin exercise this privilege to his heart's content; it seems that he also exaggerated his activities as much as possible, so engaging the curiosity—and gossip—of the nobility. Accordingly, we should perhaps say that even if the legend concerning the poem he wrote at the Shirakawa Barrier is fiction, the responsibility for creating this fiction finally lies with Nōin's own image making.

[16] [The poem just quoted became famous, often being included in collections of exemplary poems. In his *Oku no Hosomichi (Narrow Road through the Provinces)*, Matsuo Bashō gestures toward the poem on more than one occasion, never quoting it because it was too famous to require spelling out. See Imoto Nōichi et al., ed., *Matsuo Bashō Shū* (Shōgakkan, 1972), *Nihon Koten Bungaku Zenshū*, pp. 41, 341, 350, 351.—Ed.]

[17] [Nōin is mentioned in *Oku no Hosomichi* more often than any other earlier poet except Saigyō.—Ed.]

[18] See Imoto Nōichi et al., as in n. 16; or see Sugiura Shōichirō et al., ed., *Bashō Bunshū* (Iwanami Shoten [*Nihon Koten Bungaku Taikei*], 1959), p. 70.

According to another legend, Nōin's study of the way of poetry under Fujiwara Nagatō (ca. 940?-ca. 1015?) was the first case of a master-student relationship in waka. This would demonstrate that Nōin intensely desired to raise the status of waka, sometimes still considered little more than an entertaining hobby, to match that of such disciplines as studies of Confucian classics (myōgyōdō) and of Chinese poetry and history (monjōdō) practiced at the court school [daigaku]. Whether or not these legends are true, it is clear that the way of life of the aesthete-recluse was established through the efforts of Nōin, whose life was marked by a novel prejudice against the secular and the commonplace.

Nothing is known about Priest Ryōzen, a contemporary of Nōin's, except that he was a priest of the Tendai sect. The following poem, however, symbolically expresses the paradoxical way of life and aesthetic consciousness of the aesthete-recluse. It has a headnote: "Composed when moonlight was shining through openings of my dilapidated hut."

Itama yori	I have even seen
Tsuki no moru o mo	The moonlight as it filtered
Mitsuru kana	Through the roof planks—
Yado wa arashite	A hut that verges on collapse
Sumu bekarikeri.	Provides the finest place to live.
	(*Shikashū* [1151], 9, 293)

We can imagine that this poem describes Ryōzen's hut in Ohara, north of the Heiankyō [present Kyoto]. Moved by the beauty of the moonlight filtering through the gaps in his roof, he lyrically praises the virtues of dwelling in a ruined house. There is a legend that a nobleman once said, in a similar vein, "If only I could view the moon in this place of exile without having done wrong!"[19] The recluses realized that, in order to satisfy the spirit of suki, they could not avoid having to make sacrifices in their lives. In retrospect, we can see this as mental preparation for the chaotic world that was soon to impinge upon Japanese society.

[19] This story appears in *Gōdanshō*, *Hosshinshū*, and many other collections. See Hatakeda Shiro, *Nihon Setsuwa Bungaku Sakuin* (Osaka: Kyōbundō, 1976), p. 823.

The third period of the history of the aesthete-recluse came with the accelerated development of the medieval "feudal" system and the dominance of religion over other cultural elements. Reflecting the spirit of their times, the aesthete-recluses surpassed those of the previous period in number and in quality of commitment. For example, the father and grandfather, both famous poets, of Priest Shun'e, composed waka while savoring the rustic pleasures of life in a villa in Ōmi Province [by Lake Biwa], to which they escaped when they had time free from their official duties at court. In the third generation, however, Shun'e made a decisive and total break with the secular world, choosing to float freely on the waves of suki. Many poems in his personal anthology bring to mind a life of refined elegance. They offer appreciations of the cherry blossoms at the temple Hosshōji in Shirakawa, the autumn moon at the Henjōji in Hirosawa, and the wintry rain at the Chōrakuji in Higashiyama. His activities in connection with his life of suki were many and various. Not only was he always ready to participate in the poetry matches (utaawase) that were held at nobles' residences and shrines, but he also conducted the then-popular gatherings known as Hitomaro Eigu.[20] At his temple quarters in Shirakawa, on the eastern outskirts of Kyoto, he founded a literary group called the Karin'e, for which he assembled dozens of poets from both the lay and clerical worlds. The group met over a span of twenty years, from the Hōgen War (1156), the first disturbance signaling the end of Heian Japan, to the Gempei Wars (1180-1185), the series of battles that marked the beginning of the medieval period. It appears that the members of the group not only held poetry sessions but also helped each other in their personal lives. As Kamo no Chōmei wrote in the *Hōjōki*, there was a concentration of natural disasters, epidemics, and famine in this period; and with the added factor of civil warfare, social life became extremely chaotic. Under those social conditions, the Karin'e formed a strong pillar for people of culture.

[20] The great poet of the *Man'yōshū*, Kakinomoto Hitomaro (fl. ca. 680-700), came to be worshipped as a god of poetry and, beginning in the twelfth century, it became a custom to hold poetry gatherings after praying before his portrait and invoking him.

The social group most materially favored in this time of disturbances were the zuryō, lesser court officials, the governing officials in the provinces, who exploited their domains free from earlier restraints. One such official, Fujiwara Tametada (?-1136), was also a poet, and he organized numerous poetry gatherings at his estate on the outskirts of the Heiankyō. His three children also became zuryō and excelled also at waka, but they finally became recluses, though not in order of birth, adopting, as has been said, the names Jakunen, Jakuchō, and Jakuzen, and gaining the collective nickname of the "Three Jaku of Ohara," where they had their grass-thatched huts. ["Ohara" is the present pronunciation of what would normally be pronounced "Ōhara"—and was so pronounced in older times, as some poems will show shortly.]

For reasons of space, their literary accomplishments cannot be discussed in detail. The third son, Jakuzen, was the farthest removed from the court and poetry circles, but he had a close relationship with the poet Saigyō. He, living in Ohara, and Saigyō, living on Mount Kōya, often exchanged visits, and they corresponded with each other as well. In the *Sankashū*, Saigyō's personal collection, there appears a sequence of twenty poems: the first ten, all beginning with the phrase "Yama fukami" ("Deep in the mountains") were sent by Saigyō, and the remainder, all ending with "Ōhara no sato" ("the hamlet of Ōhara"), were written by Jakuzen in reply.

Sumigama no
Tanabiku keburi
Hitosuji ni
Kokorobosoki wa
Ōhara no sato.

From the charcoal
The smoke drifts upward
In a single line—
Heart-wringing loneliness
Is the hamlet of Ōhara.
(*Sankashū*, 1298)

Mizu no oto wa
Makura ni otsuru
Kokochi shite
Nezamegachi naru
Ōhara no sato.

The sound of water
Dripping at my pillow-side
Draws my attention,
For one tends to lie awake
In the hamlet of Ōhara.
(*Sankashū*, 1300)

Mugura hau	Crawled over with vines,
Kado wa ko no ha ni	The gate was already buried
Uzumorete	In the leaves of trees—
Hito mo sashikinu	And not a person comes in visit
Ōhara no sato.	To the hamlet of Ōhara.
	(*Sankashū*, 1304)

Poems such as these imagistically relate Jakuzen's reclusive life, which was filled with desolate loneliness. Turned into prose, they would serve as a description of the life in the grass hut on Hinoyama that Chōmei wrote of in the *Hōjōki*. Chōmei retired from the world at the age of fifty, and after spending five years at Ohara (like Jakuzen), he built his dwelling at Hinoyama. He immersed himself to his heart's content in his small hut and the rich seasonal beauty surrounding it. Indeed, in a corner of his heart he feared that his satisfaction with his life might actually prove a hindrance to a peaceful enlightenment. Such an emotion, which was rich in overtones, was common to all aesthete-recluses. Although I will end my historical survey at this point, it should be noted that aesthete-recluses continued to appear even after the thirteenth century, creating such literary masterpieces as *Tsurezuregusa* (*Jottings in Idleness*, 1330-1331) by Kenkō (ca. 1283-after 1352).

Saigyō as Recluse and Wanderer

The poet-priest Saigyō is known to virtually every Japanese. Although the number of Japanese who are devoted to waka is by no means small, the number of people who respond to his name is very much larger. What is the source of this mysterious attraction? The secret must certainly have some connection with the fact that he is regarded as the one at the pinnacle of the line of the aesthete-recluses. This is because a life of freedom, like that of the aesthete-recluses, has been the dream of people in both early modern and contemporary Japan. Saigyō's exemplary life has become their ideal.

Saigyō was a direct descendant of the shogun of Chinjufu in Michinoku Province, Fujiwara Hidesato (dates unknown), who performed meritorious service in suppressing internal disturbances in eastern Japan in the tenth century. Our poet was appointed a low-ranking warrior official at the age of seventeen and was selected as a member of the personal guard of the retired sovereign Toba (1103-1156, r. 1107-1123). His group of so-called Hokumen warriors not only excelled in military ability but were also required to possess a full education. Still known as Satō Norikiyo at the time, Saigyō was a highly praised rising star with superior talent in both areas. Quite a sensation followed in court society when this young warrior suddenly became a recluse at the age of twenty-two. A variety of explanations circulated to explain this incomprehensible action: disappointment in love, the influence of the doctrine of mujō, and so forth. It is not necessary to refute these suppositions. We must, however, recall that the phenomenon of the aesthete-recluse had already been well-established long before his individual act.

The unique feature of Saigyō's fifty years as a recluse can be characterized as a blending of the two styles of repose and action, as exemplified by his secluded life in his huts and his wanderings throughout the provinces. I will discuss his life and works in the context of these two ways of life.

The places where Saigyō established his grass huts (referred to as yamazato, which can mean mountain hamlet or mountain dwelling) can be enumerated as follows:

1. The outskirts of the Heiankyō—in areas such as Higashiyama and Saga, which remain popular tourist spots today. These environs of Kyoto boasted beautiful scenery and famous temples. After renouncing the world, Saigyō lived many years in these places, where he participated enthusiastically in poetry circles and gained experience in religious practice as a Buddhist novice.
2. Mount Kōya, his main home from around the age of thirty [1148] through the beginning of the Gempei Wars in 1180. This sacred place deep in the mountains was established by Kūkai (774-835), the founder of Shingon [esoteric] Buddhism, at the beginning of the ninth century. In Saigyō's time, as today, it was a prosperous center of religion. Sai-

gyō, however, did not belong to the Shingon sect; he probably built his hut on Mount Kōya out of love for the tranquility of the mountains. Of course, he read sutras, recited prayers, and practiced such disciplines as kanjin [evangelism and solicitation of offerings to temples]. Such efforts naturally gave his waka a deeply religious coloring. Nevertheless, as noted before, recluses were by no means identical with professional priests. We can imagine that Saigyō passed his days in serene isolation in the midst of the natural beauty that surrounded his hut.

3. Yoshinoyama. These remote mountains, located relatively near Mount Kōya, were a religious site for the cult of mountain worship and were famous for their cherry blossoms. As we shall see, Saigyō responded fervently in his poems to cherry blossoms and the moon above all else. So he visited Yoshino every spring to view the cherries, and sometimes he set up a hut there as well. Yoshino remains a favorite tourist spot today.
4. Zentsūji, a temple situated on the north coast of the island of Shikoku, facing the Inland Sea. At about the age of fifty [ca. 1168], Saigyō made a pilgrimage to the grave of Sutoku Tennō (1119-1164, r. 1123-1141), who had extended patronage to him when he was young. Sutoku died in exile on Shikoku after being defeated in the Hōgen War. After paying his respects to his mentor, Saigyō erected a hut at Zentsūji, the birthplace of Kūkai. We may attribute this act to his respect for Kūkai, but we cannot ignore the possibility that he was motivated by love of the view of the Inland Sea, known as one of the most beautiful seascapes of Japan.
5. Futamigaura in Ise Province. Here Saigyō lived for seven years starting in 1180. This period roughly spans the main Gempei Wars. As the site of the Great Shrines of Ise, one of the most sacred sites of Shinto, this area provided the safest refuge from the ravages of war. Moreover, the view of Futamigaura is so beautiful that it still attracts many visitors.
6. Hirokawadera in Kawachi Province. Saigyō went there the

> year before he died and set up his hut in the temple precincts. Located on Kazurakiyama, the birthplace of mountain worship, this temple was probably chosen as a result of the extreme heightening of devotion as his strength began to fail.

The sites just described show that Saigyō's grass-thatched huts were all blessed with outstandingly beautiful views of the mountains or the sea. The two great themes of the spirit of suki were love and the beautiful moods of nature, and the mountain dwellings (yamazato) chosen by Saigyō were endowed most richly with the spirit of natural scenery.[21] Writing of how much Saigyō loved nature in the mountains and how he cleansed himself by merging with it, the intellectual historian Ienaga Saburō has emphasized, "It can be said that what truly enlightened Saigyō was nature rather than the Buddha. In this respect, he was a believer in nature more than in Buddhism."[22]

As has been said, the natural phenomena holding most appeal to Saigyō were cherry blossoms and the moon.

Yoshinoyama	Since the first day
Kozue no hana o	I saw the blossoms on the trees
Mishi hi yori	At Mount Yoshino,
Kokoro wa mi ni mo	My yearning heart has seemed
Sowazu nariniki.	Separated from my body.
	(*Sankashū*, 77)

Yoshinoyama	Rather than take the path
Kozo no shiori no	Marked by twigs I snapped last year
Michi kaete	Here on Mount Yoshino,
Mada minu kata no	Shall I view the blossoms
Hana o tazunen.	Some place I have not yet seen?
	(*Sankashū*, 1883; *Shinkokinshū*, 1: 86)

[21] Saigyō wrote a great many passionate love poems even though he was a recluse. Perhaps they were composed with a mixture of reminiscence and imagination.

[22] Ienaga Saburō, *Nihon Shisōshi ni okeru Shūkyōteki Shizenkan no Ronri no Tenkai* (Shinsensha, 1973), p. 130. [Citations of Saigyō's collection, the *Sankashū*, are keyed to *Saigyō Sankashū Zenchūkai*, ed. Watanabe Tamotsu (Kazama Shobō, 1971).]

Yoshinoyama	Mount Yoshino—
Yagate ideji to	Why not stay this while with you?
Omou mi o	As my desire insists,
Hana chirinaba to	Though when they think the blossoms gone
Hito ya matsu ran.	Others may well expect me back.
	(*Sankashū*, 1122)

Harukaze no	The dream I had
Hana o chirasu to	Was of cherry blossoms fallen
Miru yume wa	In a spring breeze,
Samete mo mune no	And even after I awoke
Sawagu narikeri.	My heart remained in turmoil.
	(*Sankashū*, 150)

Hana ni somu	How has it fared—
Kokoro no ikade	The heart so palely dyed
Nokoriken	By the blossoms?
Sutehateteki to	It seemed to me I had renounced
Omou waga mi ni.	All attachments to the world.
	(*Sankashū*, 87)

A look into the meanings and tonalities of these poems reveals that blossoms were clearly something that excited Saigyō, much as a beloved woman might. Although he attempted to discard all bonds to the world, we can imagine that he found it strange that he could do nothing about his heart's attachment to blossoms.

Omokage no	It was a parting
Wasuraru majiki	Impossible to forget
Wakare kana	How sad you looked—
Nagori o hito no	As you were about to leave,
Tsuki ni todomete.	Arrested by the moon at dawn.
	(*Sankashū*, 684; *Shinkokinshū*, 13, 1185)

Kon [Komu] yo ni wa	In the world to come
Kokoro no uchi ni	I shall reveal what it is
Arawasan	In my heart—

Akade yaminuru
Tsuki no hikari o.

The radiance of the moon
That never is enough for me.
(*Sankashū*, 2036)

Itou yo mo
Tsuki sumu aki ni
Narinureba
Nagaraezuba to
Omou naru kana.

I detest this world
And am prepared to leave it,
But when autumn comes
And the moon is bright and clear
How glad I am to be alive!
(*Sankashū*, 444)

Yukue naku
Tsuki ni kokoro no
Sumisumite
Hate wa ika ni ka
Naran to su ran.

Without direction
Before the moonlight my mind
Grows bright and clear,
And what will be the end of this
Is something that I cannot tell.
(*Sankashū*, 393)

For Saigyō, the moon induced endlessly complex thoughts. At times it would symbolize a lover, as in the first poem of the series above (*Sankashū*, 684), or the truth of Buddhism, as in the second (*Sankashū*, 2036). The world, which should properly be despised, may be regretted because of the moon, while sometimes the poet cannot help but be suspicious of the outcome of such mixed desires.

Negawaku wa
Hana no shita nite
Haru shinan
Sono kisaragi no
Mochizuki no koro.

This is my wish:
That under cover of the blossoms
I may die in spring,
That day of the second month,
Just when the moon is full.
(*Sankashū*, 88)

Many years after he wrote this poem, Saigyō died as he had wished—on the night of the full moon while the cherries were in bloom. His friends were deeply impressed; not only had he died as he hoped but also on the anniversary of the day when the Buddha was said to have passed into Nirvana. This fact may have occasioned the legends about Saigyō that developed in medieval Japan. He truly was the "poet of the blossoms and the moon."[23]

As we have seen, Saigyō's life as a recluse took the direction of a union with nature. He considered natural phenomena to be tantamount to friends, and so in fact he called them. These friends included the moon, of course, also the babbling brook, the hailstones striking his window, the deer crying sadly, the pines soaring near his hut. He wrote the following poems at his hut at Zentsūji.

Hisa ni hete	For long hereafter
Waga nochi no yo o	When I have entered another world,
Toe yo matsu	Ask for me, o pine,
Ato shinobu beki	For I am one without a person
Hito mo naki mi zo.	To be moved to think of me.
	(*Sankashū*, 1449)

Koko o mata	Were I to tire
Ware sumiukute	Of living in this place
Ukarenaba	And go off again,
Matsu wa hitori ni	This pine would be left
Naran to suran.	The only person here.
	(*Sankashū*, 1450)

The pines in these poems are addressed as friends to console the poet in his isolation. This feeling of closeness is based on the Buddhist concept that "the hills, streams, grasses and trees all have Buddha-nature."[24]

This idea is also illustrated by the anecdote that claims that the poet Myōe once nostalgically wrote a letter, addressed to a "Mr.

[23] In an old manuscript of the *Sanka Shinjūshū*, which is considered to be Saigyō's personal selection of his strongest poems, there appears what is thought to be a marginal comment by his friend Fujiwara Shunzei (1114-1204): "This may also be called the *Moon and Flowers Collection (Kagetsushū)*."

[24] [The phrase, "sōmoku kokudo shikkai jōbutsu" of the *Nirvana Sūtra (Daihatsu Nehangyō)* is the most famous version of the idea in Japan; the author has rephrased it in Japanese. Apparently, it was a kind of hyperbole for the universality of the Buddha's Original Vow to make enlightenment possible for all sentient beings. The hyperbole was taken so literally by some in Japan as to reach an extreme or heretical degree.—Ed.]

Island," an island place where he had lived previously. This personification of nature demonstrates the kind of attitude that was also a vicarious compensation relieving the keenly felt loneliness that sometimes struck the recluse. Here is Saigyō again.

Sabishisa ni	If only there were one,
Taetaru hito no	Another besides me to bear
Mata mo are na	This loneliness—
Iori naraben	We would line up our huts
Fuyu no yamazato.	On this wintry hillsite.

(*Sankashū*, 560; *Shinkokinshū*, 6, 627)

Yamazato ni	Oh, for a friend
Ukiyo itowan	Who detested the world of sorrow
Tomo mo ga na	At this hillsite—
Kuyashiku sugishi	We would speak to each other
Mukashi kataran.	Of the painful past long gone.

(*Sankashū*, 2170; *Shinkokinshū*, 17, 1657; later version used)

As we can see from these poems, as well as from many others of a similar tone, Saigyō was not exempt from loneliness. Although he had summoned the determination to live in his hut, at times the isolation became so intense it was unbearable.

He embarked on wanderings through the provinces, the other characteristic of the life of the aesthete-recluse, in order to overcome the isolation and unvarying life of the hut. The Saigyō of legend imparts the impression of an eternal traveler who never remained long in one place.[25] In truth, however, he did not actually spend so great an amount of time on his travels. Yet it is a fact that, more than anyone else in his time, he actively pointed his walking stick in the direction of temples and shrines surrounding the capital region—such places as Tennōji, founded by Shōtoku Taishi (574-622) and famous since the sixth century; Shoshasan, established by a virtuous saint in the eleventh century; and Ku-

[25] The *Saigyō Monogatari* and *Senshūshō* (both thought to be works of the thirteenth century) were written on the basis of such motifs. They established the legendary image of Saigyō that has persisted long afterwards.

mano, the object of pilgrimages by all the nobility, including retired sovereigns and their consorts.

Michi no be no	At the roadside
Shimizu nagaruru	Where pure waters flow reflecting
Yanagi kage	The green willow shade—
Shibashi tote koso	It was only for a moment
Tachidomaretsure.	That I thought that I would stay.

(*Sankashū*, 2005; *Shinkokinshū*, 3, 262)

Kokoro naki	Even a soul schooled
Mi ni mo aware wa	To do without the human heart
Shirarekeri	Knows how such things feel—
Shigi tatsu sawa no	From the marsh a longbill
Aki no yūgure.	Flies into the autumn dusk.

(*Sankashū*, 515; *Shinkokinshū*, 4, 362)

Izuku ni ka	Where will it be
Neburineburite	That I shall fall and enter
Taorefusan	My long, long sleep—
To omou kanashiki	The anxious thought shows sadness
Michishiba no tsuyu.	In the dew on roadside plants.

(*Sankashū*, 916)

Full of the refreshing joy of liberation, travel also permitted one to taste with one's whole being the deeply moving sadness of things (mono no aware). And as shown in the third poem (*Sankashū*, 916) just given, travel commonly brought with it an association with the journey after death.[26] In medieval Japan, poems of travel and mujō were closely related to each other, and this connection was utilized in exemplary fashion by Saigyō. For the aesthete-recluse, no opportunity promoted the poetic spirit as much as itinerant life.

In addition to his wanderings around the capital region, Saigyō made several very long journeys. One of these was the trip to Shikoku mentioned earlier, but from a historical perspective it is most remarkable that he traveled twice to Michinoku, the most

[26] [See Nakanishi on the michiyuki in particular and on spatial conceptions of temporal matters generally.—Ed.]

distant province in Honshū, located at its northern tip. His first such trip after becoming a recluse lasted several years and was clearly the ambitious act of a youth who desired to imitate Nōin's journeys to that distant province. Saigyō satisfied his spirit of suki by writing many poems about and at famous utamakura, including the Shirakawa Barrier. The travel poems recorded in Saigyō's anthology are all prefaced with long prose headnotes (kotobagaki). The harmony of preface and poem gives a special richness to the feeling of travel. This is the secret responsible for the continual appeal of his poems to the Japanese heart. Unfortunately, many of the expressions used in the poems are so special that they cannot be rendered effectively into modern Japanese or other languages. Therefore, many examples of his craft must be omitted from this discussion.

Toshi takete	Could I have thought
Mata koyu beshi to	I would cross this peak again
Omoiki ya	After years had passed?
Inochi narikeri	And yet I have lived to do it—
Saya no Nakayama.	Saya no Nakayama once more.

(*Sankashū*, 2130; *Shinkokinshū*, 10, 987)

Kaze ni nabiku	Bending to the wind
Fuji no keburi no	The smoke above Mount Fuji
Sora ni kiete	Vanishes in sky—
Yukue mo shiranu	The matter of a destination
Waga omoi ka na.	Is nothing my thoughts know.

(*Sankashū*, 2138; *Shinkokinshū*, 17, 1613)

These two poems were composed during Saigyō's second trip to Michinoku, a few years before his death. In the former, he recalls the time he traveled the Tōkaidō some forty years earlier. He expresses his deep emotions about his long life to the utamakura, Saya no Nakayama [a place name which may be translated as "mountain of the middle of the night"]. In the smoke rising from Mount Fuji we see the state of mind of an aged man who understands the emptiness and vanity of life. Although Saigyō also composed many similar waka about his wanderings, these two poems deserve to be considered among the finest of that kind.

MEZAKI TOKUE

The Historical Significance of the Aesthete-Recluse

When the tradition of the aesthete-recluse, spanning several centuries, reached its zenith with the appearance of Saigyō, the ancient social and political structure seemed to be declining toward a total, tragic collapse. The Kampaku (Chancellor) Kujō Kanezane (1149-1207), who witnessed the greatest battles of the civil war between the Minamoto and Taira forces, consistently used the term, "the final age" (matsudai, mappō) to describe the situation.[27] He could not help but lose hope in the extreme political and cultural deterioration of the time, particularly when viewed in contrast to the tenth century, when court culture had been in full flower. His younger brother Jien (1155-1225), who held a supreme position in Buddhist circles, wrote the *Gukanshō* (1220), a history of Japan. As if in response to his brother's feeling of hopelessness, Jien gave his work a distinctive historical perspective of decline.[28] Even those at the highest level of the old order had to recognize that the law of the court and the Law of the Buddha were joined socially like the wheels of a cart and, further, that both were headed toward ruin.

Although literature existed in this situation of political and cultural collapse, it preserved its autonomy, and in the creation of works brimming with vitality, we can observe a transcendence of the crisis of the age. Under these circumstances, the aesthete-recluses drew a distinct line between themselves and the secular

[27] Kanezane's memoir, *Gyokuyō* (1164-1200), is the most detailed and accurate document recording the chaotic history of the transition from ancient to medieval Japan.

[28] Jien, a major waka poet, is second only to Saigyō in the number of his poems included in the *Shinkokinshū*. Like Saigyō, he detested the annoying intricacies of the religious world and strongly desired to retire to the life of a recluse, but he was unable to realize this wish because he was forced to consider the troubled fortunes of the Kujō family in the political realm. He was therefore not literally a recluse, but the heart of his poetry consists of religious poems that conceal the pain of not being able to renounce the world. [Jien's historical work, *Gukanshō*, has been translated as *The Future and The Past* by Delmer E. Brown and Ichirō Ishide (Berkeley: University of California Press, 1979).—Ed.]

world. By that distinction, they established an elegant way of life and wrote poetry that expressed their special views of life and nature. It was as if they had constructed an alternate world apart from that of the final age (matsudai). This naturally seems to have given them a measure of confidence. For example, Saigyō's anthology (headnote to *Sankashū*, 2103) records an experience in which he dreamed that he had heard someone say that "although all else is decaying, only this path [the way of poetry] will not change, even with the end of the world." This dream can be considered an expression of the self-confidence gained by rejecting the world and devoting one's life to the pursuit of suki.

Such pride and confidence in literature was not limited to recluses. A similar state of mind is revealed by a notation made by Fujiwara Teika (Sadaie, 1162-1421) in his diary. With regard to the civil war, he wrote in echo of Po Chü-i, "the chastisement of the red banner of the insurgents is no concern of mine."[29] Juntoku Tennō (1197-1242, r. 1210-1221) showed a similar attitude in his *Yakumo Mishō* (1234-1241), quoting Saigyō on the indestructible vocation of poetry. Juntoku had cooperated in his father Gotoba's ill-fated attempt to overthrow the Kamakura bakufu in the Jōkyū War of 1221. He was exiled to the isolated, distant island of Sado, where his unhappy life came to a close. Nevertheless, he maintained his conviction to the very end that waka at least, the essence of aristocratic culture, would exist forever, despite the political downfall of the court. It is a striking fact of history that the tradition of courtly culture persisted during the growth of political rule by the warriors. And, in examining the source of this endurance, we cannot underestimate the importance of the establishment of spiritual freedom by the aesthete-recluses. Between the feudal and religious elements that served as the underpinnings of medieval Japan, the cultural tradition of the court, with waka at its heart, maintained an independent, significant existence.

Among the elements of the culture born of the lives of the aesthete-recluses were—in addition to waka—linked poetry (renga

[29] Fujiwara Teika, *Meigetsuki* (Kokusho Kangyōsha, 1970), 1, 6; entry for the ninth month of 1180.

and haikai), entertainments (gesaku) of literary kinds, as well as the arts of tea (sadō), flower arrangement (kadō), nō, and arts such as painting and landscape architecture. All who dominated these arts wore the robes of Buddhist priests. With the passing of time, these aesthetic activities exhibited various changes both in concept and in finished works. At their root there always remained the pursuit of suki in seclusion (suki no tonsei). As a normative example of this tendency we can cite the famous words of Bashō from the opening section of his travel sketch *Oi no Kobumi* (*The Traveler's Book Satchel*, 1709): "High art is all one in nature, whether in the waka of Saigyō, the renga of Sōgi, the paintings of Sesshū, or the tea ceremony of Rikyū."[30] This may be called the most concisely expressed account of the suki no tonseisha.

Looking ahead to modern times, we can discover that the lives of the so-called "I-novelists," for example, have something in common with those of the aesthete-recluses. Although the phenomenon of the aesthete-recluse was a unique historical fact of the period of transition to medieval Japan, it also transcended historical boundaries to become a philosophical undercurrent of the Japanese people. While continuing its varied metamorphoses, it has molded many of the characteristics of Japanese literature and other aspects of culture.

[30] [*Matsuo Bashō Shū*, p. 311. Bashō actually writes that these various artistic media are all one, adding the word fūga (true art) to the beginning of the next sentence. He clearly implies that his own haikai also belongs to the category. But for all his seriousness, haikai was not so treated in classical times.—Ed.]

CHAPTER 6

MICHI AND MEDIEVAL WRITING

BY KONISHI JIN'ICHI

The Formation of Michi

The ideal known as michi, artistic vocation, is generally taken to possess great significance for the Japanese Middle Ages, although its nature has not been wholly clear. In the past I have conceived of michi in terms of the following components: specialization, transmission, a conforming ethic, universality, and authority.[1] These are not fully parallel elements, nor do they manifest themselves in the same time period: thus I would now like to consider them in order of appearance.

The word "michi" originally signified "profession," "expertise." In the *Genji Monogatari (The Tale of Genji)*, there is a phrase, "ki no michi no takumi" ("one skilled in the michi of

Translated by Aileen Gatten.

[1] The concepts I first proposed (in "Michi no Keisei to Kairitsuteki Sekai," *Kokugakuin Zasshi*, 57 [1956]) were: specialization, universality, transmission, restriction, and practicality. I revised these in a later work, *Michi: Chūsei no Rinen* (*Michi: A Medieval Ideal*; Kōdansha, 1975). [The author's terms for literary periods—e.g., "High Middle Ages"—are explained in the first volume of his *History of Japanese Literature* (Princeton: Princeton University Press, 1984), pp. 52-58. He distinguishes four periods: the archaic (zenko), the ancient (kodai), the medieval (chūsei), and the modern (gendai). He divides the medieval into three stages: early (tenth and eleventh centuries); high (thirteenth through fifteenth centuries); and late (mid-seventeenth through early nineteenth centuries), with transitional periods between.—Ed.]

wood"; "Hahakigi," 68) for which the English equivalent is "carpenter." Another expression from the *Genji Monogatari*, "koto fue no michi" ("the michi of zither and flute"; "Azumaya," 132), indicates that music was recognized as a separate field of specialization. The very presence of fields of specialization means that the knowledge or skills required could come only from individuals who had undergone specific training; such people were called "michi no hito," literally "men of michi," or "experts."[2] Specialization is the element most basic to michi, and michi cannot exist without it. Moreover, the specialization could only be one that had been tramsmitted from generation to generation. If an expert's craft—no matter how outstanding—died with him, it was not a michi. The transmission of michi, it should also be noted, was characteristically carried out through units called "ie" ("family," "house," and eventually "school"). This does not mean that hereditary houses always controlled the transmission of a given specialization: in principle at least the practice of transmission from master to disciple—a method of instruction still retained by Buddhism—would have preceded this development. Actually, the chief means of transmission was by the house unit, a fact illustrated by the famous maxim, "A man is not in truth a man until he has knowledge; a house is not in truth a house until it transmits tradition."[3]

To agree that michi is found in the act of transmission is to assume the presence of already extant material: thus michi has its roots in retrospectively considered objects. This statement need not apply solely to michi, since the Middle Ages are thoroughly diffused with the perception that models of polished beauty (ga) are to be sought in the past. What may indeed be termed char-

[2] From *Utsuho Monogatari (The Tale of the Hollow Tree)*, "Fukiage, Part 2." See *Utsuho Monogatari: Hommon to Sakuhin* (Koten Bunko, 1973), s.v. "michi no hito." Here the phrase signifies a specialist in Chinese study. In notes and in the text, when publishers and dates are omitted, the reference is to the appropriate volume number and page(s) in the *Nihon Koten Bungaku Taikei* published by Iwanami Shoten.

[3] From the Daisenji version of the *Soga Monogatari (The Story of the Soga Brothers)*. See Araki Yoshio, ed., *Daisenjibon Soga Monogatari* (Hakuteisha, 1961). Similar remarks appear in Zeami's *Fūshi Kaden* (Besshi Kuden ed.), 7, 398; and in Shinkei's *Sasamegoto*, 2, 194.

acteristic of michi, however, is an accompanying perception, the strongly restrictive view that transmission from an earlier age must communicate a conformist ethic to future generations, so that a transmission can be received exactly as it was handed down. Today people assume that, when we are given free rein to exercise creativity, our specialized knowledge or skills will improve. This is not wrong. Yet it also does not represent the only truth. Progress and improvement of a different sort are effected through the denial of one's immediate creativity. To this day, for example, an individual undergoing training in nō drama will be judged to have achieved competency only when his performance conforms precisely to that of his teacher. If the student's performance varies even slightly from his teacher's, he will be considered a novice in the art of nō. True, many nō actors thus taught are incapable of producing any but trite and stereotypical performances; but a master actor whose skills have been tempered by such training will possess an individuality infinitely more intense than that of anyone whose creativity has been freely exercised since youth. The master actor displays a freshness sufficient to make even the most seasoned nō devotee feel a well-known play is experienced for the first time ever. The conformist ethic was of course connected to the conception of "houses," and undoubtedly possessed a negative aspect: it gave rise to the practice of secret, orally transmitted tradition. One must also note, however, the substantial positive aspects inherent in this closed system. Medieval people did not perceive it as an attempt to fetter creativity, but rather, simply as the strict denial of their own small ideas in order to acquire freedom of a higher dimension.

Until quite recently, there has been a considerable number of acknowledged masters in arts transmitted from the Middle Ages. Although they belonged to different artistic spheres—nō and calligraphy, for example—in my experience, they shared one trait: despite their faithful adherence to traditional form, none gave the slightest impression of being bound by that form. In other words, artists in various fields of expertise who had become highly accomplished in one field always seemed to have attained their proficiency under similar circumstances—and this despite a total lack of knowledge about fields other than their own. This can only mean that the quality of specialization or concentration inherent in michi—a seemingly closed concept—possesses, on a higher dimension, a universality applicable to all artistic fields. My intent is not merely to state my experience concerning this fact, for the fact has been widely acknowledged since antiquity. My experience is only another instance that serves to confirm its validity. The field of performance may, like waka, receive wide respect in society, or, like horsemanship, be concerned with practical techniques, or, again, be a game like chess. But all, I have come to believe, jointly possess a universality as michi within the dimension of advanced achievement. Yoshida Kenkō (1282-1350), for example, perceived that someone who attains an advanced mastery of even a humble skill like tree climbing will experience a truth identical to that realized by masters in other artistic spheres, and his observations will include teachings apposite to the world in general. Kenkō comments on a master tree climber, "This man belonged to the lowest class, but his words were in perfect accord with the precepts of the sages" (*Tsurezuregusa*, dan 109: 179).[4] Universality is vital to michi, and, unless universal truth is ultimately attained through concentrated specialization in a given art, it is not a true michi.[5]

Even arts that, when made the objects of specialization, are of little use to society, or others that are mere games designed to pass the time, will, when fully mastered, possess a truth in common with that found in widely respected kinds of specialization. All specialized expertise possesses, then, a common authority as michi. Extremely rigorous practice and training were required of the student of a michi, regardless of the area of specialization. This could only have been due to the authority sensed within michi. We might be able to understand, up to a point, a story of a man who

[4] [Yoshida Kenkō, *Tsurezuregusa (Essays in Idleness)*, trans. Donald Keene (New York and London: Columbia University Press, 1967), p. 93.—Trans.]

[5] Attaining universal truth through specialization is a pattern similar to that presented to modern natural science, although the natural scientist differs from the "michi no hito" in two respects: (1) michi is strongly ethical, maintaining that its truths elevate and perfect the individual human personality; and (2) in grasping truth, the "man of michi" relies on immediate experience, rather than on induction based on observed experience.

stakes his life on the composition of a single superlative waka [Japanese court poetry], because it was held with such veneration.[6] But we moderns may be caught between wonder and scorn when confronted with the fact that excelling at horsemanship, a mere utilitarian amusement, was perceived to be worth the sacrifice of a man's life.[7]

Among the components of michi considered here, that of specialization apparently already existed—at least embryonically—by the Ancient Age or even earlier. The god Hōri persecutes his older brother, who, as an indication of his submissive intent, vows that he and all his descendants will serve Hōri as his "wazaoki."[8] The wazaoki were evidently an occupational group (J. "be") related by blood that performed an art similar to mime. Here we observe an awareness of something close to specialization. Furthermore, the older brother's promise, that his descendants will serve Hōri as performers of this art, signifies that this specialization would be accompanied by transmission. The specialization and transmission operative at this stage, however, were not yet elements of michi because they possessed no properties that could connect them to authority. To the contrary. It was a sign of submission to become a wazaoki, and this means that the art was practiced by people of the lowest social class. Similarly, in China the wives and daughters of captives were those chiefly assigned to the performing staff of the Music Bureau (Yüeh-fu); and professional singers in Korea were lowly people called kwandae.[9] The treatment of professional

[6] Fujiwara Nagatō is said to have died in agony because his best waka was savaged (*Shasekishū*, 5, part 2, 240).

[7] Suketomo of Shimotsuke, eager to win a horse race, commissions incantations on his behalf, which are performed on the condition that he be willing if necessary to forfeit his life. Suketomo wins the race, and thereupon dies (*Kokon Chomonjū*, 15: 385).

[8] *Nihon Shoki* ("Jindaiki," 2, 183-84). [This would represent supposed events in the Archaic Age.—Trans.]

[9] See Kishibe Shigeo, *Tōdai Ongaku no Rekishiteki Kenkyū: Gakuseihen* ("Historical Research in T'ang Period Music: the Music Bureaucracy"; 2, 190-93) on plebeians as performing personnel for the Music Bureau. A study of the conditions of eighteenth-century Korean kwandae (Kim Tong-uk, *Chōsen Bungakushi* ["History of Korean Literature"], 209-10) leads one to surmise that ancient kwandae were also plebeians.

musicians and actors as plebeians at best is a phenomenon common to East Asia from antiquity, and Japan proved no exception. Under such circumstances, it was inconceivable that specialization and transmission could possibly evolve into artistic vocation. In Ancient Japan it was not unusual for certain kinds of work to be performed by specific families on a hereditary basis. A normative example is the carrying out of Shinto ceremonies by the Nakatomi and Imbe clans.[10] Yet many more instances can be found of families (be) engaging in specific occupations: the Storytellers (Kataribe), for example, or the Interpreters (Osabe), Potters (Hajibe), or Saddlemakers (Kuratsukuribe).

If all transmitted professional occupations, regardless of type, were to be perceived as worthy, the first step in this process was probably the social recognition of one such occupation as valuable. Kangaku, scholarship along Chinese lines, proved to be the first valued occupation. The Japanese Court School (Daigaku), established on the T'ang model, was centered on specialized curricula: Confucianism (Myōgyōdō), Law (Myōhōdō), History (Kidendō, later expanded to Liberal Arts, Monjōdō), and Mathematics (Sandō). The suffix "dō" [the Sino-Japanese reading of the character for "michi"] in the curricular titles simply signified the sphere of a given specialization, one that was not necessarily in conformance with the ideal of michi. But kangaku, divided though it was into several spheres of specialization, was perceived in toto as a highly valued pursuit. This perception may be deemed an early factor in the formation of the medieval ideal of artistic vocation. It also further strengthened the connection between specialization and transmission. Families like the Sugawara, Kiyowara, and Ōe, whose principal function was acknowledged by society to be kangaku, each possessed slight but distinct differences in the content taught to their pupils. These differences served to emphasize or assert the high value of the specialization under a given family's control, and as a result, though nearly imperceptible, such differences came to acquire a great significance. Any of us today who possessed learning superior to that of other groups would probably reveal and

[10] [The latter surname literally means "Worshippers."—Trans.]

elucidate the reasons why our teachings were superior. A medieval scholar of Chinese curricula would instead have endeavored to give authority to his school by putting those superior teachings under the monopoly of his school. For example, all schools of Chinese used okototen, a code consisting of specially placed marks (whether dots or short lines) surrounding a given Chinese character, for interlinear note taking of lectures on Chinese works.[11] The code necessary to decipher these marks differed with each school. After a certain time secrecy became increasingly important, and students were forbidden to reveal the teachings of their school to outsiders. This closed system was to become the source of the secret oral tradition, a feature of the High Middle Ages. The perception of the conformist ethic was still more vital, leading both instructor and pupil to follow a teaching faithfully, precisely because it had been preserved for them from antiquity.

If the perception of specialization, transmission, and a conformist ethic had been expanded so as to include other, not greatly respected, activities, this would have signified the approach, in general terms, of the formative stage of the ideal of michi. This had yet to be accomplished. One last, vital element was necessary before the concept could become fixed so that even the lowliest spheres ultimately possess a value equivalent to that of kangaku: the suffusion of a cosmic view holding that an all-encompassing, universal truth resides even in the minutest and humblest of human activities. The attainment of this stage gave the specialized occupation an authority different in meaning from that obtaining heretofore. In other words, the components of michi—specialization, transmission, a conformist ethic, and universality—followed a process whereby the most basic element, specialization, was successively joined through derivation or accretion by other elements, and gradually increased in authority with each stage. This formative process might be expressed as in the diagram, be-

[11] This marking system was apparently invented by monks. Each powerful temple had its own marking code. The Confucian scholarly families seem to have followed the ecclesiastical example: the Sugawara and the Ōe each had its own characteristic marking code, known respectively as Kanketen ("Sugawara code") and Gōketen ("Ōe code").

FIGURE 3

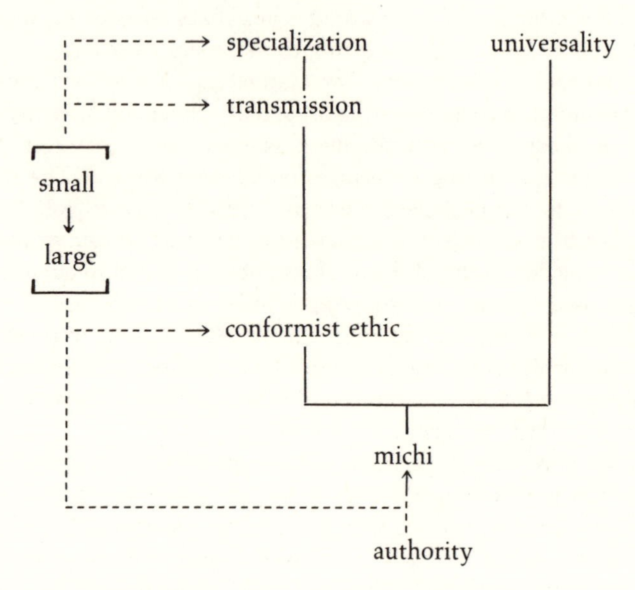

ginning from the bottom. No single element given in the figure can comprise michi on its own; michi becomes an operative concept only when all these elements are present together.

Background for the Formation of Michi

The medieval concept of michi was slow to develop, despite a tradition, harking back to the Ancient Age or earlier, of continuous transmission of a given specialized function by specific families or occupational kinship groups. This delay may well have been due to the spread of Sinified ideas into aristocratic society. The guiding principle in Chinese government was the broad acquisition of knowledge, by which measure literati were evaluated. Specialized work was therefore not respected, and those who pursued it belonged to a social class lower than the literati.[12] Since this perception also came to predominate in Japan, people involved in specialized work probably would have had difficulty summoning up a life-sacrificing passion for their vocations.

The only exception, as noted earlier, was kangaku. The raison d'être of the literati was the study of the Confucian Classics (Ching), the Philosophers (Tzu), the Histories (Shih), and the Anthologies (Chi), and so the Japanese aristocrats, too, were obliged to accord a high value to such study. The *Utsuho Monogatari* (ca. 980) candidly portrays a Court School student with the Sinified name of Tō Ei who diligently pursues his studies despite crushing poverty ("Matsuri no Tsukai," 110 [431]-114 [447]). This may well reflect contemporary realities. Aristocratic society in early medieval Japan differed from its Chinese counterpart, however, in its lack of connection between education and high government service. In China a man might win appointment to ministerial rank on passing the higher civil service examinations. In Japan, however, the government careers of the high nobility were generally determined by family status.[13] For this there is little evidence of a passionate dedication to kangaku in Japan, at least among the sons of the powerful. The Court School professors who appear in the *Genji Monogatari,* consequently, are described in a manner close to caricature ("Otome," 278-80). In Japanese society, kangaku lacked the authority accorded it in China. This lack became more severe in direct proportion to the degree of success enjoyed by the governmental system known as the Fujiwara regency. Even during

[12] The function of high government officials (kuan)—members of the literati class—was to deal with the general principles of government; specialized administrative duties were carried out by lower officials called li. Similarly, music that required specialized training was seen as the function of technicians (kung), and assigned to the lowest artistic stratum.

[13] Sons of powerful houses were accorded preferential treatment, in accordance with family status, from their first appointment on, and received higher official rank than did the average appointee. This practice was called "on'i," "ranking by indebtedness" (i.e., obligation felt toward the young appointee's influential forebears). Professional advancement in later life was also frequently determined by family status. Sugawara Michizane (845-903) was the first man from a scholarly family to hold ministerial rank. He was also the last.

this period, however, the minor aristocracy must have perceived that acknowledged expertise in kangaku would improve their chances to obtain good government positions, even if possibilities were limited. And because Japanese intellectuals of all ranks devoted themselves to kangaku, middle- and low-ranking aristocrats like Tō Ei who specialized in the Chinese curricula doubtless enjoyed considerable social support and respect. It was precisely due to such circumstances that the Sugawara and Ōe families were able to establish themselves securely as kangaku schools.

Waka was surely the next specialization to follow kangaku as a valued pursuit. Through the extraordinary efforts of Ki no Tsurayuki (d. 945) and his circle, waka was able to achieve a position equal to that of Chinese poetry. The fixing of its new status must have required considerable time, since the institution of waka schools does not appear until the end of the twelfth century. Tsurayuki and his circle, needless to say, perceived waka as a worthy specialization, but that was only their view. The high aristocracy seem to have regarded even Tsurayuki as a sort of waka artisan from whom one might order a quantity of poetry for the decoration of folding screens and expect prompt delivery of good products. A somewhat later figure than Tsurayuki, Sone no Yoshitada (fl. ca. 985), believed that no poetry gathering was worth convening that did not include him, the foremost waka poet of the day. Yoshitada invited himself to one such affair, only to find that it was closed to people of his humble status. He was consequently ejected and thoroughly humiliated (*Ōkagami*, "Commentaries"). If the ideal of michi had been operative at this time, even lowly waka poets would have been welcomed at formal gatherings. By the twelfth century, the situation had begun to change: Minamoto Shunrai (?1057-1129) and Fujiwara Mototoshi (1056-1142), neither man of high rank, became leading figures in waka circles and were constantly invited by the high aristocracy to poetry gatherings. It should also be noted that Fujiwara Shunzei (1114-1204) was a pupil of Mototoshi (according to Kamo no Chōmei [1153-1216], *Mumyōshō*), a fact indicating that the practice of transmission from master to pupil had been added to the earlier practice of transmission through "houses" made up exclusively of blood relatives.

During the twelfth century, the Rokujō branch of the Fujiwara was shaped into a school of waka by Fujiwara Akisuke (1090-1155) and his sons Kiyosuke (1104-1177), Shigeie, Kenjō (fl. 1161-1207), and Suetsune (1131-1221). In seeming response, Shunzei created the Mikohidari school, which was to become the most powerful of all waka schools. The establishment of artistic vocation was close at hand.

In addition to fairly authoritative specializations like kangaku and waka, by the twelfth century various other arts came to be perceived as worthy. In its sections on music, magic, military arts, equestrian arts, court kickball, and painting and drawing, the collection of setsuwa [more or less didactic stories], *Kokon Chomonjū* (comp. 1254) tells how remarkable these arts are when practiced by masters and adepts, and also records the enormous self-sacrifice in training required for the high attainments. These passages must reflect a realization that a high value was attached to arts possessing skilled practitioners. Many of the masters and adepts who appear in this setsuwa collection, moreover, lived in the twelfth century, and we may infer that a general awareness of the high value of all kinds of art had apparently evolved by then.

This awareness did not arise solely from the lower classes—for whom a rise in rank was impossible—in their desire to gain some measure of glory through specialization in art. A respect for specialization reached the highest social levels as well. From his youth, the cloistered sovereign Goshirakawa (1127-1192), no less, worked unstintingly at mastering the popular songs known as imayō (new style), so that he might transmit a correct singing method to future generations.[14] His efforts can be logically explained only if they are seen as stemming from an acknowledgment that great value

[14] "Thus a great many people, men and women both, studied singing with me," writes Goshirakawa, "but all abandoned their study while their art was yet imperfect, and now there is no one to succeed me. What a pity that, despite many years of devotion to my art, I have no students, to whom I might securely transmit it!" (*Ryōjin*, "Kudenshū," 10, 460). The *Ryōjin Hishō* originally consisted of 10 fascicles each of songs and instructions (kuden) on training and performance. Approximately 10 percent of the original corpus survives.

resides in the act of specialized artistic transmission. The art of imayō was practiced mainly by dockside singer-prostitutes (asobime) and itinerant female entertainers (kugutsume)—although aristocrats also sang such songs. Imayō singing thus occupied an even lower social status than the performance of instrumental music.

Goshirakawa's compilation of the *Ryōjin Hishō* in twenty fascicles may be seen as indicative of a heightened tendency, beginning in the twelfth century, toward the codification of knowledge transmitted from the past.[15] For this tendency to grow, the conviction was necessary that even worthless pursuits, if practiced earnestly and industriously, would lead to religious enlightenment. Goshirakawa wrote his "Unique Instructions in Imayō Performance" (*Ryōjin Hishō*, "Kudenshū," 10, 469) because, he states, "Even secular literature, if transformed [i.e., comprehended in a different way], will surely become a factor extolling the Dharma and a link to the preaching of the Buddha's Word." His declaration is based on a passage from Po Chü-i's (772-846) "Postscript to My Loyang Anthology, Presented to Hsiang-shan Temple":

> I have long cherished one desire, that the secular literature I have written in this life and the faults occasioned by my wild words and fancy language be transformed, for worlds to come, into a factor extolling the Dharma and a link to the preaching of the Buddha's Word.[16]

These lines, which also appear in song form in the *Wakan Rōeishū* (2,200), were very celebrated. Goshirakawa probably refers to the song, which was well known in Japan at the time, rather than to Po Chü-i's own text. Now, Goshirakawa's statement, removed from the context of Po's "Postscript," was undoubtedly interpreted as signifying that all linguistic compositions, even those frivolous pieces that veer from the path of righteousness, should be preserved so that they might provide future impetus for attaining the su-

[15] Exemplified by the *Ruiju Utaawase Maki*, a 12th-century compendium of all waka competition texts extant at the time; see *Heianchō Utaawase Taisei*, ed. Hagitani Boku (Dōhōsha, 1979).

[16] [See ch. 5, n. 9.—Ed.]

preme truth of the Dharma. One important reason why Goshirakawa rigorously practiced and eventually mastered the once plebeian imayō, endeavoring to communicate a correct method of performance to future generations, may be his conviction that one might follow the same paths to enlightenment by singing imayō or by reciting the *Lotus Sutra*.

Practical logic cannot account for the idea that plebeian songs are ultimately identical to the sutras as a means of expounding the truth inherent in the Dharma. Such concepts were possible, however, in the logic of Tendai Buddhism, a new school of thought for contemporary intellectuals. Tendai is characterized by its doctrine of Ten Worlds Concommitant (Jikkai Gogu). The "Ten Worlds" refers to the worlds of Hell, Hungry Spirits, the Animal, Asuras, the Human, the Celestial Beings, the Arhats, the Self-Enlightened, the Bodhisattvas, and the Buddhas. Each of the Ten Worlds has an independent existence: an inhabitant of the Human world, for example, might after death be reborn in the world of Hell or the world of Celestial Beings, depending on past conduct as a human being. Thus the Human world is separate from the other nine worlds. While recognizing the mutual exclusivity of the Ten Worlds, Tendai teaching also conceived of each world as simultaneously containing within itself all other nine worlds. For instance, the world of the Buddhas is not limited to Buddhas alone. Since it contains within itself the other nine worlds, a Buddha can on occasion manifest himself in human form, and, conversely, a dog or cat from the Animal world can become a Buddha. Thus one world is the Ten Worlds, and the Ten Worlds are a hundred worlds. According to such logic, plebeian songs share certain features with celestial music and the Buddha's teachings; and a thorough knowledge of the art of imayō might well lead to birth in the Pure Land.

The doctrine of Ten Worlds Concommitant—that one world is the Ten Worlds, and the Ten Worlds a hundred worlds—can be reduced to the more general reasoning that one is many and many are one. When this logic is applied on a practical plane, it evolves into the characteristic Tendai doctrine of Endonkai, the Perfect and Immediate Precept. Hinayāna Buddhism requires that its religious train themselves to observe all the precepts determined for each sex, two hundred and fifty for monks, and three hundred and forty-eight for nuns. This is called Gusokukai, the Observance of Multiple Precepts. Mahāyāna Buddhism is not quite so exacting, although it does require that all the important precepts be observed—those forbidding murder, theft, fornication, falsehood, and consumption of alcohol. But the doctrine of the Perfect and Immediate Precept, first advanced by Saichō (767-822), was unique to Japan: it stipulates that if one perfectly fulfills a single precept, all the rest will be contained in it. When this reasoning is applied to the various specialized arts within society, the result is an idea that, by attaining the innermost meaning of an art, one would encompass within that art the innermost meaning of all other arts. This concept represents nothing less than a bond between specialization and universality, the stage at which michi is established.

Thus the twelfth century apparently contained the potential for forming the medieval ideal of artistic vocation, although the stage of linkage between specialization and universality may not have been reached by that time. With the thirteenth century, however, michi had become clearly established. The following passages appear in *Shōbō Genzō Zuimonki* (ca. 1235), a record of the teachings of Dōgen (1200-1253):

> A man who is born into a certain family and engages in its profession [michi] should know that he must be diligent above all in his family's work. If he learns a profession in addition to his own, one that he knows is not within his scope, he is acting totally in error (2, 334).

> Rather than a man—monk or layman—pursue several areas of study without mastering a one, he should perfect a single pursuit, becoming so expert in it that he can give public performances. How much more does this apply to nonsecular matters: Buddhism has been studied since time began, but never thoroughly. To this day, therefore, our scholarship has been inadequate. Then again, we students of Buddhism are not greatly gifted. A monk who approaches the vast, sublime subject of Buddhism by studying several aspects at once will fail to understand a single one. Even concentration on one

> aspect alone cannot guarantee its thorough mastery in the space of this life, since a man's natural gifts are inherently poor. Scholastic monks must definitely specialize in a single area of study (2, 344).

Dōgen's teaching—that one cannot master all the areas of specialization within Buddhism and should instead concentrate his powers on a single specialty—was premised on the possibility of attaining the innermost meaning of Buddhism through a thorough knowledge of "a single pursuit," which would be equivalent to mastering "several aspects." This passage is alive with the logic of "one is many and many are one." This also applies to Dōgen's teaching that someone engaged in the "family's work" is not to meddle in a michi other than the family specialty. Dōgen's statement, "a monk who . . . stud[ies] several aspects at once will fail to understand a single one," clearly resembles a dictum of Kenkō, even in its mode of expression:

> If you are determined to carry out one particular thing, you must not be upset that other things fall through. Nor should you be embarrassed by other people's laughter. A great enterprise is unlikely to be achieved except at the sacrifice of everything else (*Tsurezuregusa* [dan 188], 245).[17]

Zeami similarly asserts that "he who wishes to excel in the michi of nō must, above all, not practice other michi" (*Kaden*, "Introduction," 342). "Do not practice other michi" is an important precept in the medieval ideal of artistic vocation. Behind the injunction lies a conviction that persistence in gaining a thorough knowledge of one's own michi should result in the acquisition of its innermost meaning, a meaning common to all michi. With the establishment of this conviction, the finishing touches have been added to the ideal of artistic vocation.

It might be well to note that the michi ideal was perfected in the thought of Dōgen, the founder of the Sōtō branch of Zen Buddhism. Tendai Buddhism offered the possibility of effecting the concept of michi in the twelfth century. But by the thirteenth

[17] [Keene, trans., p. 161.—Trans.]

century Tendai was in decline, and new branches of Buddhism derived from Tendai had taken the lead. Among these, Zen, which was considerably modeled on the Tendai concept of contemplation (shikan), possessed as one of its central tenets the logic that "one is many and many are one." I would like to think that Zen thus took the place of Tendai in providing the impetus whereby the ideal of michi was perfected. Sōtō Zen, unlike the Rinzai school of Zen, has no tradition of kōan [paradoxical or seemingly obvious questions that would stimulate a moment of enlightenment (satori)]. Instead, it teaches that satori can be attained through the performance of everyday actions—tidying one's house and garden in the early morning, gathering firewood and drawing water, and eating meals in accordance with strict etiquette. This approach is at one with the ideal of michi, which holds that the precepts of the sages are to be found even in the act of climbing a tree.

The Relation of Michi to Expressive Ideals

As discussed in these pages, michi was of course related to High Medieval expression; but this relation was not always the same in every practice. I have previously considered the characteristics of High Medieval expression to be: retrospectiveness, subtlety, profundity, and fragmentation.[18] These characteristics are markedly present in the ga [higher, esteemed] practices of the High Middle Ages and are consequently difficult to link to the zoku [lower, disesteemed] genres. Connections with michi are limited to the former practice.

Literary retrospectiveness—or, more precisely, a retrospective orientation—is a stance in which the writer is always aware of the connection between his or her work and preexisting expression. This is most strikingly recognized in diction. The normative state-

[18] Konishi Jin'ichi, "Chūseijin no Bi: Karon o Chūshin to shite" ("Medieval People and Beauty: Centering on Poetic Treatises"), *Kokugo to Kokubungaku*, 30 (1953). [Here, and in what follows, the reader will recognize close if implicit connections with Mezaki's chapter.—Ed.]

ments are Fujiwara Teika's (1162-1241) that waka poets "should employ ancient diction" in their compositions, and his more concrete stipulation that "Waka diction must not diverge from usage found in *The Collections of Three Eras*.[19] Exceptions are diction used by great masters and poetry by the ancients that appear in the *Shinkokinshū*; such usage is equally acceptable" (*Eika Taigai*, 114).[20]

In the thirteenth century, poetic conception and design largely resembled those of earlier ages. Considerable perseverance is required of any person worthy enough to attempt to read through the last thirteen royal anthologies, beginning with the *Shinchokusenshū* (ca. 1234). Of these thirteen, even the *Gyokuyōshū* (1313) and the *Fūgashū* (1345), deservedly considered to be fresh and innovative collections, contain a great many waka that adhere to poetic stereotypes. This tendency would probably either bore or enrage modern readers. But before we rush to condemn it, we must first carefully consider the fact that the poets represented in the last thirteen anthologies composed typical waka because such poetry was believed desirable. To these poets, expression that conformed to earlier types possessed positive value. Such set types were to become still more striking, on rather different terms, for renga [linked poetry]. It is difficult indeed to discover any original concepts or diction in the several thousand extant renga compositions.[21] The author of the seventeenth-century treatise, *Renga Hajakenshō*, emphasizes that renga can only consist of the linking of commonplace verses.[22] This view shares certain features with the transmissive presumption basic to michi.

[19] [*Sandaishū*, a reference to the first 3 royally commissioned waka anthologies, the *Kokinshū* (ca. 905-20), the *Gosenshū* (951), and the *Shūishū* (ca. 985).—Trans.]

[20] [The *Shinkokinshū* is a waka collection compiled by Teika, among others, in 1206. It includes work by poets of the Ancient Age, like Kakinomoto Hitomaro (fl. ca. 680-700), as well as works by the compilers and their contemporaries. Teika recommends emulating only the diction used by the former group.—Trans.]

[21] Since research is incomplete, the precise number is unknown. There could be well over 10,000 renga sequences extant somewhere.

[22] The *Renga Hajakenshō* was written by a renga master named Saijun; nothing is known of his life. The only surviving text is a woodblock edition dated 1693. There is no revised edition in modern print.

Renga composition required not only the perpetuation of past concepts and diction but a conventionalized, set treatment of subject matter as well. "Spring rain" ("harusame") might serve as an example. Although heavy rain sometimes falls in spring, in renga, "spring rain" must always be portrayed as falling soundlessly, gently obscuring the poet's view. Such characteristics are called the "hon'i [essence] of spring rain."[23] Every frequently used renga subject has its specific hon'i. This was made possible by the limitation of subject matter treated in renga to that most frequently used in preexisting waka. If renga had not been limited in its subject matter, its hon'i would probably not have been developed. Hon'i may be described as a set form employed in the treatment of a poetic subject. One of the major characteristics of the arts that evolved in the High Middle Ages is the creation of compositions made up of an assemblage of specific, set forms. The unit parts (called shōdan, small stages) that make up a given nō libretto—from the shidai, michiyuki, issei, mondō, shodō, kakeai, kuse, and nakairi down to the kiri—each possesses its own modality. All are specific, set forms within a larger configuration. Nō music is also made up of various specific forms: ageuta, sageuta, kuri, sashi, and waka, to name a few. The performers' movements are similarly ordained. Performers must sing and move in accordance with predetermined norms. One would not be exaggerating much in saying that the nō performer has no scope, in terms of form, to exercise his creativity. Such extremely impersonal forms are supported by the conformist ethic—the idea that supreme art can arise only through the rigid observance of form.

By the twelfth century there was a clearly perceptible inclination to preexisting expression. This is reflected in the judgments delivered in waka competitions, where statements like "familiar expression" and "frequently used expression" are employed without exception in a positive sense. For instance, *The Palace Minister's Waka Competition of 1118* records that one of the judges, Mototoshi, nominated the following poem, by Fujiwara Tamezane

[23] See Yamada Yoshio, *Renga Gaisetsu (Outline of Linked Poetry)* (Iwanami Shoten, 1937), pp. 129-36, for details.

(dates unknown), as the winner of round twelve, on "Late Chrysanthemums":

Oku shimo no	If the frost
Nakaramashikaba	Had not touched the chrysanthemums,
Kiku no hana	Would their flowers
Utsurou iro o	Be of the lightly faded colors
Kyō mimashi ya wa.	That are visible today?

Mototoshi's reason for selecting this poem was that its last two lines contain a "somewhat familiar expression" (*Heianchō Utaawase Taisei*, 6, 1769). Another example, this time involving some negative judgment, appears in *The Waka Competition of the Kamo High Priestess of Rokujō*, for the round entitled "Cormorant Fishing on the River" (*Heianchō Utaawase Taisei*, 4, 994).

Kagaribi no	The fishing flares
Hima shi nakereba	Burn everywhere upon the water:
Yoru shi mo zo	Nighttime though it is,
Ukawa no soko wa	The river where the cormorants fish
Kakurezarikeru.	Is illumined to its depths.

> The judgment: It is reasonable enough to have a poem in which the reflected light of flares makes the water seem aflame; but it is impossible to see a riverbed clearly illuminated. On the other hand, the poet is correct in employing frequently used expression.[24]

These judgments can only represent the criterion that a beautiful turn of speech is one that is consonant with past expression. This retrospective orientation is not unique to the High Middle Ages, since the standard informs all medieval expression based on the ga aesthetics. But it is in the High Middle Ages that retrospective orientation plays a leading role.

The differing characteristic of subtlety accompanies retrospective

[24] [Cormorant fishing takes place at night: flares, contained in iron baskets and suspended over the water from fishing boats, attract the fish, which are caught by tame cormorants. The birds are tethered to lines held by the fisherman; a ring round the cormorant's neck prevents it from swallowing any but the smallest fish.—Trans.]

orientation and, like the latter, predates the High Middle Ages. Single-minded dedication to frequently used expression is not likely in itself to yield fresh impressions and evoke intense emotion—such an approach contains absolutely nothing new. And since newness is life for literary expression, its absence can only signify a withering of expression. Thus frequently used expression, while thought desirable, was necessarily to be accompanied by something new. Yet newness was most appreciated in nearly imperceptible amounts. This approach is predicated on (or demands) a thorough acquaintance by both composers and audiences with frequently used expressions and a capacity for sensitive response to the slightest change in such expression. Just as, on the stillest of mornings, one can clearly hear leaves rustle as they fall, so would people accustomed to mutual composition and reception of the same expression be capable of clearly distinguishing minute expressive novelty. Excessively accentuated expression would undoubtedly have struck the sensitive recipient as disagreeable or even painful.

Some of the most typical nō masks—such as the "young woman," "Zō, "Ōmi woman," "Magojirō," and "girl's face" masks—would all look, to the uninitiated, like approximately identical masks of young women's faces.[25] How much more indistinguishable, then, would be an ordinary "Zō" mask, a "knothole Zō," and a "somber Zō"![26] On the other hand, anyone familiar with nō masks and well

[25] The "young woman" ("wakaonna") mask depicts the face of a woman in her early twenties; its nonspecific beauty makes it adaptable to various roles. The "Zō" mask (named for Zōami, an early fifteenth-century nō actor and mask maker who is said to have carved the prototype) communicates noble and refined beauty and is used only in roles depicting supernatural women and high-ranking noblewomen. The "Ōmi woman" ("Ōmi onna") mask expresses voluptuous beauty, suitable for such roles as that of the lustful Shirabyōshi dancer protagonist in *Dōjōji*. The "Magojirō" mask is named after Kongō Magojirō, a sixteenth-century nō actor and mask maker who is said to have created the prototype by carving the likeness of his dead wife; the mask communicates a sense of sorrow. The familiar "girl's face" ("koomote") mask depicts a woman in her late teens, radiant with health and most appealing.

[26] The "knothole Zō" ("fushiki Zō") is a kind of Zō mask treasured by the Hōshō school of nō. The tiny knotholes in the wood from which the mask is made exude a sap that subtly alters the mask's coloring, giving it—to the expert eye—greater dignity than an ordinary Zō mask. The "somber Zō ("naki Zō"), true to its name, has a graver expression than is found on ordinary Zō masks.

endowed with sensibility will easily recognize the grace of the "young woman" mask, the restraint and elegance of the "Zō," the allure of the "Ōmi woman," the melancholy beauty of "Magojirō," and the lovableness of the "girl's face." And such a person would vigorously protest the impropriety of any attempt to clarify a mask's grace or elegance by further accentuating its expression by some unheard of novelty.

Renga is also based on the assumption that its audience will sense a wealth of expression in the sublest of points. Those who see renga as mere repetition and accumulation of set expressions must also perceive the act of listening to or reading renga, like that of viewing nō, as tedious unto death. The truth, however, is that renga audiences consist solely of people capable of experiencing great pleasure at the most minute expression of newness: thus when it is their turn to compose, they refrain as best they can from presenting unusual verses, and instead offer ones of scant interest. This is evidence of the affective-expressive postulates (Earl Miner's theory): the composer or performer intentionally suppresses what he would wish to express, leaving it to his audience to sense and absorb what he has suppressed (or perhaps more).[27] A nō audience, then, tends to be made up of people who have spent at least some time studying the actual techniques of nō, because anyone who has not will have no idea where a performer has displayed his subtle innovation. In other words, a nō audience can be said to consist generally of people who, regardless of individual proficiency, are capable (either seemingly or in fact) of joining the cast as actors. The case is clearer for renga: no one incapable of composing renga will participate as a member in a renga group. The practice of audience members also serving as performers or composers (in the case of poetry composition in Chinese or Japanese) has already been recognized as characteristic of the Early Middle Ages and has much in common with the stance of retrospective orientation.

[27] Earl Miner, "Towards a New Conception of Classical Japanese Poetics," *Studies on Japanese Culture*, 2 vols. (Japan P.E.N. Club, 1973), 1, 99-113. [Or, for a more accessible account, though with less Japanese evidence, see "On the Genesis and Development of Literary Systems," *Critical Inquiry*, 5 (1979), 339-53, 553-68. The author here interprets the thesis his own way.—Ed.]

The characteristic I call profundity, however, did not appear until the High Middle Ages, and so its connection to michi is stronger than that of the first two characteristics. "Profundity" signifies a stance that searches out the most essential presence of an object, rather than grasping that object through superficial perception. This is literary activity performed at a deep level of awareness, and it can be understood only at a deep level of awareness. The following waka, from Teika's *Shūi Gusō* (comp. 1213-?1237)[28] will serve as examples:

<table>
<tr><td>HARU
Naniwagata
Akeyuku tsuki no

Honobono to
Kasumi zo ukabu
Nami no irie ni.</td><td>SPRING
The Bay of Naniwa:
The moon that moves with breaking dawn
Casts a faint glow
Upon the very mist afloat
Above the waves within the cove.
(2, 1509)</td></tr>
<tr><td>NATSU
Yukinayamu
Ushi no ayumi ni
Tatsu chiri no
Kaze sae atsuki
Natsu no oguruma.</td><td>SUMMER
Straining as it goes,
The bullock's every footstep
Raises up the dust
In the breeze that stirs up hot
Summer in my little carriage.
(2, 1525)</td></tr>
<tr><td>AKI
Tabibito no
Sode fukikaesu
Akikaze ni
Yūhi sabishiki

Yama no kakehashi.</td><td>AUTUMN
The man in travel,
His sleeves blow this way and that
In the autumn wind
Where the evening sun shows desolate
The mountain's suspension bridge.
(2, 1535)</td></tr>
</table>

[28] *Shūi Gusō* in Reizei Tameomi, ed., *Fujiwara Teika Zenkashū*, repr. ed. (Kokusho Kangyōkai, 1974), using Reizei's numbers.

FUYU

Hashitaka no
Kaeru shirafu ni
Shimo okite
Onore sabishiki
Ono no shinohara.

WINTER

The windhover's wings
Show as it returns whitened spots
Where frost has settled;
Oh, know how its desolation deepens
Ono and its stand of bamboo grass.[29]
(2, 1555)

A waka poet of the Meiji Period might have misinterpreted these poems as examples of objective portrayal. All four were composed, however, on the same day, the eighteenth of the Ninth Month, 1196. The spring, summer, and winter poems are clearly not concerned with immediate, actual scenes. The autumn poem, moreover, was composed at the house of the Palace Minister, Gokyōgoku Yoshitsune (1169-1206), and so it, too, is not a depiction of a scene before the poet's eyes. Nevertheless these waka proffer reality—a reality, however, different in significance from that apprehended by the senses of sight, hearing, touch, smell, and taste, or depicted in accordance with such apprehension. The reality conveyed by these waka serves to draw the reader near to the most elemental way of being possessed, as the seemingly objective poetic phenomena are made to convey subjectivity. The reality involved pertains to a deeper stratum than usual.

This expressive stance apparently arose out of an esteem for hon'i. The practice of composing waka on given topics reached its height in the twelfth century, and was accompanied by experimentation with various poetic styles in accord with one's assigned topics. The chief object of concern was to capture the essential presence of the topic (its hon'i). To attain this end, a poet was required to adopt a contemplative stance, concentrating and focusing the mind on the elemental aspects of the topic. (This stance surely originated with Shunzei.) Teika's poetic style inherits this approach.

[29] [The profundity or yūgen that is spoken of is primarily that of conception (kokoro no yūgen), but there are also verbal counterparts in the adjectives concluding the fourth lines of the summer, autumn, and winter poems. Each applies—as the translations are meant to show—to what precedes and follows.—Ed.]

The contemplative approach of Shunzei and Teika eliminated the distance between poetic object or topic and poet, rejecting superficial psychological capturing of a subject. Instead of that, the poet was obliged to focus on deep thoughts, encountering the essential reality of the subject to hand. This expressive procedure differs profoundly from the wittiness of the *Kokinshū* style, in which the poet deliberately alters the original status of the poetic subject personally remade. The contemplative expressive approach involves the bracketing of a poet's individual impressions and drawing near to the very essence of the subject. Once the essence has been regained, the poet will recommence grasping forms manifested on a more superficial level of awareness. As a result, these poems often give the average reader a sense of profound mystery and difficulty, whereas poetry grasped only on a superficial level of consciousness is easily understood. The sense of profound mystery conveyed by the contemplative stance is called "yūgen." Because Teika's four waka are so descriptive that they might be mistaken for realistic poetry, they are perforce difficult to evaluate as yūgen; but expression using a radical contemplative stance generally tends toward yūgen. So it is that the process of restoring a poetic subject to its essence has some important features in common with michi—those that link a person, by the concrete, individual task called specialization, to a formless, universal truth.

Nō is the normative art for this profound expression. *Izutsu*, for example, is a very famous play and yet a most tedious drama if viewed superficially. Its plot is nearly identical to that of other nō plays with young woman protagonists, and one may safely say that it contains no highly dramatic scenes. The spectator wishing to receive a deep impression from *Izutsu* must, above all, sense the presence of the moon on stage. This moon is not simply a celestial phenomenon: it symbolizes the theme of this play, the purity of first love.[30] *Izutsu* is based on a story from the *Ise Monogatari* (ca. 950), but the plot of the original story is not presented on the nō stage. The only events performed in *Izutsu* are the visit

[30] One may take as the ultimate source the story in the *Ise Monogatari* (dan 23)—a depiction of a woman who, because she never loses the purity of her first love, eventually triumphs over that human attachment.

of a traveling priest to the ruined temple of Ariwaradera, his encounter with an unearthly woman and, subsequently, his beautiful dream. Yet the audience first senses the presence of autumn in the plumegrass placed onstage, and then, as the word "moon" appears over and over again in the libretto, begins to feel that moonlight is flooding the world of the nō. This very moonlight is the focal point of *Izutsu*. The moonlight manifests the purity of a love that budded in childhood and was never lost in maturity. One will, however, lose sight of *Izutsu* if one approaches it with the attitude that "purity," symbolized by moonlight, should be found and closely scrutinized within a given performance. The process of understanding that A is a symbol of B represents no more than a superficial judgment, and the "purity" grasped thereby will evoke only shallow emotion, emotion that can be fully expressed by words. The emotions I experience during a master actor's performance are beyond my powers of explanation and description. They can be felt only when my superficially conscious judgment has been stilled, and I have been assimilated into the performance itself. This method of directly experiencing the essence without recourse to the medium of intellect was probably the product of a spirit common to the realm of michi as well, since in michi the movement of a brush in the simple act of writing is connected to universal truth.

The characteristic of fragmentation, like that of profundity, did not appear until the High Middle Ages. Renga provides a normative example of fragmentation, but the characteristic is conspicuously present in waka as well after the thirteenth century. There are examples in waka by Yoshitsune.

Aki zo kashi	It must be autumn!
Koyoi bakari no	And will I not be spared tonight
Nesame ka wa	Being roused from sleep?
Kokoro tsukusu na	Do not disquiet my whole heart,
Ariake no tsuki.	O moon in the dawning sky.

Kyō kurenu	Today is at an end.
Asu mo karikon	Tomorrow let us hunt again
Katanohara	In these Katano fields.

Kareno no shita ni / On the ground of withered moors
Kigisu naku nari. / It must be pheasants that cry out.[31]

In both poems the forward movement is broken—so much so as to make them appear anomalous in Japanese poetry, one of whose chief characteristics (according to Yoshikawa Kōjirō) is a continuous flow of words. This tendency toward fragmentation takes the form of a division: the first half of the poem is reserved for emotion, and the second for natural description.

When waka are disconnected in thought as well as syntax, the reader must bridge the gap, or the poem will not be whole. Here are two examples.

TOPIC UNKNOWN
by the priest Jakuren

Sabishisa wa	As for loneliness,
Sono iro to shi mo	To say that it is one color
Nakarikeri	Is impossible.
Maki tatsu yama no	Black pines rise upon the hills
Aki no yūgure.	In the autumn twilight.
	(*Shinkokinshū*, 4, 361)

Night of the Thirteenth, in the Ninth Month of Kenkyū 3 [1192]
[*by Teika*]

Musubikeru	You gave your pledge
Chigiri mo tsurashi	To a love now heartlessly forgot.
Aki no no no	In the autumn fields
Sueba no shimo no	The frost on the tips of branches
Ariake no kage.	Tinges with moonlight in the dawn.[32]

For such poems, reposing with simple intellectual explanation leads to comprehension that something is not completely expressed. But that will be the only result. No emotions will be kindled. The lover's reproachfulness must be directly sensed as the frost on the tips of branches brightened by a dawn moon. If full understanding

[31] Yoshitsune's poems are 1, 834 and 4, 2117 as in Katayama Tōru, ed., *Akishino Gesseishū to Sono Kenkyū* (Kasama Shoin, 1976).

[32] *Shūi Gusō*, as in n. 27: extra part, and no. 3140.

is to be achieved, solely ratiocinative comprehension must be suspended. This poetic premise indicates a marked departure from the *Kokinshū* style, where the focal point of interest lies in intellectual comprehension. The hallmarks of fragmented expression become still clearer when a break occurs between the waka and its topic, rather than within the waka itself, as in these poems treating religion allegorically.

The Discrimination of Merits
[*by Teika*]

Tobu tori no	Where the birds fly,
Asukagawa kaze	In Asuka the river breeze
Sore mo ga to	Blows just as it will,
Sode fukikaeshi	Setting my sleeves fluttering
Hana zo furishiku.	In a shower of cherry blossoms.[33]

"Be Vigilant at All Times to Quell Erroneous Thoughts"
[*by Hanazono In*]

Kari no tobu	The wild geese fly
Takane no kumo no	Toward a lofty peak where clouds
Hitonabiki	Drift in a single bank;
Tsuki irikakaru	The moon rises up to hang
Yama no ha no matsu.	In a pine on the mountain's ridge.[34]

(*Fūgashū*, 18, 2052)

Considered apart from their topics, these poems appear to be simple descriptions of nature. The poets anticipated, however, that readers would sense the unstated connection between the poem and its topic without recourse to intellectual busy work. Just as in *Izutsu* the audience senses the purity of a first love in the waving plumegrass and the moonlight, so the realization of fragmented expression presumes a profound understanding by its readers.

[33] Ibid., 3, 2750. [Teika's headnote or title reproduces the title of the seventeenth chapter of the *Lotus Sutra*, in which the Buddha describes the twelve stages of merit that will accrue to those who venerate the teaching of the sutra.—Trans.]

[34] Hanazono's headnote reproduces a line from the *Engakukyō (The Sutra on Perfect Enlightenment)*, as in the standard compilation of sutras, *Taishō Shinshū Daizōkyō*, 17, 917.

Originally a characteristic of Chinese poetry, such fragmented expression came to dominate the finest Japanese poetry. With the poet's contemplative comprehension, this fragmentation seems to have developed into the rich expression we have been observing. What I have called fragmented expression was surely connected with the poet's contemplative stance, just as the conception of michi was imbued with an implied universality.

CHAPTER 7

❖

LANGUAGE IN CRISIS: OGYŪ SORAI'S PHILOLOGICAL THOUGHT AND HIRAGA GENNAI'S CREATIVE PRACTICE

❖

BY SUMIE JONES

> "When *I* use a word," Humpty Dumpty said, in rather a scornful tone, "it means just what I choose it to mean—neither more nor less."
> "The question is," said Alice, "whether you *can* make words mean so many different things."
> "The question is," said Humpty Dumpty, "which is to be master—that's all."

Language and Two Interpreters

As between a word and its utterer, "which is to be master" is no simple question. Their mutual dependence—neither comes into existence without the other—makes each master and servant, simultaneously, to the other. In action vis-à-vis the listener or reader, their positions move in a seesaw fashion: while the utterer can employ, manipulate, and even create a word, a word is capable of carrying off, imprisoning, tricking (as in the case of an unintended pun), and even exposing (as in the case of a Freudian slip) its utterer. In the act of extended writing, the writer stands in the same seesaw relationship with the grammar, syntax, form, structure, and style that accompany combinations of words. Whether the purpose is to instruct or to delight the reader, this act consists of a sustained struggle to be master of language. The struggle is a frustrating one, because of the complex nature of language and the fact that language is the prime vehicle of communication.

In both theoretical and creative writing, language provides the writer with immense possibilities: an effective choice and arrangement of words may not only accurately convey the idea or transmit the experience but may even create the system for a new kind of thought or literature. It is due to the charm of language that a theory can convince the reader better than factual evidence or that a poem can move the reader more intensely than experience in real life. On the other hand, a written work is dictated by the inherent limitations of language: there is not always a ready word or syntactical system for everything to be expressed, and there is no absolutely universal meaning for every word or expression. What is written is bound to leave gaps in communication and openings for misunderstanding. Hence the theoretician and the literary artist are blessed by the expressive features of language and, at the same time, burdened by its inadequate and misleading aspects. In response to this dilemma, the conservative attitude would be to forbid a word to mean more than one thing, as Alice wishes to do in her reproachful question, or to close language against interpretation. The liberal one would be to take advantage of the very mutability of language, as Humpty Dumpty declares he does, or to open it to interpretation. Thus the world divides between Alices and Humpty Dumpties. Alice's attitude points to a solution that is possible only conceptually, and Humpty Dumpty's represents a general understanding that constitutes the basis for literary art. A comparative examination of theoretical and creative responses to the dilemma of using language may reveal an essential element of the culture they represent.

I have chosen the cases of Ogyū Sorai (1666-1728) and Hiraga Gennai (1728-1780) for the present inquiry not only because they represent in extreme the two attitudes mentioned but also because of their importance in the culture of the mid-Edo (or Tokugawa) period, when problems of language were particularly complex. The two men have much in common. Both served the feudal bakuhan [governmental system of fiefs] authorities and officials, each attracting, albeit to very different degrees, the attention of the most powerful politician of the time, Sorai that of Yanagisawa Yoshiyasu, Grand Councillor, 1698-1709, and through him the shogun Tsunayoshi, 1680-1709; and Gennai that of Tanuma Okitsugu, Grand Councillor, 1772-1786. And both are suspected, by later scholars, of grand political ambitions that were never fulfilled.[1] Both ended as masterless and family-less free agents, Sorai as scholar-teacher (only nominally in the service of the Yanagisawa household after Yoshiyasu's retirement), and Gennai as projector-promoter-author. More importantly, in their work they demonstrated a similar spirit: essentially self-taught in their special fields, both were founders, discoverers, and inventors of methods and techniques. Sorai, head of the Ken'en School of learning and founder of Kobunjigaku, or Philology of Classics, revolutionized classical learning by questioning the Neo-Confucian interpretations of texts and by establishing a theory of reading and interpretation. Gennai, widely acknowledged as the founder of the gesaku (playful composition) genre of fiction, not only created a unique writing style for comic fiction but also introduced the use of Edo dialect in popular jōruri plays.

The two men were also alike in the scale of their activities and achievements, which extended far beyond the boundaries of their respective specialties. Sorai's writings encompassed nearly all fields of culture: literature, philology, intellectual thought, politics, law, history, military science, and music, to name a few. He was not only a theoretician-critic but also a social commentator, dictionary-compiler, classical-style poet, as well as tutor-secretary to government officials and teacher to the students of his Ken'en School. Gennai's career was no less expansive. As a scientist-philologist, he compiled catalogues in mineralogy and botany as well as writing poems, plays, essays, and fiction. His activities in areas outside

[1] See, for example, Bitō Masahide, "Kokkashugi no Sokei to Shite no Sorai," in his edition, *Ogyū Sorai, Nihon no Meicho*, vol. 16 (Chūō Kōronsha, 1974), pp. 30-31; and, Jōfuku Isamu, *Hiraga Gennai, Jimbutsu Sōsho*, 161 (Yoshikawa Kōbunkan, 1971), 217-18.

literature and scholarship extended, in an eclectic fashion, much farther than Sorai's: he created Japan's first electric generator and the first piece of asbestos fabric as well as one of the earliest examples of Western-style oil painting; he organized exhibitions of natural products and conducted projects in mining, salt production, sheep breeding, as also pottery production; and he also taught painting and writing. In essence both men represent the type of wide-ranging and prescient genius that emerges in times of extreme change, and, therefore, both were prevented from achieving prominence in any institutional capacity by the conservative and anachronistic feudalism of the Edo period. Neither Sorai's political teachings nor Gennai's projects "for the sake of the nation's wealth"[2] had any effect on the politics and economy of their time. Their frustration in this area, however, may well have stimulated their chief contributions to Edo culture: Sorai's conceptual paradigm and Gennai's literary world.

Although Gennai was trained in classical studies, this cannot be attributed to the Ken'en School of thought. Nor are there factual data to prove Sorai's influence on Gennai's writing.[3] Although it is possible to suppose a general and indirect relationship between Sorai's thought and some of Gennai's pronouncements on various topics, parallels in this area will only show that Sorai's system of thought had, by Gennai's time, become part of the cultural climate. This essay, isolating the two figures from partisan categories and considerations of influence, will focus on one connecting point: the awareness of both men of the crisis of language in their time.[4]

[2] The phrase is Gennai's favorite to describe his industrial and commercial endeavors. See, for example, *Hōhiron*, Part II, 1777, in Nakamura Yukihiko, ed., *Fūrai Sanjin Shū, Nihon Koten Bungaku Taikei*, 55 (Iwanami Shoten, 1961), 243.

[3] Gennai briefly studied Chinese classics at the Seidō, the government-supported hotbed of Chu Hsi thought and learning against which Sorai established his conceptual system, and Japanese classics with Kamo Mabuchi (1697-1769). Although there are certain elements of Chu Hsi morality and Mabuchi-like nationalism in Gennai's writings, they are obscured by his religious and philosophical eclecticism.

[4] I follow the methodology proposed by Tetsuo Najita for the study of Edo thought in his "Method and Analysis in the Conceptual Portrayal of Tokugawa Intellectual History," in Tetsuo Najita and Irwin Scheiner, eds., *Japanese Thought in the Tokugawa Period* (Chicago: University of Chicago Press, 1978), pp. 3-38. "Crisis" is also Najita's key concept in characterizing eighteenth-century Japan.

The Mid-Edo Crisis

Despite the impression of general stability created by centralized shogunate rule, the sakoku (isolation) policy, and a strict class system, the Edo period abounded in conflicts and contradictions. Repeatedly proclaimed reforms and frequently issued edicts are evidence of the government's struggle during two and a half centuries to establish and reaffirm its authority over three conflicting forces: the traditionally powerful daimyo class, the newly established merchant class, and the impoverished and desperate farmer class. The government could not resolve the conflict between the land-based feudal structure and the rapidly developing money economy, on both of which it depended. The neo-Confucian ethic it tried to impose failed to curb the universal acquisitiveness that dangerously increased the amount of credit within the economy. The inferior coins repeatedly minted in order to increase government funds only confused the market and damaged the government's financial credibility. Confiscation of personal property in the name of frugality laws, and obliteration of debt—desperate measures for reducing government deficits and samurai debts—had little effect other than ruining some merchants and financiers. Farmers were exploited to the point of starvation. The government's managerial failures brought on farmers' rebellions and city residents' riots during the latter half of the Edo period, and antishogunate movements toward its end.

Signs of failure were visible earlier, but it took Ogyū Sorai—"the first crisis thinker produced by Tokugawa feudal society," as Maruyama Masao calls him[5]—to read the signs of danger as early as the Genroku era (1688-1703), the "Golden Age" of the Edo period. He noted that the feudal system was crumbling, as Japan rapidly moved away from a land-based economy, and was withering at the top as political leaders neglected learning, leaving space for new powers to rise from below.[6] When the Shogun Yoshimune

[5] Maruyama Masao, *Nihon Seiji Shisōshi Kenkyū* (University of Tokyo Press, 1952), translated by Mikiso Hane as *Studies in the Intellectual History of Tokugawa Japan* (Tokyo and Princeton: University of Tokyo Press and Princeton University Press, 1974), p. 134; hereafter, Maruyama.

[6] For Sorai's criticism of the Reforms, see his *On the Era of Tranquility Policies*

introduced the Kyōhō (1716-1736) Reforms in order to encourage cuts in government spending, frugality among citizens, and learning on the part of samurai, it was, in Sorai's view, already too late.[7] The situation was different in the Hōreki and Meiwa eras (1751-1764; 1764-1772), when Hiraga Gennai was active. Whatever effect the Kyōhō Reforms had had, Yoshimune's policies were made obsolete soon after his death, and, as if to fulfill Sorai's prediction, the incompetence of the shogun Ieharu gave way to the rise of Tanuma Okitsugu from the lowest samurai rank to the position of Grand Councillor, in which capacity he ran the country. Not being a full-fledged member of the class, Tanuma showed little respect for samurai authority. Family names and the right to wear swords—privileges hitherto limited to the samurai class—were granted to merchants who made sufficient contributions, and bribes were eagerly received in exchange for favors that compromised the dignity of samurai rule. During the so-called Tanuma Era, it did not require a perceptive thinker to detect the government's moral corruption and the decline of the feudal hierarchy. To a feudalistic and physiocratic critic like Sorai, this would have seemed a disaster.

Tanuma succeeded, however, in the areas where Yoshimune had not—land development, expansion of industries, and development and control of exchange brokers' guilds. The success eased the problems of the government treasury as well as the economy of the nation as a whole, chiefly by way of newly risen capitalists. Gennai was on the side of Tanuma's bullionism, and he attributed all his activities, except the literary ones, to his motive of contributing to the "wealth of our nation." Not only his projects in various industries but also his scholarship in mineralogy and botany had the purpose of developing natural products within Japan, thereby diminishing imports. By calling Tanuma "the big boss who knows all sides of life,"[8] Gennai expressed his appreciation of the sense of freedom and adventure that Tanuma's capitalistic

---

(Taiheisaku) and *Discourse on Politics (Seidan)*, presented, respectively, in 1716 and in 1722 to the shogun Yoshimune, in Imanaka Kanji and Naramoto Tatsuya, eds., *Ogyū Sorai Zenshū*, 6 (Kawade Shobō Shinsha, 1973), 141-66 and 9-140.

[7] Maruyama, pp. 133-34.

[8] *Hōhiron*, Part II, *Fūrai Sanjin Shū*, p. 249.

government allowed its citizens. The diametrically opposite attitudes of Sorai and Gennai on the political and economic issues indicate not so much the difference between the earlier and the later parts of the mid-Edo period as differences between the two men: one a highly conceptual thinker, and the other, a pragmatic man of action.

The mid-Edo period was a time of unresolved incongruities, fundamental conflicts, and rapid changes. The term, "crisis," however, can be applied here only metaphorically. The term refers not to a length of time or process but to "the point of time," as Webster's *New International Dictionary* says, "in which a decisive change one way or the other is impending." It is the moment when a conflict reaches the extreme, or when the existing force is threatened with extermination by an alien force. It must be noted that a crisis is recognized as such only when viewed from the standpoint of the existing force that wishes to continue. In a sense, Edo feudalism was pushed into a cul-de-sac by new forces, although the bakufu (Edo government by the military aristocracy) managed to maintain the existing system by making minor changes rather than a "decisive" one, thereby prolonging the state of danger. Therefore the mid-Edo period may be best characterized by the term, "crisis," with its connotation of an intensity normally attributed to a moment rather than a period of time.

In a similarly metaphorical sense of the word, the Japanese language was also in crisis. The political, economic, and social conflicts of the time had an extraordinary effect on the state of the language. Under Tokugawa rule, the tennō (sovereign) reigned in name only, so that terms like "kōkoku" ("royal country"), frequently used to refer to Japan, were without substance. The honorific "mi" in "miyo" (era) was no longer thought to apply to the tennō but was attributed to the shogun. Moreover, as the Grand Councillor and other officials became powerful, the shogun's dwindling authority over his samurai subordinates came to resemble that of the tennō. Haga Tōru reports that the Samurai Code of Behaviour (buke shohatto), promulgated by each shogun, lost its high authority after Yoshimune.[9] The hierarchy and distinctions

[9] *Hiraga Gennai, Asahi Hyōdensen*, 23 (Asahi Shinbunsha, 1981), 205.

of the four classes *shi-nō-kō-shō* (samurai, farmer, artisan, merchant) lost their validity as the importance of farmers in this scale was ignored and samurai sought favor of merchants, some even abandoning their privileged class. *Shi-nō-kō-shō* was just as meaningless a phrase as "the Era of Tranquility" (taihei no yo) and other slogans of the Edo period. The samurai could no longer be defined as military men; they were, in fact, landlords and politicians. To merchants, government officials were bribe-hungry nuisances, and to samurai merchants were suppliers of money on credit. To farmers the daimyo and his retainers were a devouring gang of tax collectors, to whom in turn the farmers were merely sources of revenue. Obvious gaps opened between words and facts. As hitherto well-defined words lost their meaning, ambivalence and obscurity prevailed.

Another element of the language crisis of this period arose from the heavy cross Japanese culture had borne since the beginning of its dual system: the use of Chinese ideograms for meaning and Japanese syllabaries for sound. In addition, the scholarly and official practice of writing entirely in the Chinese language and the literary tradition of using classical Japanese, written chiefly in Japanese letters, further complicated the situation. As Noguchi Takehiko suggests, this duality, added to the remoteness of the classical languages from highly developed everyday speech, brought about a great crisis during the mid-Edo period.[10] Noguchi has in mind the Genroku era, evidently to spotlight Ihara Saikaku (1642-1693) who made the first step through the barrier by establishing colloquial Japanese as a literary language. The state of the crisis continued in the Hōreki and Meiwa eras (1751-1771), only with increased intensity. The growth of schools of classical studies, the newly developed field of classical Japanese studies (kokugaku, or national learning), the newly introduced Western sciences and the Dutch language—all added to the complexity of scholarly vocabularies and writing styles. Moreover, the Edo dialect was being developed into a separate category of colloquial language. The pomp and glory of the Yoshiwara, the licensed quarters in Edo,

[10] *Shōsetsu no Nihongo, Nihongo no Sekai,* 13 (Chūō Kōronsha, 1980), 17-18.

introduced a whole system of pleasure-quarter jargon. In short, while the feudalistic class-based distinctions in language persisted, the capitalistic development of the city of Edo expanded the Japanese language immensely during the mid-Edo period. The population expansion brought in a great variety of regional and class dialects. Economic prosperity was accompanied by the rise of new occupations and occupational hierarchies with their jargon, and the growth of technology, sciences, and the arts brought about finer distinctions than ever in the citizens' language.

On the one hand, this expansion of language enriched Japanese culture. The impressive diversity and sophistication seen in the works of intellectual thought and of literature of this period would not have been possible without this linguistic phenomenon. On the other hand, the very richness of the language made communication far more difficult as specialization came to be required more than ever. Scholars understood only their colleagues, since the various schools defined terms differently, and only connoisseurs could converse with courtesans, since each pleasure district had its dialect and each tea house its jargon. While expanding to express the increased diversity of life, language excluded large groups of people from each specialized area of communication. And even within the specialized area newly invented words and newly assigned meanings made language increasingly fluid. For the intelligentsia, who would naturally aspire to communicate on a universal and permanent level, the problem must have been especially acute. It was, indeed, a time when "talented individuals might have been able to say, but not write, what they wanted to convey."[11]

The Japanese language, an existing force with an inertia to continue, thus faced a crisis, the point in which a decisive change was called for. For writers in more abstract theory and in literature, continuation of the authority of the language was of vital necessity. Sorai and Gennai shared an awareness of the crisis, and each endeavored to save the language from the dangers threatening it. While dealing with the written and spoken features of the Japanese

[11] Ibid., p. 18.

language, the "langue" of their time, each discovered problems inherent in "langage" itself. The radical changes they proposed were not merely for the survival of Japanese as a useful vernacular but for the continued validity of language itself. Their proposed solutions are diametrically opposite to each other because of their differing views of the nature of the crisis of language. Sorai saw that the manifest meaning of a word was obscured by interpretations and that the spokenness of language was made obsolete by interpretive reading. In his view, language was losing its authority, as words lost their close associations with meaning and sound. Hence he chose to recompose the "original" content of words by eliminating what he considered irrelevant accretions that had developed through the process of misreading and misinterpretation and by restoring authentic sounds of words in the act of reading. For Gennai, on the other hand, the crisis consisted of the threat of political, social, religious, and scholarly conventions that chained language to official labels. In his view, language was losing its freedom to exercise its own power to mean. In order to reaffirm this power of language, he endeavored to decompose it into meaningful elements—sounds, transcriptions, syntax—encouraging multiple readings and interpretations. They are alike in their awareness of the separation between spoken and written language and of interpretability as the inherent nature of language.

Sorai's Linguistic Imperium

Like all other Confucian scholars, Sorai was primarily an interpreter of classical texts. His uniqueness lies in his new theory of reading and interpretation. The intellectual outlook of the Tokugawa period had much in common with that of post-Renaissance Europe as described by Wilhelm Dilthey:

> Henceforth people were separated by their language, living conditions, and nationality from classical and Christian antiquity. Interpretation thus became even more than in ancient Rome a matter of translating an alien spiritual life through

> the study of grammar, monuments, and history. And in many cases this new philology, learning, and criticism had to work with mere second-hand reports and with fragments. So it had to be creative and constructive in a new way. From this period, a considerable hermeneutic literature survives. It is divided into two currents, since classical and biblical writings were the two greatest forces which men of that time sought to appropriate. . . . But the ultimate, codification of hermeneutics stems rather from biblical interpretation.[12]

In Edo Japan, interpretive efforts abounded in religion—Buddhist and Shinto—as well as in Chinese and national studies. Chinese studies constituted the field where scholarly discourse was most polemical and intense. Confucian texts and materials derived from them were variously analyzed in a fashion similar to biblical interpretation in the West: the fragmentary and foreign nature of the materials posed problems and opened possibilities, just as in Christian studies. There were conflicts between new trends and the orthodox interpretation of the Chu Hsi School [or shushigaku], rivalries akin to those between Catholic and Protestant interpretations in the West. Individual efforts on both sides were certainly "creative and constructive."

The Chu Hsi School, following Ch'eng Ming-tao (1032-1085), Ch'eng I-ch'uan (1033-1107), and Chu Hsi (1130-1200), interpreted texts by linking natural law with moral values. Its exegeses offered a scientifically logical scheme for the universe by which to justify the feudal structure and samurai moral norms. By referring contemporary questions to ancient texts they reconciled feudalism and rationalism, the two conflicting elements of the Edo period. The chief contribution of the opposing movements, Itō Jinsai's (1627-1705) semasiology of the classics (kogigaku) and Sorai's philology of the classics (kobunjigaku), was to liberate text from dogma. In insisting upon reading literature as nothing but literature, history purely as history, and so on, they diverted scholarly attention

[12] Dilthey, "The Rise of Hermeneutics" (1900), tr. Frederic Jameson in *New Literary History*, 3 (1972), 237; hereafter, "Hermeneutics."

from secondary to primary matters—human sentiment, in Jinsai's case, and fact and form in Sorai's—thus opening texts to generally humanistic approaches. Sorai's amoral modernism was more radical than Jinsai's humanism in attributing validity exclusively to text themselves and more widely humanistic in conceptualizing all aspects of culture through his interpretation.[13] Sorai fits perfectly Dilthey's description of Friedrich Schleiermacher (1768-1834), whom Dilthey regards the founder of modern hermeneutics: "a mind where a virtuoso practice of philological interpretation was united with a genuine capacity for philosophical thought."[14] With similar qualifications, Sorai created the first example of modern hermeneutics in Japan.

Sorai's theory of reading and interpretation was based on his keen awareness of the fact that the materials for scholarship were written in an ancient and foreign language. In Japan, since the earliest days of importation of Chinese culture, scholarship had developed a system called wakun (Japanese recitation) for reading Chinese. That is, by the aid of syntactical, grammatical, and phonetic notations, the word-order was changed to follow Japanese syntax, Japanese grammatical accessories were added, and Chinese characters were pronounced in Japanese equivalents or approximations, so that texts were read as though they had been written in Japanese. It was a clever system for bridging two languages, which shared, if nothing else, a large number of Chinese characters. Because of the isolation policy permitting only official interpreters to speak directly with Chinese visitors and traders, opportunities were rare, indeed, for Japanese to learn Chinese. Thus, wakun was the only way of reading Chinese, and one was admitted to the scholarly profession by mastering this reading system.

Teaching consisted largely of tutoring students how to read particular texts in this fashion. In short, reading aloud in wakun was equal to comprehending the meaning of the text, and knowing

[13] See Maruyama as well as Yoshikawa Kōjirō, "Jinsai Tōgai Gakuan," in Yoshikawa and Shimizu Shigeru, eds., *Itō Jinsai Itō Tōgai, Nihon Shisō Taikei*, 33 (Iwanami Shoten, 1971), 565-621, and his "Sorai Gakuan" in Yoshikawa et al., eds., *Ogyū Sorai, Nihon Shisō Taikei*, 36 (1973), 629-739.

[14] "Hermeneutics," p. 240.

the wakun pronunciation meant knowing the word. Hence wakun gave the Japanese the illusory impression that it was Chinese as well as Japanese, when in fact it was neither. This system, despite Sorai's objections, is still widely used in classical Chinese education and scholarship in Japan. Ishikawa Jun exclaimed in 1954 after reading Sorai, "What, then, is this that we have been reading?"[15] This is just the response Sorai expected from his contemporaries. His own answer had been that wakun is a "dialect" belonging to "what language I do not know" (Preface to *Translation as Method [Yakubun Sentei]*, c. 1715, V, 16, and *Introduction to Poetry Composition [Shibun Kokujitoku]*, 1735, V, 621).[16]

In order to awaken a true sense of language among contemporary readers numbed by the wakun practice, Sorai repeatedly exposes the foreignness of the language in which classical texts are written: "Characters [logographs] are part of the language of the Chinese people. Chinese is different in nature from the Japanese language. And even within the Chinese language, there are differences between the ancient and modern varieties" (*In Response to Questions [Sorai Sensei Tōmonsho]*, 1724, VI, 203). Hence, he declares, "wakun is not a way of reading, as it is thought to be, but one of translation" (Preface to *Translation as Method*, V, 16). The use of the word "translation" (yakugo), normally used for an incomprehensibly foreign languge such as Dutch during Sorai's time, denies the accepted status of the Chinese language as a quasinative tongue among Japanese scholars and establishes wakun as something distant from the original.

Even as translation, wakun is inadequate because the system was established by ancient courtiers who had a "meticulous preference for elegant and sonorous words" (*Introduction to Poetry Composition*, V, 623), and who misrepresented the simple language and familiarly human events that, in Sorai's view, dominate all Confucian texts:

[15] "Wakun," in *Ishikawa Jun Zenshū*, 9 (Chikuma Shobō, 1962), 470.

[16] The Roman and Arabic numbers after quotations from Sorai refer to the volume and page numbers in Imanaka Kanji and Naramoto Tatsuya, eds., *Ogyū Sorai Zenshū*, 8 volumes (Kawade Shobō Shinsha, 1973-).

> People in modern times imagine that texts were created by ancient Chinese after some complicated thinking. This is a gross misunderstanding. These texts are no different from our contemporary story books. They were written in the language they used in daily life (Preface to *Guide to Translation [Kun'yaku Jimō]*, date of first publication unknown, revised edition, 1766, V, 369).

In brief, as a method of reading, wakun is guilty of obscuring the spatial and temporal distance between text and reader, and, as translation, it is guilty of creating unnecessary distance. Learning and teaching by means of wakun is as frustrating as "scratching one's foot through the shoe" and "teaching swordsmanship by means of a fan" (*Introduction to Poetry Composition*, V, 621 and 620).

To resolve the frustration, Sorai first proposes "translation into the daily and common language of the Japanese people" (Preface to *Method*, V, 18). Two of his earliest works, *Translation as Method* and *Guide to Translation*, are classical Chinese dictionaries that give (besides definitions in scholarly Japanese and examples of usage) contemporary and colloquial Japanese equivalents. For example, the entry on the word "wu" (mochi; kutsu) includes the classical Japanese "Nakare" ("Thou shalt not") and the colloquial "suru na" ("Don't"). And the one on the phrase "pu yü" (fugu) lists the classical "gu narazu" ("not foolish") as well as the colloquial "baka de wa nai" ("not a dumb-bell"; *Guide*, V, 415 and 399). These equivalents are of the sort that, in fact, Saikaku had not achieved in a sustained fashion in his narrative style, and they indicate the dictionary compiler's intense desire to bring the content of Chinese words into his own linguistic world. As modern scholars point out, Sorai's involvement with problems of language bears an important relation to the whole of his thought system.[17] But it seems particularly important to note that Sorai began as a dictionary compiler. Describing himself as "a worm who abandons himself in a pile of letters" (*Composition*, V, 624), he scrutinizes

[17] See, for example, Hino Tatsuo, *Sorai Gakuha* (Chikuma Shobō, 1975), pp. 5-6.

Chinese characters in order to discover the precise content of each. His own way of organizing words is not by appearance or sound but by meaning.[18] The two dictionaries mentioned are those of confusables, their chief feature being fine distinctions between similar words. The whole of Sorai's thought is based on his close adherence to individual words and his belief in distinctions between any two given words.

In addition, the dictionary structure provides his writings with basic form and method. Many of his arguments are presented as replies to questions, as with *In Response to Questions* and numerous letters collected in *Sorai Shū*, 1746. In these, each question is briefly noted as the topic at the head of a letter or a passage so that the whole work is structured like an encyclopedia of Confucian learning. Here, too, the essential method is distinction: he develops his argument by separating misconception from facts. His *Commentaries on the Analects (Rongo Chō)*, 1740, is a voluminous work in which he challenges existing interpretations of Confucian texts both in China and in Japan, discussing each text section by section, each section under the heading of the first sentence in a passage. Every entry lists early and modern interpretations, as in a dictionary, and argues for his own special interpretation, which is distinguished from the rest by references to specific words in the text.

His chief theoretical works—such as *Explanations of the Way (Bendō)*, and *Explanations of Terms (Bemmei)*, both published in 1740—may be regarded as extended dictionaries. The former redefines the term "Way" on the basis of his readings of texts and

[18] [The author's point may be elaborated for specialists and nonspecialists alike. For the former, Sorai's organization of a dictionary by entries according to meaning of words can be set in context by Yamada Toshio, *Nihongo to Jisho* (Chūō Kōronsha, 1978). For nonspecialists, it is easier to explain two kinds of dictionaries in use today in Japan. There is one kind using the hiragana syllabary when one knows the pronunciation of a word but wishes to look up its meaning or how to write it in one or more Chinese characters. The other kind involves looking up Chinese characters or their meaning when one does not know the pronunciation. It is then necessary to determine by lists and experience the number of strokes required to write elements and any additional strokes. Here is a reason why the author's point in the next sentence is so telling.—Ed.]

the latter does the same with a larger number of Confucian terms such as "Virtue," "Wisdom," "Sage," and so on. By redefining—Sorai would have said "by reconstructing the original content of"—existing Confucian terms, he not only draws distinctions between words and meaning and between preceding interpreters and himself but also develops his own idiosyncratically amoral, institutional, and formalistic philosophy. Categorical organization itself was a common practice among Confucian scholars, but the idea of distinctions as a method of argument and definitions of words as rhetoric is Sorai's own. His system is built on manipulation of language by his categorical arrangement of words and assignment of a single and concrete meaning to each word.

Sorai's intellectual paradigm has been well elucidated by Yoshikawa Kojirō and Maruyama Masao.[19] Here it may suffice to consider a few of his definitions and distinctions. The "Way," according to him, is not the unknowable way of the universe or an unassessable course of individual virtue; it is "the way of governing the world," the political system created by the ancient rulers Yao and Shun (*Explanations of the Way*, I, 413 and 414). The term "Sage" is defined as "one who creates" ("sakusha"), and refers specifically to each of the ancient rulers—three before Yao and Shun, Yao and Shun themselves, and five after them—each so called not because of their moral superiority but because of their creations, or "inventions," as Mikiso Hane translates Maruyama's term, "sakui" (*Explanations of Terms*, I, 427).[20] The term "Matter" ("mono") refers to specific facts established by the Sages for teaching later rulers how to govern, not to some abstraction hitherto considered central to Confucius's teachings (*Explanations of Terms*, I, 458-59). "Gentlemen" are, instead of virtuous men or those well versed in Confucian learning, people in political positions, since they are "those who govern the ones below them" (*Explanations of Terms*, I, 459). Sorai's definitions strip words of moral and metaphysical implications and reduce them to concrete objects, to actual social positions and events, thus closing openings for interpretation. And the definitions are locked in with one an-

[19] Maruyama, as in n. 5; Yoshikawa, as in n. 13.

[20] Maruyama, pp. 94-96.

other in such a way as to form a cohesive and concrete world view. Matters that defy such concrete explanations are to be distrusted: Sorai often refers to Buddhism and Buddhist scriptures as things beyond human comprehension and thus unsuitable for scholarship.

Sorai's recognition of the variable nature of reality—frequent references are made in his works to the variety and changeability of human character, language, and history—leads him to treat Confucian concepts as a regulating system for dealing with that reality. For Sorai the heart (kokoro), or the spiritual and psychological functions of a human being, are "shapeless, hence unmanageable," and can be "regulated only by ritual" (*Explanations of the Way*, I, 417). Similarly, facts and events should replace argument, which is merely "shapeless, hence without a standard . . . and being based on individual points of view, how can it be applied to the Way of the ancient rulers and Confucius?" (ibid., I, 417-18). By dissociating Heaven ("ten") from the human world, the ruler from the ruled, facts from arguments, and standard from specific cases, Sorai draws a sharp line between public or "large" matters and individual or "small" ones, the former being definite and constant and the latter, ambiguous and variable (*Explanations of Terms*, I, 439). Hence, to Sorai the validity of Confucianism lies in the fact that it deals objectively and concretely with an objectified and standardized reality; its texts are records of such concrete and permanent matters as historical events, ritual manners, and forms of writing.

The general idea here is that truth would be wholly knowable were it not for the varied and variable nature of the language in which it is communicated. The modern scholar is isolated from the factual content of Confucius's teachings because language, as well as fact itself, has "branched out" to become more complex and ambiguous (*Introduction to Poetry Composition*, V, 631-34). Truth seems to float in the form of the person of Confucius, clearly visible and immobile in the pure, calm waters upstream in the gigantic river of the Chinese language, while Sorai struggles to keep afloat in the rapidly flooding and muddy waters downstream in the nearby river of Japanese. Building a channel between the two rivers, by way of colloquial translation, does not guarantee

Confucius's swimming down to the modern part of the other language. Even if he does, his body will be blocked from Sorai's view by a mass of irrelevant interpretations, and the muddiness of inflectional and other variations in modern language. For these reasons, Sorai dismisses the idea of a channel. And in spite of his theory of colloquial translation and his partial practice in his dictionaries, he did not translate an entire text into colloquial Japanese. He proposes to plunge into the nearest part of the other river and swim upstream. While translation, like wakun, attempts to bring Confucian texts closer to the reader, his proposed method of immersion in the Chinese language aims at bringing the reader closer to the material.

The description just given is an extension of Sorai's own metaphor: "Furthermore, what is ancient is the source and what is modern is an end. How can one, while floating in the stream, know its source? Our modern books constitute an ocean. There is no hope for one who sinks in it ('Letter to Chiku Shun'an')."[21] The extended metaphor of the swimmer and two rivers may show the dynamics of Sorai's understanding of the nature of the relationships among text, language, and reader. The modern reader is crippled by particularized language and ramified reality. In Japan he is doubly taxed by the fact that his culture never had a standard reality in the form of "Sages" and that his language is far more particularized than modern Chinese in degree of inflections and number of synonyms.[22] Sorai sees reading as a translingual and transhistorical act in which the reader must overcome the problems of the foreignness of a text's content and language and the mutability of contemporary reality and language. The problems are minimized if the reader moves toward "the source," leaving behind the impure and complex reality of actual contemporary surroundings. As Sorai himself demonstrates, the classical Chinese language and the Confucian writing style are simple and concise in contrast

[21] *Sorai Shū*, in *Ogyū Sorai, Nihon Shisō Taikei*, vol. 36, 527.

[22] For Sorai's notions of ancient vs. modern languages and of Chinese vs. Japanese, see the preface to his *Translation as Method* and the first section of his *Guide to Translation*, V, 16-23 and 369-76.

with the complexity and wordiness of a modern language and its styles.

What Sorai seeks in a text is, however, not the actual facts of ancient Chinese history or the actual language of the Chou Dynasty. Both reality and language are seen as something normative, "created" for the sake of succeeding cultures. As pointed out earlier, Sorai believes that "matter" (mono) was "established by the Sages for the purpose of teaching," and that its constituents, "facts" and "events," were also "invented" by them. Likewise, language was such an invention:

> Ever since people came into being, there were words wherever there were things. Because there were words, ordinary people were able to refer to things. But this was possible only with things that had shapes. As for things that had no shapes, since ordinary people could not recognize them by sight, the Sages established words for them (*Explanations of Terms*, I, 421).

Sorai's definitions of terms, which constitute a large part of his theses, have the purpose of reaffirming the original creators' intentions in the language and content of a text, and ultimately of constructing a meta-reality and a meta-language for the sake of reading and learning. Hence, his method of reading "by a direct understanding of the Chinese language by way of the Chinese language" (*Introduction to Poetry Composition*, V, 621) aims at the mastery of this meta-language and meta-reality.

Since a Confucian text is to be comprehended within itself and ancient Chinese is to be learned on its own terms, Sorai's theory operates in circular patterns. For example, comprehension of words is the means for, and purpose of, comprehension of reality, while reading is the means for, and purpose of, mastery of language. Drawing his line between reading and comprehension, Sorai describes a circle. In the Preface to *Translation as Method*, he recalls that as a child he used to be puzzled by the ancient saying, "Read one thousand times, and the meaning will automatically reveal itself," and wondered how the ancients had been able to read without already knowing the meaning (V, 16). The passage is intended to illustrate the impression given by the wakun practice that "reading means comprehension, and without comprehension one cannot read." "Reading" here refers to recitation by the wakun method, and "comprehension" means the ability to transpose Chinese into wakun Japanese. Sorai denies the validity of the old formula by saying that if one reads in Chinese, one can, indeed, read (or recite) the text without ever knowing the meaning of the words. While promoting reading in Chinese, however, he arrives at the same formula of reading and comprehension. On the one hand, he notes that, "unless the meaning-of-words [gi] is known, the meaning-of-the-whole [i] is not comprehended" and asks, "How can one know the Way without knowing Chinese characters?" (*Introduction to Poetry Composition*, V, 620 and 626). On the other hand, he repeatedly accuses Confucian exegetes of misunderstanding terms as result of ignorance of the Way (*Explanations of the Way* and *Explanation of Terms*).

The formula here matches Dilthey's hermeneutic circle: "The whole of a work is to be understood from the individual words and their connections with each other, and yet the full comprehension of the individual part already presupposes comprehension of the whole."[23] Whereas Dilthey proposes reading the whole once and then reflecting on parts as resolution of the logical circle, Sorai suggests repeated and quantitative reading "skipping characters that are not comprehended until their meanings come naturally" (*In Response*, VI, 203; and *Introduction to Poetry Composition*, V, 617-18); or, "deducing meanings of characters from usages in other texts" (*In Response*, VI, 173). Sorai's approach seems to aim at a larger, intertextual "fore-understanding," to use Frank Kermode's term, on the part of the reader.[24]

Sorai's "fore-understanding," however, is not a passive act of accumulating knowledge from texts but an aggressive one of stepping into the language and content of the text and even assimilating himself with the author of a text. He insists that the ability to

[23] "Hermeneutics," p. 243.

[24] Kermode, *The Genesis of Secrecy: on the Interpretation of Narrative* (Cambridge, Mass. and London: Harvard University Press, 1979), pp. 70-72; hereafter, Kermode.

write in the same language and style as in the text is required for comprehension:

> Especially, since we carry out our study in this country, and since our Sages are Chinese and our texts are written in the Chinese language, we will not be able to grasp the Way of the Sages unless we come to possess the sentiment of the Ancients who composed the texts at the time of composition. This can be achieved only when we are able to compose poetry and prose in their language (*In Response*, VI, 197).

Not surprisingly, therefore, the essential part of Sorai's method of composition is close imitation. His advice is to collect words and expressions from texts on slips of paper and divide them into baskets according to periods and styles so that appropriate ones can be pulled out for use (*Introduction to Poetry Composition*, V, 631). By composing in this fashion, one acquires a style in which sentiments are expressed as though by the remote classical author.

Sorai's belief in style and form is such that he held that, when this understanding is reached, one automatically "possesses" the feelings of the original author. And the original author is often seen by Sorai as speaking rather than writing. In writing practice, for example, "we produce words from out of our own fingers so that ancient texts will seem to be coming out of our own mouths" ("Letters to Kutsu Keizan" *[Kutsu Keizan ni Kotauru Sho], Letters of Sorai*).[25] Sorai's idea of, and practice in, Chinese pronunciation and his habit of presenting his theory in the form of verbal lectures may reflect his belief that Confucian texts were initially spoken. Naoki Sakai rightly suggests that Sorai's theory aims to "re-occupy the position from which the author should have spoken."[26] Only by participating with the original author as well as the ur-textual narrator can the reader comprehend the text. Sorai's personal practice not only with Chinese speech but also with ancient Chinese music and dance—two of the important topics in Confucian texts—

[25] Yoshikawa Kōjirō et al., eds., *Ogyū Sorai*, p. 529.

[26] "The Status of Language in Eighteenth-Century Japanese Thought," an M.A. thesis (University of Chicago, 1980), p. 15. This thesis deals conceptually with the matter of language in Sorai's thought.

may imply that he also believed in acting out the content as a method of comprehension. Reading is an act of stepping into what Sakai calls the "interiority" of the text by assimilation with the acts of acting, narrating, and writing.[27]

For Sorai incomprehension causes discomfort and comprehension brings satisfaction (*Introduction to Poetry Composition*, V, 627). Total comprehension, or the blissful state of "interiority," is the goal of his theory of learning:

> Our philology of the classics requires us not merely to read but also to produce words out of our own fingers so that the classical text will seem to be coming out of our own mouths. Only then can we meet with the ancients in the same room and exchange greetings with them without the formality of introduction. We will no longer need to wander about outside the gate fearfully watching the pleasure of the guards. How delightful it will be! ("Letters to Kutsu Keizan," p. 529).

The reader "meets" the text in the exclusive and stationary space of a "room," where the variability of language and reality is transcended. The reader is not only close to a text but is on an equal footing with it. Conversely, what makes impossible this ideal condition of stasis and equality—what makes a text remote from the reader—is presented as "the formality of introduction" and as "the pleasure of the guards." "Introduction" here is translation, which stands, as previously stated, close both to text and reader but between them. The "guards," however, represent a more harmful barrier, namely, interpretation. Unlike translation, interpretation stands outside the interiority of a text—because it is based on limited knowledge of the text's language and thrives on embellishments and distortions—but harmful for the reader because of the power of its whim. Sorai's definitions of words in *Explanations of the Way* and *Explanations of Terms*, as well as his textual commentaries such as those on *The Analects*, consist mainly of corrections of errors in earlier and contemporary interpretations. But beyond such practical criticism, he explores the nature of the act of interpretation.

[27] Ibid., pp. 3-32.

"Interpreters, says Frank Kermode, "usually belong to an institution, such a guild as heralds, toastmasters, thieves, and merchants have been known to form," and as members they have "the right to affirm, and the obligation to accept, the superiority of latent over manifest sense." He goes on to say that, in the history of interpreting a text, the inadequacy of preceding interpretations is always assumed, so that "the first person to misunderstand the content of the gospel of Mark was the man who wrote it."[28] The Chu Hsi School of Confucian thought is regarded by Sorai as such a questionable guild that favored and guarded the superiority of latent sense. The questionable quality comes from the fact that interpretations are based on interpretations:

> The Way is difficult to comprehend and difficult to explain. It is because the Way is vast. Scholars of later ages have called whatever each could see "the Way." Theirs are all fringe definitions. The Way is the way of Ancient Kings. Since Tzu Ssu and Mencius, scholars formed a Confucian School to compete against the hundred other schools. . . . The later scholars, pleased to find their explanations easy to understand, chose to define the Way according to their words, which were originally used for the purpose of attacking outsiders (*Explanations of the Way*, I, 413).

Here Sorai establishes the origin of Confucianism as its founder's polemical attempt at rendering other schools of thought—most notably, in this case, the Lao Tsu School—obsolete.

In other words, Sorai finds the earliest interpreters of Confucian texts guilty of violating the texts by purposeful coloring. The later ones are yet farther removed from the original texts: "over the years Confucian studies have divided into schools and sects, fighting against one another, becoming increasingly numerous and smaller" (*Explanations of the Way*, I, 413). "Small," refers not to the size of each sect but to the scale of its understanding of a text: the universal, or "large," matter of Confucian thought is made increasingly particularized, or "small," by interpretation. The history of Confucianism is that of interpretations breeding

[28] *The Genesis of Secrecy*, pp. 2, 17.

interpretations, so that Sorai's contemporary scholarship is densely populated by increasingly degenerate descendants of the questionable ancestors, Tzu Ssu and Mencius.

The redeeming factor, however, is that the original texts are held to be transparent. Their meaning should be manifest once interpretations are dismissed. For, unlike Kermode's St. Mark, Sorai's Confucius was not an interpreter, nor even an author: "Confucius," says he, "was not one who created" (*Explanations of the Way*, I, 413). Confucius is to be taken as an innocent recorder of the "Way of Ancient Kings," whose meaning was perfectly clear in his own time in China:

> His teaching was intended for all people in the world. Among people there must have been numerous dull and foolish ones and few wise and bright ones as there are now. Hence, the Way and teachings of the ancient Sages could not have contained such incomprehensible arguments as the later Confucians attribute to them (*In Response*, VI, 204).

The six works attributed to Confucius—the *Book of History*, *Book of Songs*, *Book of Music*, *Book of Changes*, the *Spring and Autumn Annals*, and the *Rites of Chou*—are isolated by Sorai from the rest of the canon of "classics" of Confucian studies as the only authentic texts. This is not only because they are supposedly by Confucius himself, but also because they are accounts of public events and procedures, or, in Sorai's word, "techniques" ("waza"), such as historical events, ritual procedures, or manners of musical performances. Thus Confucian texts are public in their intent ("for all people of the world") as well as in content. "Arguments," or interpretations, violate the public nature and purpose of a text as they present the content in their own "private ways" ("jikoryū") by adding their own "private meaning" ("gai"), which places philosophical meaning on a higher level than the very words of a text (*In Response*, VI, 204). All exegetes are guilty of "creating extratextual meaning" (*Explanations of Terms*, I, 495).

So the "interiority" of text is a public arena and to be approached by a private reader only in a public or normative manner. For this reason, Sorai's theory puts much emphasis on form, style, and rhetoric. His catch phrase, "kobunjigaku," given here as "philology of classics," indicates this emphasis. The phrase has been translated and interpreted variously. Mikiso Hane translates it as "study of old phrases and syntax," and Samuel Hideo Yamashita as "study of ancient literary styles," while Yoshikawa Kōjirō interprets bunji as stylized language or rhetoric.[29] The words "ko" ("old," "ancient," "classical") and "gaku" ("study," "learning") are simple enough, but Sorai utilizes multiple meanings—rather against his principle of allowing one meaning to a word—for the other two, "bun" being "sentence," "writing," as well as "decorated," or "sublime," and "ji" being "words," "phrases," as well as "arrangement of words." As a result, none of these interpretations is incorrect and none complete.

There are two focal points in his catch phrase: one is language itself, as opposed to moral implications, and the other is form—of facts, of language, and of text. What Sorai advocates is the study of words (or characters) themselves and the study of form through which to reach Matter, or the invented reality of a text. The act of reading is one of acquiring the text's content by way of its form. Reading, Sorai says, does not improve one's moral nature but helps one to acquire the text's fūga, or elevated beauty, which, in turn, affects one's actions (*In Response*, VI, 196-97). The term "fūga," in Sorai's terminology, refers not to any quality of beauty, such as elegance, but to the form of beauty, or the correct style, in which "facts" are formed, "techniques" applied and texts written, so that it is form through which all these elements are to be comprehended and acquired. Sorai often quotes Mencius on the question of form and content: "If someone wears Yao's clothes, says Yao's words, and acts Yao's actions, then, he is Yao" ("Letter to Kutsu Keizan").[30] Content is content, or "fact" becomes "fact," by virtue of the form it takes. Conversely, when there is form, content automatically enters like air into a container. The acqui-

[29] Maruyama, p. 76; Yamashita, "Nature and Artifice in the Writings of Ogyū Sorai (1666-1728)," a paper presented at the University Seminar in Neo-Confucian Studies, Columbia University, May 7, 1982, p. 6; and Yoshikawa, "Sorai Gakuan," p. 653.

[30] Yoshikawa Kōjirō et al., eds., *Ogyū Sorai*, p. 531.

sition of form normalizes and stabilizes the reader into a special kind of implied reader who speaks like the author-narrator and acts conceptually in the fashion of the text's content.

Imitation and repeated practice are chief methods of acquiring the proper form: "Learning is the act of making something one's own habit by practicing it and achieving dexterity" (*On the Era of Tranquility Policies [Taiheisaku]*, 1716, VI, 158). This method of "habituation" as Samuel Hideo Yamashita aptly calls it, aims at a natural and unconscious assimilation with the author and reality of text.[31] Habit, formed in quantitative and repeated reading and writing, seems to acquire an energy of its own which, in turn, accelerates further reading and writing, finally to penetrate, by the law of inertia, as it were, into the interiority, carrying the reader with it. Once the reader is in the interiority, the text's content is automatically transferred to the reader. Sorai often uses the terms, "to shift" ("utsuru"), "to come" ("kitaru"), and "to arrive" ("itaru") to describe this phenomenon. The acquisition of the text's form is described as "fūga shifting on to you" (*In Response*, VI, 196). And writing practices are taken to be purposeful: "so that skills will naturally shift to you" (ibid., VI, 203). The ultimate effect of reading is seen as the "coming of Matter":

> When one practices something for a long time and comes to retain it within himself, it is called the "coming of Matter." In the beginning of one's study, Matter is not yet one's own: it is as though Matter were somewhere else refusing to come over. At the accomplished stage of study, Matter becomes one's own: it is like Matter coming over from somewhere else to reach one. As this process requires no effort, it is called the "coming of Matter" (*Explanations of Terms*, I, 458).

Once the reader moves toward the text by way of reconstructing its form by acquired habit, the text approaches; and the transference of the text's reality is automatically and painlessly accomplished between text and reader.

[31] "Compasses and Carpenter's Squares: A Study of Itō Jinsai (1627-1705) and Ogyū Sorai (1666-1728)," a Ph.D. diss. (University of Michigan, 1981), p. 251.

Psychoanalysis postulates that the memory of a lost past is unconsciously recalled in acting out that past.[32] Sorai's theory of reading aims at recalling the memory of the ur-reality of human history, or what Jung would call the memory of the cultural past of the tribe, by forming a habit in which acting-out is automatic. Since the memory does not belong to an individual reader, its constituents are made accessible by the static meta-language of text. Sorai's theory is not merely Alice's conservatism pushed to the extreme but an artificial contraption for making language and reality fit each other precisely. In practice, however, Sorai does not necessarily follow his rules to the letter. His use of multiple meanings has been mentioned earlier. His alleged definitions are also trapped by the multiple nature of language: the formula "A is B" necessarily replaces the word "A" with the word "B," inevitably violating the singularity of the relationship between a word and its content. He is guilty of interpretation like everyone else. Thus, in practice, this theoretical Alice turns into Humpty Dumpty. This trick of Sorai's may indicate something inherent in the nature of language in actual practice. This, however, will be observed more clearly in the case of an unapologetic practitioner of Dumptyism, Hiraga Gennai. While Sorai, the theoretician, traces language to its conceptualized "source," Gennai, practitioner, witnesses it at its living "end." The width and muddiness of the river at the mouth is his reality. Gennai swims back and forth, largely crosswise, mixing by his strokes and splashes waters coming from a variety of origins. His question is not what language is or ought to have been but what it is like and what it can potentially do.

Gennai's general stance is no different from Sorai's: that of a public speaker and teacher. As he satirizes human nature and society by parodying scholarly and religious treatises, his fictional topics are large—the ways of learning and religions, the political system, the meaning of life. His vocabulary is highbrow—taken

[32] See Sigmund Freud on the subject of transference, especially as in James Trachey, tr. and ed., *An Outline of Psycho-Analysis* (New York and London: W. W. Norton, 1969), pp. 32-35.

from religion, scholarship, and literature—and his created world consists, not of private sentiments, but of objectified patterns of human behavior, categorically represented by professional, hierarchical, and regional types. Rather than diary, memoir, or other personal narration, he chooses seemingly objective means such as history (as in *Rootless Grass [Nenashigusa]*, Part I, 1763, Part II, 1769) and biography (as in *The Dashing Life of Shidōken [Fūryū Shidōken Den]*, 1763). Most frequently, he parodies the scholarly question-and-answer format either in the form of commentaries on topical news—the rumor about the drowning of a famous actor (*Rootless Grass*), the scandal about the love affair between a stage star and the widow of his colleague ("Comments on the Scandal" [*Tonda Uwasa no Hyō*], c. 1778), the sensational fame of a fart artist in town (*Treatise on the Art of Farting [Hōhiron]*, Part I, c. 1774, Part II, c. 1777), etc.—or in the form of responses to a student's questions—whether there could be a tree on which money grows, as in old folk songs ("Money Tree" [*Kane no Naru Ki*], 1780), or whether the rock-like formation then recently discovered could be a skull once belonging to a mythical mountain spirit (tengu), as popular belief claimed ("An Expert Opinion on the Tengu Skull" [*Tengu Sharekōbe Mekiki Engi*], 1777). Within these general frameworks, Gennai often uses: definitions and etymologies (for terms like "idiot" and "braggart"); debates (the pros and cons of homosexual and heterosexual practices, for example); or instructions (for instance, how to enlighten oneself out of the benighted Buddhist faith by visiting famous pleasure quarters). Although the intended effect is comedy and satire, these strategies themselves are identical with Sorai's. And, in spite of the twisted uses of words and logic that poke fun at serious histories and exegeses, his ultimate goal is the enlightenment of the ignorant public by correcting the errors of received opinion.

For example, in "Comments on the Scandal," Gennai questions the "scandalousness" of the affair by pointing out its public benefit—the fellow will keep the rest of the men of Edo safe from the danger of this particular femme fatale. The absurd perspective ridicules the larger, institutional core of society—in this case the narrow-minded neo-Confucian morality and the government's severe laws concerning sexual behavior, which give rise to standard and individual responses—with a "What scandalous behavior!" and so on. Thus Gennai's works are structured as treatises, like Sorai's, and written, like Sorai's, for polemical and pedagogical purposes. As with Sorai, the narrator is a teacher/disputant, and the implied reader is a group of students and opponents in dispute. This formal characteristic, not to be found in later authors of gesaku, the genre invented by Gennai, is inseparable from the way he uses languages.

For Gennai, literary writing is not a private, spontaneous act, as tradition would have it, but a public function that requires artifice:

> I might say that I, too, being weary of leisure, am at the ink slab all day, aimlessly recording this and that which happens to come to mind. But that would be a complete lie. This spell of rainy weather has prevented the manufacture of gold-painted leather products, an invention of mine which has exhausted my minuscule supply of ingenuity, leaving me with much leisure and no money ("Comments on the Scandal," p. 270).[33]

By quoting the famous opening line of the fourteenth-century classic, *An Essay on Idleness [Tsurezuregusa]*, and calling it a lie, Gennai denies the idea of literature as personal pastime. Writing is a commercial enterprise, regardless of the nature and amount of profit in such activity in his day, to replace his leather production during the rainy days. Like all commercial activities, it addresses itself to the public and requires "ingenuity" on the part of the participant. It is certainly "not a reflection of highbrow taste (fūga) nor of artistic whim (share)," as it is with Yoshida Kenkō, the author of *An Essay on Idleness*. Although Gennai never claims to have increased "the wealth of the nation" by means of creative writing, his work in that area seems to be regarded by him as similar in nature to his industrial and commercial enterprises. Inventive ideas and ingenious skills are paramount features of his writings as well as of his inventions and projects.

[33] The page numbers in parentheses after quotations from Gennai's works refer to those in Nakamura Yukihiko, ed., *Fūrai Sanjin Shū, Nihon Koten Bungaku Taikei*, vol. 55 (Iwanami Shoten, 1961).

As has been said, Gennai's writing is, to all appearance, no less public than Sorai's in nature and form. Like Sorai, Gennai demonstrates a strong sense of distinction between the public and private in human reality. Unlike Sorai, however, he distrusts the public aspect. Truth is the ugly and irrational human reality that is hidden behind official appearances. Life and the world consist of the front side ("omote") and the back ("ura"), and truth lies in the latter: "Priests nowadays, although officially [on the front side] wearing a countenance that reeks of incense, have fun in private with courtesans" (*Shidōken*, p. 43). Again:

> Not knowing that the New Year's pine tree is a milestone on our journey to death, people celebrate it as a symbol of felicitation. Not realizing that the New Year's redsnapper is nothing but the corpse of a fish, they relish it as something auspicious (*Rootless Grass*, Part II, p. 101).

The author's task is to "probe" ("ugatsu") for the hidden truth. For that purpose, the assumed correlation between form and content—a priest's piety or the symbolic meaning of New Year decorations and delicacies—must be denied. Truth is knowable and showable only when the ostensible meaning of the form is destroyed. Thus in *Rootless Grass*, for example, the medical profession represents the skill of killing, and the public institution of Hell is seen to follow the sexual drive of its ruler, Emma. The negative replaces the positive, and the private, the public.

If truth lurks on the back side of official appearance, anything that is contrary to the appearance, be it a word, an institution, or a profession, ought to be the true content of the label. Thus truth is falsehood, and a lie is the only means for expressing truth. The world, for Gennai, consists of liars:

> "Were there no lies in this world,
> How people's words would gladen us!"
>
> said a poet. Indeed, there are no more truthful courtesans than there are square eggs, as they say. Lies are all around us: Buddhism dubs them parables, military science calls them

> strategies. The world is full of flattery and toad-eating, and our social life consists of pleasantries and minced words. Lie, trick, falsehood, technique, deception, design, scheme, artifice. . . . Words may vary, but it is one and the same falsehood that smoothly wraps up the world. The only certain truth in our lives is that those who are born are bound to die (*Rootless Grass*, Part II, 101).[34]

This passage plays upon the question of truth and falsehood that was ever-present in the social and intellectual scenes of Gennai's time. On the social level, courtesans were largely considered as experts in amorous techniques and tricks (terentekuda) or professional lies, rarely possessing sincerity (jitsu), and connoisseurship in pleasure was divided between those who savoured skills and those who cherished feelings.

In intellectual theory and literary criticism, the words "kyo" and "jitsu" were used to contrast falsehood and truth, or fiction and fact. Literary artifice and imagination were considered to be kyo, while facts and factual realism were considered jitsu. The dominant concepts of the time were Chikamatsu Monzaemon's definition of theatrical art as occupying the border between kyo and jitsu and Itō Jinsai's categorization of sentiment or emotion-laden narration as kyo and event or objective description as jitsu.[35] Gennai's view is that art lies in the reversal of truth and falsehood, rather than in the border of the two or in a balance between the two. He explains the art of fiction-writing in the following manner:

[34] The poem quoted by Gennai is an anonymous one collected in the 4th "Love Poems" section of the *Kokinshū* (14: 712). By playing on the ambiguity of the words, "yo" (the world, life, love relationship) and "hito" (a person, people, others, a lover, my lover), the poem conveys a lover's indirect complaint as well as making a general statement. The translation in this essay emphasizes the general statement. An alternative rendition, with emphasis on the amorous implications, may be:

> If there were no lie between lovers
> How your words would delight me!

[35] See Nakamura Yukihiko, "Kyojitsu Himakuron no Saikentō," in his *Kinsei Bungei Shichōkō* (Iwanami Shoten, 1975), pp. 128-54.

"To call a needle a pole is a plain lie, and to use a pole as a pole is an artless truth, but to take a chopstick and use it as a pole is truth in a lie."[36]

If all human beings are liars, and reality is a pack of lies, as the earlier quotation suggests, art, as well as philosophy and religion, must represent human nature and reality in lies, or tell the truth of the lies of reality in the form of lies. Hence Gennai refers to great achievements in cultural history as "the Buddha's fraudulence, Lao-tse's and Chuang-tse's balderdash, and Lady Murasaki's zillion lies" (Preface to *Rootless Grass*, Part I, p. 37). This acknowledgment, however, is two-faced. On the one hand religion, philosophy, and literature, represented by these masters, artfully tell "truth in a lie," but on the other, their works, being respectable classics, are in the suspect domain of the public, or the "front side" of reality, so that truth is to be sought on the "back side" of it. Hence truth and lie become interchangeable—"a truth in a lie" may turn into "a lie in truth." Whatever ultimate truth there may be will reveal itself involuntarily by way of double or multiple negatives.

On this view, writing and reading become complex and suspicious acts like a commercial negotiation between a cunning seller and a thrifty buyer with the merchandise out of sight and perhaps unsuitably wrapped. The seller keeps the merchandise wrapped in order to make the sales pitch effective and the buyer's expectation high. The buyer accepts this because it is the only accepted method of negotiation, and because it may be possible to get more than the seller believes is offered in a moment of forgetting the precise object in question. The seller tells lies and speaks in riddles and double negatives, while the buyer responds in guesses. When wild imagination and association are left loose in their verbal exchange, the merchandise may be forgotten by both of them, reducing the negotiation to sheer nonsense. The only redeeming factor in this strange situation is that both the seller and the buyer are very clever and know each other's ways. The seller assumes that the

[36] Ōta Nan'yō, ed., *Ichiwa Ichigen*, Book 45, *Shokusanjin Zenshū*, 5 (Yoshikawa Kōbunkan, 1908), 439.

buyer, occasionally, reads through lies and riddles and the buyer assumes there is a certain pattern in the confusing remarks made by the other. Their mutual trust, as well as the cunning of each, prevents merchandise from being neglected entirely, so that the negotiation is kept going back and forth between sense and nonsense. Gennai's narrator is a Rabelaisian one, who alternates between claiming some hidden meaning and higher intentions and denying all such claims. The reader negotiates with the narrator, both for the value of possible meaning and for the sheer pleasure of verbal negotiation.

While maintaining, like Sorai, the role of champion of enlightenment, Gennai seeks to "probe" into the lie of lies by destroying the public values that champions are expected to uphold. Soraiesque strategies of argument are employed for destroying the reliability of written texts and the singularity of meaning, just in case there are such things, by mixing incongruous words, meanings, and matters. Gennai's definitions are not used to restrict meaning but to multiply it. The formula is often the reverse of that in Sorai's dictionaries: the familiar expression is defined by an official or scholarly one, in the fashion of a dictionary of vulgar terms. It is the scholar who needs to be enlightened in the common language, or in the reality on the "back side." The expression, "to raise one's own bean paste" ("miso o ageru"), equivalent of "to toot one's own horn," is defined as "a colloquialism of Eastern parts meaning vainglory" (Preface to *Rootless Grass*, Part II, p. 99). By the use of words of Chinese origin—"jiman" ("vainglory"), "tōto" ("Eastern Capital"), and "zokugen" ("colloquialism")—and by the reference to Edo as the "Eastern Capital," the definition shows a greater need of definition than the expression it purports to define. The definition is followed, in the tradition of scholarly commentaries, by an analysis of the origin of the expression and a listing of examples of its use. This passage is an elaborate parody of scholarly commentaries: a great variety of expressions that refer to bean paste are put to actual use, and words related to bean paste—salt, beans, fermentation, soup, odor, etc.—are woven, in puns, into the history of human culture and language and Gennai's place in it. Vainglory is explained in terms of bean paste, and vice versa, all matters high and low are discussed as vainglory and in bean-paste language, so that the entire world and its history become a mass of ill-smelling brown substance that is vainglory. The dictionary à la Gennai is a counter-dictionary stretching words to all possible meanings and at the same time erasing distinctions between words and between meanings. One becomes many and different becomes the same.

A similar principle operates in Gennai's catalogues. As a literary device, listing goes back to ancient poetry. Edo literature, particularly, shows a strong inclination toward enumeration as is evident in the abundance of examples of pastiche and parody of Sei Shōnagon's aesthetic catalogues in her *Pillow Book (Makura no Sōshi)* (late tenth or early eleventh century). Gennai's use of the device, however, also derives from his own scientific habits. As noted by Haga Tōru, who calls Gennai's gesaku work "The Catalogue of Humanity" ("*Jinrui Hinshitsu*"), after the title of Gennai's scientific catalogue, *Catalogue of Materials (Butsurui Hinshitsu)*, Gennai presents human nature and reality categorically, and his narrative often takes the form of lists.[37] The finical precision and distinction of his botanical and mineralogical catalogues are ostentatiously present in these lists of different human types and behaviors. At the same time, the mechanical and egalitarian character of scientific enumeration is put to full use, so that unequal levels and incongruous categories are equated with one another. A summer festival at the Sumida River in Edo is described in a catalogue of the attire and behavior of people who gather to watch fireworks, where all types, professions, and classes are enumerated mechanically, therefore equitably, so as to become a general "cloud of dust" (*Rootless Grass*, Part I, pp. 78-79). A list of synonyms of the word "idiot" ("baka") is followed, in the manner of the bean-paste definition mentioned above, by a narrative demonstrating uses of these terms, except for the absence of puns, as though to indicate a definitive singularity in the idiocy represented by all the terms. Such words as "softhead" ("untsuku"), "nincompoop" ("berabō"), and "dupe" ("tawake") adorn the narrative of

[37] *Hiraga Gennai, Asahi Hyōden Sen*, 23 (Asahi Shimbunsha, 1981), 213.

the circumstances that inspired the composition of this biography: the sensational popularity of Shidōken as a comic lecturer, and the enthusiasm of the publisher about a book on the subject. Here the acts of narrating, listening, writing, publishing, and reading are ostensibly distinguished by the words modifying them; and, since the words are synonyms, all are impartially equated as variations of idiocy (Preface to the *Dashing Life of Shidōken*, p. 157).

Gennai's lists are Rabelaisian, long and exuberant, indulging both author and reader in the joy of enumeration. As in Rabelais, in the case of a lawyer's bag and a penitent's hood in the Gargantuan catalogue of things with which to wipe one's bottom (*Gargantua and Pantagruel*, Book I, Chap. 13), so Gennai nonchalantly tosses unexpected items into the list. Even when there is a detectable move from the ordinary to the absurd, directing the reader from a mundane narrative to satire, the list is too elaborate and fast-moving for a reader to know just where absurdity begins.

Gennai's lists fall into three types. The first offers lists of synonyms—as in the case of the word "idiot" discussed above. The second consists of inventories of things observed—as in the one of people who gather to watch fireworks cited above. The third involves reasons in debates—as in, for example, those of harms and benefits of homosexual love (*Rootless Grass*, Part II, pp. 124-37). Each list consists of a medley of varied vocabulary, ideography, meanings, and sounds. An audio-visual rhythm is created by the repetitions and variations of syntactical patterns and grammatical units as well as the poetic 5-7 and 7-5-syllable schemes and the mechanical beat of enumeration. This flow is what makes the reader unwittingly accept, or willingly suspend—until too late—his disbelief in the incongruous association of the items and agree upon reflection with satirical implications of that incongruity.

There is, therefore, a conspiracy between the author and language to trick the reader into accepting the hidden truth, or a conspiracy among all three to trick truth into revealing itself. But truth here, even when revealed, is not reducible to a logical statement. Whatever sense there might be in the text, that sense is at constant risk of erasure by the mechanical beat and sonorous sound of Gennai's prose. In this way, Gennai's text is a battle between words and sounds, a seesaw game between sense and nonsense in which the author and the reader collaborate in spasms, inscribing and erasing sense. "Whatever is followable" is, indeed, "on the way to being aceptable," as Kermode states.[38] But the followability here lies not so much in the capacity of language to say as in its ability to do, and what is accepted includes not only what the text says but what it does.

Like all parodists, Gennai mixes styles. What is called "Hiragaburi," or "Hiraga style," consists of assortments of languages (Chinese and Japanese, with occasional uses of Korean, Sanskrit, and Dutch in phrases); kinds of diction (scholarly, classical, poetic, colloquial, etc.); dialects (regional, hierarchical, as well as occupational), and literary styles (classical tale, essay, jōruri play style, etc.). The most dominant, however, is the kambun yomikudashi (Chinese read in Japanese), a style in which actual or imagined Chinese sentences are transposed into Japanese. Chinese characters are employed, often accompanied by use of a Japanese syllabary on the side to denote pronunciation and to provide grammatical accessories. It is a written form of wakun recitation: sentences are written out to be recited as they are, instead of guiding the reader back and forth by syntactical notations along Chinese sentences. An elevated style is maintained by a conventional presupposition of an original Chinese text. Gennai also seems to assume, conventionally, a verbal recitation, thereby creating an informal and conversational tone. The presence of Chinese characters adds to the formal tone, and the Japanese syllabary to the informal aspect.[39] Much of the body of official and scholarly writing of the Edo period was in this style. For scholars this style was an appropriate vehicle for addressing friends informally and yet in a dignified fashion or for making philosophical matters accessible to students. Gennai

[38] Kermode, p. 118.

[39] [In what precedes, the author refers to Gennai's extraordinary, witty juxtapositions of "Chinese" and "Japanese" readings—often at radical variance—effected by various graphic means. And she later comments on puns as well as other means that may yield bizarrely different meanings. Such strains on characters and sounds often make Edo titles exasperatingly difficult to translate. Those who read Japanese will find examples later in the chapter.—Ed.]

makes comical and satirical use of the duality of the style—the formal vs. informal, the high vs. low, the classical vs. modern. In particular, Gennai's discovery of the separation between writtenness and spokenness in the kambun yomikudashi style constitutes the essential feature of his fictional writing.

Because Gennai's prefaces chiefly parody those of scholarly treatises and follow classical Chinese rhetoric closely, the duality of his prose is more conspicuous there than in his narrative descriptions. A typical instance goes as follows:

> There are fools who do not neglect to gulp down their daily dose of ginseng just as they are about to wring their own necks, but there are those who devour blowfish stew and live to a ripe old age. If some serving girls get themselves bastards from a single fling, there are lackeys who keep their noses intact through countless bouts with the cheapest whores. Is it not—if I may use big words—all the will of Heaven? (*Treatise on the Art of Farting*, p. 229)[40]

In the original, this passage is a remarkably correct example of classical Chinese parallel prose. Each of the first two sentences consists of two thesis-antithesis subunits, and the last sentence is the synthesis. The taking of ginseng, the magical health aid, and suicide by hanging oppose each other, while eating blowfish stew, the deadly poisonous delicacy, and living a long life oppose each other. And the first unit about the man who takes care of his health and kills himself is diametrically opposed to the second unit about the man who lives long in spite of eating blowfish stew. The nouns, "ginseng" and "blowfish stew," the verbs "to gulp" and "to devour," the verbs, "to wring the neck" and "to live long," and nouns "fool" and "man" (translated as "those"), are paired, either in contrast or in parallel, to create a tight connection between the two clauses that constitute the first sentence. The parallel between the words "fool" and "man" is an irony typical of Gennai. Since the two words in the matching syntactical positions are not ob-

[40] Translation by William F. Sibley, entitled, "On Farting," unpublished, p. 1. The last sentence has been modified by me.

viously opposed in meaning, they must be, by rule, synonymous with each other. The reader makes the equation: fool = man, or man = fool, arriving at the generalization that all men are fools, one of Gennai's most frequently expressed opinions.

The second sentence functions in the same manner, contrasting the serving girl's misfortune with the good fortune of the whoremonger, each being a case of a counter-logical operation of destiny. Destiny is represented by two hidden actors, lurking in the "back side" of the surface phenomena: masters who impregnate their serving girls and whores who inflict diseases upon their customers. The parallel structure puts the two into the same category of ill fortunes, so that respectable masters become the same sort of public menace as whores are thought to be by sober citizens. The final sentence begins with an apology in colloquial Japanese, "though it may sound bombastic," and suddenly soars to the height of classical diction in the latter half, "Ah, is it not the will of Heaven?" The latter part consists of six Chinese characters that should be read, according to Gennai's phonetic transcriptions, not in a Japanese equivalent but in Chinese readings (kan'on): this play of Japanese and Chinese shows us what an English translation cannot, that there are two parts in opposition to each other: one Japanese and colloquial and the other Chinese and formal.

In these three sentences, while the Chinese characters, Chinese sounds, and the Chinese rhetorical structure create a dignity reminiscent of classical philosophy and history, a very casual tone is set by the Japanese sound and syntax as well as by the depiction of contemporary Japanese life. These Hiraga-buri sentences create absurdity and achieve satire by pulling apart, as far as possible, word and meaning, written language and spoken language, and form and content. In the process, however, the sentences also pull together words in different categories, separate language and forms, and realities of incompatible sorts. These three sentences say, if anything, that life is death and death life, masters are whores and whores masters, human reality is low and absurd but, at the same time, the lowness itself is dignity. Ultimately, sameness is differences and difference sameness. Here is the original:

人参(ニンジン)呑で縊る(クビクク)癡漢(タハケ)あれば、河豚汁(フグジル)喰(ク)ふて長寿(ナガイキ)する男もあり。一度で父(テテ)なし子孕(リラ)む下女あれば、毎晩夜鷹(マイバンヨタカ)買ふて鼻(ハナ)の無事なる奴(ヤツコ)あり、大そふなれど嗚呼(アア)天(テン)歟(カ)命(メイ)歟。

The Hiraga-buri narrator has two voices—that of a classical scholar and that of a gossipy little man in the neighborhood. The two speak of reality in ways incongruous with each other, sometimes simultaneously and other times in turns, as described. They never speak in unison, but occasionally the two voices become a harmonious duet. The following is Gennai's metaphorical representation, in normal reading of the characters, of the world's indifference to his numerous talents:

数説(なんぼくど)いても戸に(といたに)激する(ごろつく)菽(まめ)焉(よ)。

That is,

"Shibashiba toite mo to ni gekisuru shuku."

With Gennai's phonetic guidelines, we read it, "Nanbo kudoite mo toita ni gorotsuku mame yo." (Preface to "The Secret History of a Withered Dick" [*Naemara In'itsu Den*], c. 1768, p. 259.) The official text says," Although I repeatedly lecture to persuade, I am (ignored) like beans hitting the door." "Shibashiba" represents the classical wakun reading of the Chinese expression meaning "frequently." "Toite" is an inflected form of the verb, "toku," to lecture or to explain, as with an ancient Chinese scholar to a ruler. "Gekisuru," to act violently, and "shuku," beans, are terms common, respectively, in classical Chinese histories and poetry. A classical Chinese end-word is attached, to be taken silently, according to the wakun system. The phonetic reading represents a colloquial translation of this Chinese-style sentence. Each word, except for the equivalents of prepositions, is put into a colloquial

Japanese equivalent, with the end-word translated as "yo," or "I tell you." But the phonetic readings do not necessarily correspond with the normal Japanese readings of these words. The word "toku" turns into "kudoku," to make love verbally, and "gekisuru" into "gorotsuku," to make a rattling noise, as well as to hang around aimlessly. The door is changed to "toita," door-board, a word normally associated with casually constructed doors of tool sheds or back entrances. This vocal reading, however, is an almost straight quotation from a popular song of the time:

> Nanbo kudoite mo toita ni mame yo;
> Isso anna yatsu wa shineba yoi.
>
> (All my sweet-talk is nothing but beans
> against a doorplank;
> Such a wench should be dead!)

Although Gennai's line appears to be a classical text with erroneous Japanese reading, it is, in fact, a colloquial song accompanied by a classical Chinese translation. In this parody of the wakun system, the visual and vocal readings provide two separate images of Gennai: one of an unappreciated genius whose views are not accepted by those in power, and another of an unattractive and perhaps penniless man who hangs around noisily at a woman's back door. The first image had been prominent in classical Chinese literature since Ch'ü Yüan, and the latter is a familiar one in the contemporary Edo life with its emphasis on the glory of the pleasure quarters. Thus the sentence reads in two separate ways, contrasting and at the same time equating the official cause with the private one of Gennai's frustration, as well as the conventional sublime culture with the popular one throughout human history. The separation between Chinese and Japanese and the distance between the writtenness and spokenness of language are used to signify two meanings simultaneously. And the simultaneity equates the two separate levels of actions: the heroic or public tragedy of a historical genius and the trivial and private predicament of an unpopular man.

Gennai's parody of the kambun yomikudashi style presupposes

that a text is not always read in the way it is intended to be read. It assumes interpretation in the act of reading. In the sentence discussed above, the scholarly text gives an official statement, or reality on the "front side," while the debased and faulty vocalization—typically by an uneducated Edoite—reveals, quite unwittingly, the other side of reality. Thus this sentence enacts the separation between the acts of writing and reading, indicating that signification takes place in the superimposition of what the text may be intended to say and how the reader interprets it. In contrast to Sorai's belief in reading without interpretation, Gennai invests meaning in the fusion of static text and dynamic reading, or what Sorai would call "private interpretation." The schema is operative not only on the linguistic level but also on the conceptual one, extending beyond specific sentences. "The Secret History of a Withered Dick," for example, is a cultural history of China and Japan, describing its major events in sexual terms. Contemporary vulgarisms in reference to sexual organs are transliterated in Chinese characters of religious and scholarly nature while highbrow terms are sometimes accompanied by blasphemous and debasing readings. And the whole of the work is unified by the general image of the world being populated by nothing but male and female sexual organs. The excellence of cultural achievements is represented by phalli not finding appreciation in the form of welcoming receptacles. Linguistic and conceptual superimpositions erase geographical, historical, and other categorical distances so that the high and public achievements are pulled down to the level of the low and private acts of sex, while sexuality is elevated to the level of philosophy and religion and expanded to a historical, universal dimension.

In more extensive works, the superimposition of reverse upon obverse controls the narrative structure in a more complex manner. *Rootless Grass* depicts the commotion in Hell because of its ruler's infatuation with Kikunojō, a female impersonator of the kabuki stage. The story involves this world as Hell's spies are dispatched to investigate the actor's surroundings, and Emma, the infernal ruler, is led by passion to visit the world himself. The two worlds represent the obverse and reverse of reality: life and death, reality and hearsay. Contemporary life in Edo is plausibly described, while Hell is represented as oral tradition has long established it, down to a detailing of methods of punishment for sinners. This world is seen as "truth," and Hell as "lie." However, Hell is made to resemble this world: the problems of overpopulation and lack of labor are intense and are solved by land development, automation of penal methods, and mass-production of necessary materials for punishments. The government system and the corruption of officials and landlords recall the Japan of the Tanuma Era. This world is represented as a concrete world of private citizens in Edo, which is nothing but an extension of Hell's domain, much resembling neighborhoods in Hell. In this sense, this world and Hell are equated. In fact, obverse and reverse are interchanged as Hell becomes the official and public system, while this world becomes a private sector of that system.

It is on the private side that true human sentiments reveal themselves. The sincere love between Kikunojō and his assassin is contrasted with Emma's selfish infatuation with the actor and his institutionalized pursuit of him. The love scene of Kikunojō and the assassin is described in the style of Heian courtly romance, in keeping with the emotional nature of the scene, or with kyo in Itō Jinsai's terminology. But kyo, by Gennai's definition—as "lie"—also appears in the unreality of the two characters involved: Kikunojō is an actor and the assassin is a kappa, a mystical primate, disguised as a young man. "Truth" is thus told in a "lie," or the reverse, while Emma and his world, or the obverse, become only ostensibly "true," much as institutions—the Tokugawa government, the feudal system, religion, scholarship—were ostensibly honored as valid during the Edo period.

What these various characters represent, or whether they represent, are also complex questions. Names of actual persons living during Gennai's time are used, and to that extent these characters are officially "true." But those are all actors, and they behave in the narrative as they would on stage, so that they represent fiction, or "lies." Emma is a deity, therefore unreal, but he may reveal, on the "back side," Mizoguchi Naonori, a feudal lord who acquired notoriety by his infatuation with the actual Kikunojō. On the other hand, Mizoguchi Naonori may be the façade of a shōgun who sits at the top of the Tokugawa hierarchy. Hell is this world, or more specifically, Edo Japan. The "back side" reveals that Japan under the Tokugawa rule is Hell. But even this message is obscured by the jolly tone of the text and obstructed by the absurdity of the context. The more the reader probes, the more frequently the view changes, back and forth between obverse and reverse, truth and falsehood, public and private. The text is wide open to interpretation, so that meaning is repeatedly inscribed and erased. The exhilarating impression made by Gennai's writings derives not only from grandiosity of vocabulary or topics but from suggestions of multiple meanings that stimulate the reader to exercise a power and freedom of interpretation. The suggestions are not made by the author's manipulation of language alone: language itself has the power of such suggestion, since a word, according to Gennai, is already open to interpretation. Inoue Hisashi (1934-), who has revived Gennai-like gesaku in modern fiction, identifies the essence of gesaku composition as "the awareness that one is using language and perhaps that one is also being used by it."[41] This applies to the reading of gesaku as well. Both reading and writing gesaku involve a conscious exercise of this awareness of the relationship between such acts and language.

In contrast to Sorai's fūga, what is transferred from Gennai's text to the reader is fūryū, contemporary reality described in a contemporary language. At this time, the term "fūryū" generally referred to good taste or stylishness according to contemporary standards. In comic literature, the term signified comic and absurd aspects of modern life. Gennai uses the term in both senses. The title, *The Dashing [Fūryū] Life of Shidōken*, implies that this is a comic biography of someone whose life was comic as well as that this is a stylishly written biography of a man of fashion. The writing and the life it describes are both to be taken simultaneously as absurd nonsense and normative models. Gennai the rebel and Gennai the teacher are both present in his use of the term. Thus

[41] "Gesaku Tōzai," a dialogue with Takahashi Yasunari, *Kokubungaku: Kaishaku to Kanshō*, 44 (1979), 12.

Gennai's fūryū is not merely the reverse of Sorai's fūga, ramified and unfollowable reality as opposed to correct and normalized reality, but it also contains the reverse of that reverse as well—something tenable but hidden behind the unfollowability of reality. While Sorai's fūga is based on congruous connectedness of form with content, Gennai's fūryū assumes a variable connectedness between the two, such that a congruous connection is only expected to occur accidentally.

The Two Alternatives to Linguistic Crisis

As with Sorai's philological thought, Gennai's writing is transcultural and interlingual. The communicable yet fallacious nature of translation is part of the basis for the duality of Gennai's style. As a scholar, however, Gennai did not devote himself to serious translation. Translation from Dutch probably was the only field of new studies of his time where Gennai did not make a pioneering contribution. When *Kaitai Shinsho* (1774), a Japanese translation of a Dutch book of anatomy commonly known as *Anatomische Tabellen* (1734), was completed to mark the first achievement in this area, Gennai regretted this lack in his scholarly career:

むき過ぎてあんに相違の餅の皮
名は千歳のかちんなる身を

Mukisugite an ni sōi no mochi no kawa
Na wa senzai no kachin naru mi o.[42]

Or,

Eager to peel off the dough, I found unexpected filling;
The dough itself could have been the glory of ages.

Like all translations, this English version represents only a part of what the original poem says in the maze of wordplay. Haga

[42] *Ichiwa Ichigen*, Book 2, in *Shokusanjin Zenshū*, 4 (1965), 56-57.

Tōru's interpretation is that Gennai was "anxious to grasp the content of Dutch books, but, against his expectations, the language was too hard to handle; so he ended by not reaching the content, thereby failing to leave his name to posterity."[43] There are several other ways of paraphrasing this poem. Haga's is particularly interesting because his interpretation of the dough and filling of a rice cake as language and content allows the poem to illustrate the status of language in Gennai's fiction. In the first line, "an ni sōi no" is an idiomatic expression meaning "against expectations," but "an" (speculation) is a homonym of "an" (bean filling), so that the phrase also means "different from filling." In the second line, "senzai" (one thousand years, eternity) recalls "zenzai" (sweet bean dish), and "kachin" (rice cake) recalls "kachi" (victory). "Na" signifies both name and fame, and "mi" (self, person) is homonymous with "mi" (the solid content in a soup). Hence the second line is to be read in two ways:

1. (The dough) could have borne the name of "rice cake," content of a zenzai dish.
2. I could have had the fame of being the one whose victory is eternal.

Full explanation (if that is possible) involves the contrasting images of a filled rice cake and zenzai. In the former, thick red bean paste is wrapped in rice dough, the bean filling being the most attractive part or the main point of eating a filled rice cake. In the latter dish, according to Edo custom, sweet cooked red beans are poured over rice cakes, the cake part being the essence of the dish. By alluding to zenzai, the poem refers to the "back side" of what is conventionally recognized as a filled rice cake, thereby demonstrating how the outer form and the inside content are interchangeable.[44] Hence the poem's message may be that "One

[43] *Hiraga Gennai*, p. 389.

[44] Elsewhere, Gennai uses a similar metaphor of a rice cake filled with red beans and a red bean cake with rice filling to illustrate the relationship between recognition and talent: talent is either apparent or hidden but recognized only when it is apparent. In this case, too, he plays upon the interchangeability of the appearance and content. ("Treatise on the Art of Farting," Part II, p. 251.)

seeks too eagerly to penetrate language to grasp the content, but content without its language may prove not worth the trouble; put words in a different context, they will become content, and what appeared to be content will prove to be nothing but a context for words." If meaning lurks in the "back side" of a word, a word hides behind meaning. "Reality" keeps popping up either as "content" or as "language." Thus language and meaning constitute a typically Gennai-esque pair like those of truth and lie and of public and private. Each such pair consists of a contrasting yet interchangeable "front side" and "back side," in a twisted connection like the two sides of a Mobius strip.

Ogyū Sorai's concept of the relationship between language and meaning may be compared in terms similar to a perfect rice cake that has been chosen and isolated from all the other rice cakes that have ever existed. The materials are authentic, and the shape, flavor, and color as they should be. The form faithfully signifies its content, so that the cake is eaten in good faith, as a whole. Eating this cake means tasting all possible cakes, because the normative essence of all cakes exists in this one. Gennai's practice, on the other hand, resembles a whimsical rice cake that is to be eaten playfully or suspiciously. The dough and the filling may be incongruously combined, to be eaten separately, or combined differently to be eaten as a new delicacy. Between Sorai and Gennai, the essential difference lies in the conception of the relationship between language and meaning. This is the basis for their diametrically opposed attitudes in all the matters illustrated here. Sorai restores the authentic definition by elimination. Gennnai destroys it by expansion. While Sorai goes back to the "source" for authenticity, Gennai turns to the future by way of showing possibilities. If Sorai inspired trust in the act of reading, Gennai inspires distrust. The theoretician and the artist represent the two opposite responses to the interpretability of text: Sorai seeks to restore the authentic, but lost, core of a text by eliminating interpretation, while Gennai seeks to nurture the latency of the text by opening it to interpretation.[45] Sorai moves toward singularity,

[45] See Frank Kermode, "Secrets and Narrative Sequence," in W.J.T. Mitchell, ed., *On Narrative* (Chicago: University of Chicago Press, 1980), p. 82.

simplicity, and clarity, while Gennai is inclined to multiplicity, complexity, and distortion.

There are facile explanations for the differences. Conceptual theories are inclined to normative simplicity and clarity, whereas art thrives on multiplicity and distortion; or, Sorai reflects the ethical righteousness and faith of the time of the Kyōhō Reforms while Gennai represents the free and at the same time uneasy atmosphere of the Tanuma Era. Essentially, however, the differences derive from the fact that one speaks about language while the other speaks it.

For all their differences, however, what is striking is the shared spirit of the two: they are both rebellious student-teachers of language. Sorai emerged in Edo as *l'enfant terrible* of Confucian studies, having learned classical Chinese not in any established school but in isolation during his father's exile. The language Gennai mastered was the colloquial Edo dialect: although born and raised in far off Sanuki, he demonstrated his mastery of Edo language in *Rootless Grass*, Part I, six years after his arrival in the city. The regularity, definiteness, and brevity inherent in classical Chinese may explain these features in Sorai's concept of language, and the varied and fluid nature of contemporary Edo language may account for Gennai's demonstrations of the multiplicity and mutability of language and reality. What is more important, however, is the fact that in each case the awareness of the nature of language is based on independent study of a foreign language. By comparing classical Chinese with contemporary Japanese, or by comparing the new Edo dialect with the established scholarly language, each discovered the hitherto hidden aspects in the nature of language in general: the distinction between form and content, the separation between spokenness and writtenness, and the dynamics of language in the acts of writing and reading.

Sorai's conceptualized Chinese and Gennai's Hiraga-buri are revolutionary languages created on the basis of this discovery. Sorai's theory of kobunjigaku and his concept of fūga teach not only that text is followable and reality knowable but also that language has, in its nature, something that inspires and facilitates an endless succession of interpretations that, in turn, inspire a desire in the user of language for followability and knowability. Gennai's writing style and his fūryū enact the variability of reality and fluidity of language, thereby teaching the reader to experience the way in which one is irresistibly led into the complexity of text, thereby to discover the eternally redescribable nature of reality and the eternally reinterpretable nature of language. In the face of the disturbing crisis of language that they encountered and exploited, the two teachers offer comfort with differing emphases: Sorai stresses the satisfaction of being aware of the possibility of the ultimate comprehension beyond all possible interpretations, and Gennai stresses the pleasure of the process of eternal reinterpretation. Their teachings represent the two sides of the same structure: the true if double nature of language as it reveals itself in a state of crisis.

THE AUTHORS AND TRANSLATORS

The Authors

Sumie Jones is assistant professor of Comparative Literature and East Asian Languages and Cultures at Indiana University. Her major scholarly interests include eighteenth-century East-West comparative literature, literature and the visual arts, literature and film, and Tokugawa (Edo) literature. She was educated in Japan and the United States, receiving her Ph.D. from the University of Washington for her thesis, "Comic Fiction in Japan During the Later Edo Period." She has published chapters or articles on Natsume Sōseki, Eugene O'Neill, and Tanizaki Junichirō. She has participated in numerous conferences and seminars and has received various grants and appointments, including a Bunting Fellowship at Radcliffe College in 1982-1983. As co-organizer of an international conference (the first ever held on the subject), "The World of Genji: Perspectives on the *Genji Monogatari*," at Indiana University in August 1982, she received an award from the Council for the Advancement and Support of Education. She is completing a study of later Edo fiction.

Konishi Jin'ichi is Professor Emeritus of Tsukuba University, where he retired as academic vice president. He is a Doctor of Letters. His very numerous publications include a study of a Heian collection of songs, *Ryōjin Hishō Kō* (1941); an edition and commentary on a major treatise by the founder of Shingon Buddhism in Japan and also a major poet in Chinese, Kūkai, *Bunkyō Hifuron Kō* (1949-1953); a study of nō treatises, *Nōgakuron Kenkyū* (1961); a biography of the most famous renga poet, along with an account of renga canons and commentary, *Sōgi* (1967); and an annotated edition of one of the great poetry matches, *Shinkō Roppyakuban Utaawase* (1976). He is presently writing the fourth volume of his *History of Japanese Literature* (*Nihon Bungeishi*; first volume in English published by Princeton University Press, 1984; second volume in press). He has held numerous positions in the United States. These include appointments as visiting professor to Stanford University (1957-1958); senior specialist at the East-West Center, the University of Hawaii (1967); Visiting Scholar at Princeton University (1980); and member of the Council of Scholars at the Library of Congress (1982 and 1983). He won the Japan Academy Prize for literature (1951) at the unusually young age for a humanist of thirty-six; and at present he is the sole Japanese who is Honorary Member of the Modern Language Association of America.

MEZAKI Tokue is a professor of cultural history of early and medieval Japan, teaching at the University of the Sacred Heart, Tokyo. He is a Doctor of Letters. His books include one on itinerancy, *Hyōhaku—Nihon Shisōshi no Teiryū* (1965); a biography of a major Heian poet and critic, *Ki no Tsurayuki* (1961); a treatise on Heian culture, *Heian Bunkashiron* (1968); and a study of the priest and poet Saigyō, *Saigyō no Shisōshiteki Kenkyū* (1978). In recognition of the last book, he won in 1979, the first year the award was granted, the Kadokawa Academic Prize Honoring Minamoto Yoshi (Kadokawa Minamoto Yoshi Kinen Gakujutsushō). Readers of his chapter will see reflected in it the interest he finds in considering together literature and history, belief and art.

NAKANISHI Susumu is Professor of Japanese Literature at Tsukuba University. His interests center chiefly on early Japanese literature, thought, and history. He has sought to obtain the interest of the Japanese public in its earlier literature by various television and radio appearances. He has visited the United States several times, including teaching at Princeton University and lecturing elsewhere. He has written many books, some very popular, others highly learned. Many center on the great early collection of Japanese poetry, the *Man'yōshū*, and its principal poets. Some of these include a comparative study of that collection, *Man'yōshū Hikaku Bungakuteki Kenkyū* (1963); a detailed study of the collection in historical terms, *Man'yō Shi no Kenkyū* (1968); and studies of two principal poets of that collection, *Kakinomoto Hitomaro* (1968);

and *Yamanoe Okura* (1973). Some of his books have ranged over Japanese literature, dealing with specific topics; for example, so-called madness, *Kyō no Seishinshi* (1978); and the images of snow, moon and flowers, *Setsugetsuka* (1980). He won the Yomiuri Newspaper Literary Prize in 1963 and the Japan Academy Prize in literature in 1970.

NOGUCHI Takehiko is Associate Professor of Japanese literature in the faculty of letters at Kobe University. He was educated at Waseda University and at the University of Tokyo. He has written, apart from his novels, a number of critical and historical books. They include studies of Mishima Yukio (1968), of Ishikawa Jun (1969), of Ōe Kenzaburō (1971), and of Tanizaki Junichirō (1973). He has written also on Edo writers. These books include as subjects poetry and truth in Edo literature (1971), the historian Rai San'yō (1974), the Confucianist and historian Tokugawa Mitsukuni (1976), historians of the Edo period (1979), and the idea of evil in Edo literature (1980). He has also written a book about the language of prose narrative fiction from the Edo period to modern writers (1980). His writings have earned him three awards: the University of Tokyo May Festival Prize (1967), the Kamei Katsuichirō Prize (1973), and the Academic Award from the Suntory Foundation (1980). He has held visiting positions at three North American universities: Harvard (1970-1972), Princeton (1975-1976), and British Columbia (1982-1983).

Makoto UEDA is Professor of Japanese and Comparative Literature at Stanford University. His interests include literary theory, East-West literary relations, Japanese poetry, and modern Japanese literature in its various kinds. These subjects are reflected in his various books, which include: *Literary and Art Theories in Japan* (1967); *Matsuo Bashō* (1970, 1982), a number of books in Japanese, among which is an annotated study of Japanese critical pronouncements, *Nihon no Bungaku Riron* (1975); and studies of the literary ideas of modern Japanese writers of prose fiction and of poetry—*Modern Japanese Writers and the Nature of Literature* (1976) and *Modern Japanese Poets and the Nature of Literature* (1983). He has held awards from the Fulbright Commission, the Canada Council, the Social Science Research Council, the American Council of Learned Societies, and other bodies.

Earl MINER, compiler and editor of this book, took his academic degrees in Japanese and English at the University of Minnesota. He is the first Townsend Martin, Class of 1917, Professor of English and Comparative Literature at Princeton. His interests include seventeenth-century English literature, classical Japanese literature, and comparative poetics.

THE TRANSLATORS

Aileen GATTEN is a fellow of the Center for Japanese Studies at the University of Michigan. The subject of her Ph.D. thesis for that university was the *Genji Monogatari*. Her publications include articles on that work and other narratives in its wake. She is the chief translator of the first three (of the five) volumes of Konishi Jin'ichi's *History of Japanese Literature* (in progress; first volume published 1984; second in press).

Matthew MIZENKO teaches Japanese language and literature at Amherst College. He did his academic work at Columbia University and Princeton University. He is chiefly interested in modern Japanese literature, especially in Kawabata Yasunari, on whom he has published in Japanese.

Yoshiko Yokochi SAMUEL is an assistant professor of Japanese language and literature at Wesleyan University. Her academic work was done in Japan and in the United States, culminating in a Ph.D. (dissertation: "The Life and Works of Ōe Kenzaburō") at Indiana University. Besides language teaching, she is interested in study of Japanese and comparative literature, Asian folklore, and the performing arts. She has a wide variety of teaching experience in these and other subjects.

Bob Tadashi WAKABAYASHI did his undergraduate work at UCLA. After six years' study in Japan at the Tokyo University of Education and the University of Tokyo, he took his Ph.D. at Princeton University in 1982. His chief field of interest is the history of Japanese thought and culture in the eighteenth and nineteenth centuries, the general field of his dissertation. He has been a Lecturer at Princeton University, Visiting Lecturer at Columbia University, and Research Fellow at the Japanese Institute at Harvard University. As this book is in proof, he is lecturer at Harvard.

JAPANESE NAMES, TERMS, AND A HISTORICAL TABLE

The handling of Japanese names begins with those of some authors of this book. Our usage is consistent not with Japanese usage but with the country in which the person teaches. For Mezaki Tokue, who teaches in Japan, Mezaki is the surname and Tokue the given. For Makoto Ueda, who teaches in the United States, Ueda is the surname (although when he publishes books in Japanese he is known as Ueda Makoto). The order of names on the title page reflects these differences, since it is alphabetical by surname.

There are several practices used for historical Japanese. That used here is to omit the medial "no" traditionally used of pre-Edo individuals, except for individuals whose surnames have one or two syllables: So Ono no Komachi or Ki no Tsurayuki, but Fujiwara Michinaga. For some women the practice differs. Properly speaking, Sei Shōnagon does not have "Sei" as a surname but Kiyowara (the "Sei" being the Sinified reading of "Kiyo"). "Shōnagon," or "Junior Councillor," is a title appropriated from a male relative. For men, we use familiar designations, but our Fujiwara Shunzei will be found in many biographical dictionaries as Fujiwara no Toshinari. A few highly regarded poets were granted Sinified readings of their personal names. Shunzei is one; and although Fujiwara Michinaga was a poet of sorts and a great potentate, he was not a great enough poet to be termed Fujiwara Dōchō. We have omitted religious titles, using instead simply the religious name: "Saigyō" rather than "Saigyō Hōshi." For writers after the major waka poets, the given "names" are normally pen names or styles. And both for waka poets and post-waka writers, we have usually referred to the individuals by the given name or style after first giving the name in full: first Matsuo Bashō, and then Bashō. There is simply no easy or consistent way to handle these matters, as is explained in part in the first chapter. Pedantically speaking, "Kakinomoto Hitomaro" should be "Kakinomoto no Asomi (no) Fitomaro."

If there is doubt as to surname, the index contains entries under alternative surnames, except for priests and for women (when, as with Sei Shōnagon, custom rules it out). In these matters, it is possible only to specify the method used and hope that readers adjust to the method explained.

Either by a parenthetical description or by context, we have tried to make clear the meaning of various Japanese terms. It is not easy to do so simply, whether for those who know the meanings already or for those to whom the terms are outlandish. Where there is doubt, a reader can refer to *The Princeton Companion to Classical Japanese Literature* by Miner, Hiroko Odagiri, and Robert E. Morrell. The preface to that work also explains the handling of titles, romanized Japanese, periodizing, etc. here.

A Historical Table

There are several kinds of periodizing of classical Japanese literature, although these are more a matter of names than of period units. In terms of location of government and with some adjustments of, or decisions as to, arbitrary breaks, this is the the pattern followed for this book:

Legendary	pre-539
Historical	539-645
Yamato	645-712
Nara	712-794
Heian	794-1186
Kamakura	1186-1336
Nambokuchō	1336-1392
Muromachi	1392-1573
Azuchi Momoyama	1573-1603
Edo	1603-1868

One alternative to this division involves more or less the same periods but names relating to powerful ruling families (e.g. for

Heian, Fujiwara; for Edo, Tokugawa). There are also smaller divisions (e.g. Early and Late Fujiwara). There is another scheme of quite alternative names. A common version follows:

Ancient (kodai)	to 794
Ancient-Medieval (chūko)	794-1186
Medieval (chūsei)	1186-1603
Recent (kindai)	1603-1868

There is one definition of "medieval" that goes back to 645 and another to 1868. When the term is used in this book, it designates the dates in the immediately preceding table.

The index includes a large number of Japanese terms with brief glosses and references to discussion in one or more chapters, along with cross references to or from English versions.

INDEX

WORKS are entered under authors' names, when known, with translations of titles where feasible and conventional. Sovereigns are designated as Tennō or, if cloistered and better known so, as In. Exalted priests are entered by their familiar religious name (Kūkai, Priest) rather than by special title (Kōbō Daishi). Citations are given under the Japanese term or title, with a cross reference from an English version. Commas are entered between surnames and given names of those residing outside Japan.

LIBRARY OF CONGRESS CATALOGING IN PUBLICATION DATA

Main entry under title:

Principles of classical Japanese literature.

"Based on a conference sponsored by the Joint Committee on Japanese Studies of the American Council of Learned Societies and the Social Science Research Council"—P.

Includes index.

1. Japanese literature—To 1868—History and criticism—Theory, etc.—Congresses. I. Jones, Sumie. II. Miner, Earl Roy. III. Joint Committee on Japanese Studies.

PL726.1.P75 1985 895.6'09 84-42895

ISBN 0-691-06635-3 (alk. paper)